The Campus History Series

University of Rio Grande and Rio Grande Community College

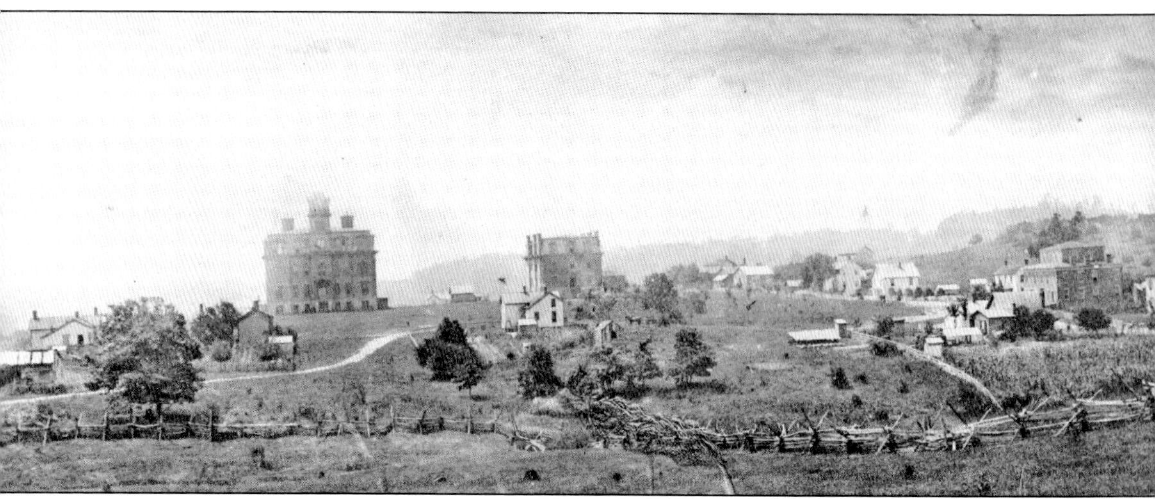

Established in 1876 on a 10-acre plot of ground in the western part of Gallia County, Ohio, in the southeastern corner of the state and the beginning of the foothills of the Appalachian Mountains, Rio Grande College consisted of two buildings. Separated by 12 miles from the nearest railroad line and with no good roads, the location was chosen partially because of the isolation. Young Christian college students could study and learn away from the temptations of the world. The town grew up around the college, which was sometimes referred to as "the blackberry patch" because of its remoteness. (Courtesy of the Jean Lloyd Cooper Archives at the University of Rio Grande.)

On the Cover: Davis Cottage, formerly the home of Pres. John Merrill Davis, could accommodate up to 25 girls. They often became a close-knit group. Pictured here about 1951 eating crackers in bed are, from left to right, Willavene Sheets, Gloria Norris, Josine Thomas, Maria Leach, Faye Neal, Joan Conway, Bea Queen, Marcelline Wilson, and Doris McFann. The home was used as a dorm until 1957. (Courtesy of the Jean Lloyd Cooper Archives at the University of Rio Grande.)

Cover Background: An aerial view shows the Rio Grand campus around 1964. (Courtesy of the Jean Lloyd Cooper Archives at the University of Rio Grande.)

The Campus History Series

UNIVERSITY OF RIO GRANDE AND RIO GRANDE COMMUNITY COLLEGE

JACOB L. BAPST AND IVAN M. TRIBE
FOREWORD BY MICHELLE JOHNSTON, PHD

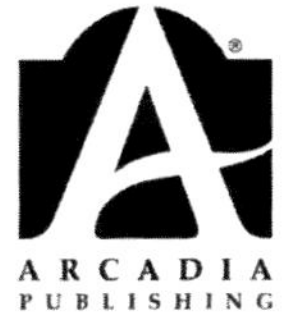

ISBN 978-1-4671-2542-0

Published by Arcadia Publishing
Charleston, South Carolina

Printed in the United States of America

Library of Congress Control Number: 2017930432

For all general information, please contact Arcadia Publishing:
Telephone 843-853-2070
Fax 843-853-0044
E-mail sales@arcadiapublishing.com
For customer service and orders:
Toll-Free 1-888-313-2665

Visit us on the Internet at www.arcadiapublishing.com

Contents

Foreword

People—above and beyond everything else, this depiction of Rio Grande, as a college and as a university, is all about people. What you will see on these pages is the very fiber, the lifeblood, the heart and soul of an educational institution that has faced incredible challenges and achieved remarkable successes. As you become acquainted with the students, faculty, staff, administrators, and friends of Rio presented in this book, you are experiencing at least a glimpse into what we believe comprises our legacy and upholds our traditions. If you look closely at the buildings and the landscapes, imagine the faces that were the reason and the reasoning behind the bricks and mortar. A number of excellent and thorough books chronicle the ups and downs, the ins and outs, and the heydays and darker days of Rio Grande. This work adds to the collection by bringing those narratives forward through rich photographs and extensive visual artifacts. In every way, the people of Rio Grande—past, present, and future—are the vessels of change that sustain the presence of an institution of higher learning like none other in the United States.

A historical portrayal of Rio Grande sorely misses the mark if the deep veins of struggle and sacrifice are masked. Through the masterful selection of photographs and artifacts, authors Jacob "Jake" Bapst and Ivan Tribe do not shy away from the underbelly of strife and toil that is part of the fabric of Rio Grande. Equally, they capture the power and the pride that balance and propel this one-of-a-kind place. Ever since our doors opened in 1876, Rio Grande has strived to provide high-quality education to students—whether they are from Appalachia, the far reaches of our nation, or across the globe. You will see that commitment to quality and openness throughout this volume.

As a proud member of the Rio family, I am forever grateful for the blood, sweat, and tears that Jake and Ivan poured into the compilation of this book. Their perseverance, dedication, talent, and ever-present curiosity are emblematic of the identity that has characterized Rio Grande for over 140 years. Their love for Rio Grande is infectious and contagious. I have no doubt that you will catch the Rio "bug" through their artful and engaging presentation of the University of Rio Grande and Rio Grande Community College. Pass it on!

—Michelle Johnston, PhD
President of the University of Rio Grande and Rio Grande Community College

ACKNOWLEDGMENTS

This particular work on Rio Grande has largely been a labor of love. It has been possible because of the numerous historic photographs and other data housed in the Jean L. Cooper Archives of the Esther Allen Greer Center (Allen House), which also contains files of the *Grandion*, student newspapers, and other material concerning the University of Rio Grande and Rio Grande Community College's past.

Assistance has come from the president of the University of Rio Grande/Rio Grande Community College, Dr. Michelle Johnston, who provided the foreword and much encouragement, along with alumni director Annette Ward, who provided unlimited access to archive contents. Nearly all of the images contained herein come from that source, although some came from Chad and Angela Lambert, Erik and Megan Miller, Stacy Vaughn Hutton, Carol Cremeans, and Michael Thompson. Josie Bapst and Deanna Tribe also provided assistance.

For those who wish for more information about Rio Grande's colorful history—which often has been a struggle for survival—other books may prove useful. These include *Rio Grande: From Baptists and Bevo to the Bell Tower*, by Abby Gail Goodnite and Ivan M. Tribe (2002), as well as the latter's more interpretive chapter in *Cradles of Conscience: Ohio's Independent Colleges and Universities*, by John Oliver et al. (2003). Older and hard-to-find works include *The First Fifty Years of Rio Grande College*, by Perry D. Woods (1926); *A History of Rio Grande College*, by Benjamin Evans (1939); *The Haning-Atwood Vision*, by Anna Pabst (1969); and *Lamp of the Hills*, by James Sherman Porter (1978). For the extensive Bevo Francis story, see *One Basketball and Glory*, by Newt Oliver (1969); *His Records Stand*, by Juanita Daily (1995); or *Shooting Star: The Bevo Francis Story*, by Kyle Keiderling (2005).

Introduction

In 2016, Rio Grande completed 140 years as an institution of higher learning. In those fourteen decades—first as a college and then as a university—it has provided schooling for thousands of students, a majority of whom would probably not have otherwise had an opportunity for such an education. Like other colleges, Rio Grande falls short of perfection. Keeping the doors open has usually been a financial challenge, yet the Rio staff typically did the best they could with their limited resources. Thus they fulfilled a characteristic often identified with the best of Appalachian hill-folk while nurturing and attending a school that often operated on a monetary shoestring. It is a college with a name that people in more distant locales often misidentified with a river on the Texas border.

The name "Rio Grande" (Rye-o Grand) originated in 1846 when the Post Office Department moved to establish an office in Raccoon Township in Gallia County. The name Adamsville, used for a small hamlet nearby, had already been taken, so the locals chose a name then current in national news when Gen. Zachary Taylor's army opposed the enemy in the Mexican War. About the only notable event happening locally in the next quarter century took place in 1850, when a zealous Free Will Baptist minister, Ira Z. Haning, preached a revival that resulted in the formation of the Calvary Baptist Church. Nehemiah and Permelia Atwood—an affluent, childless, middle-aged couple who prospered while running a wayside inn and tavern a couple of miles away—ranked among the more prominent new converts.

Reverend Haning and nearby fellow ministers desired to promote education and had already started a couple of academies in the area: Atwood Institute in Albany and Randall Academy in Berlin Cross Roads. But they hoped for a full-fledged college and that Atwood philanthropy would support it. Nehemiah Atwood died in 1869, according to tradition uttering "Permelia, build the college" as his last words. Within a year, the widow Atwood married Harrison Wood, a cousin of her late husband, but persisted in following Nehemiah's wishes. In 1871, surveyors platted a townsite with a 10-acre "college green" in the center on Atwood property; the plat was filed on July 6, 1874. Three months later, construction began on a building that would become Atwood Hall. Rio Grande College opened for business on September 13, 1876. A few months later, workmen completed a second building, known as the Boarding Hall, which provided housing for some 72 students. Since many of the students lacked secondary school experience, most enrolled in the Preparatory Department. No students actually received four-year degrees until 1883, when four were graduated. Two, Ida and Rebecca Haning, were daughters of Ira Z. Haning, who had died in 1878. The Collegiate Department had been divided into two sets of course work: classical and scientific.

Through the passing decades, Rio Grande College endured numerous trials and tribulations. The first followed the death of Permelia Atwood on March 9, 1885, when 29 of her relatives filed a lawsuit in an effort to break her will. The college trustees hired two of the best law firms in the region—Grosvenor and Jones and Wood and Wood, the latter being brothers-in-law of I.Z. Haning. After some years of litigation and appeals, the Ohio Supreme Court upheld the will in 1896. Under the first president, Ransom Dunn; his successors, A.A. Moulton and John M. Davis; and other Free Will Baptist ministers, Rio Grande followed the desires of its founders. In 1911, Free Will Baptists merged into a larger Baptist denomination and the curriculum turned more toward teacher training.

Other tragedies continued to take a toll. In 1917, the Boarding Hall burned down, and in 1937, another fire destroyed Atwood Hall. During the Depression, Rio Grande became a de facto junior college, and it did not confer bachelor's degrees again until 1940. Teacher training continued to dominate, with enrollments typically becoming much larger in the summer as area teachers in the one-room rural schools continued to pursue certification and degrees. At the end of the 1930s, Rio became a self-help school on a model similar to the highly successful Berea College in the Kentucky hill country. Three new buildings went up, largely built by student labor, and the school operated a farm and dairy, but the intervention of World War II took most of the male students. Enrollment fell in the fall of 1944 to only 33, of which 24 were girls. A brief student renaissance, augmented by the GI Bill, swelled numbers to 209 in the spring of 1948 and crippled the self-help plan, and by 1950, the whole scheme was virtually abandoned. Unfortunately, the American Baptist Convention was about to do the same, putting more support into the larger and more affluent Denison University.

In the fall of 1952, enrollment fell to 94. The end seemed near when an atypical near-miracle occurred. Led by flamboyant basketball coach J. Newton Oliver and long, tall player Clarence "Bevo" Francis, Rio Grande gained national attention on the roundball courts. Francis accumulated phenomenal point totals, twice exceeding 100 points in a single game, and the team had an undefeated 39-0 season. Critics scoffed at the weak teams on the Rio schedule, but the next year the team did almost as well with a schedule that included wins over relative giants like Wake Forest. The Oliver-Francis era burned out after two years, but it provided a sufficient boost that enabled the school to enter into a small but steady growth period. New buildings went up, including modern dorms, a library, and a gymnasium. In 1969, after seven years of determined effort on the part of Pres. Alphus Christiansen, Rio received full accreditation from the North Central Association of Colleges and Schools. By 1969–1970, enrollment reached a new high of 850, surpassing the pre–World War II peak of 517 set in 1921–1922.

Another problem soon followed. After the all-volunteer Army replaced conscription, enrollment dipped again, although much less drastically than in earlier crises. Enrollments fell to 589 in the fall of 1971. An increased scholarship program, followed by a truly novel plan, stemmed the decline. The real innovation consisted of the creation of a tax-supported levy in the four counties of Gallia, Jackson, Meigs, and Vinton and the creation of a community college district. The levy passed in June 1974, and in 1977–1978, enrollment reached 1,085, rising to 2,160 in 1992–1993. Numbers since that time have remained near that figure. In 1989, the private college altered its name to the University of Rio Grande.

Through good years and hard times, Rio Grande has endured. In 1926–1927, the annual budget was only $34,000. By 2015–2016, for Rio Grande Community College (RGCC) and the University of Rio Grande (URG) combined, it was $40 million. Many institutions in Appalachian Ohio, such as the Albany Manual Labor University, Alfred Holbrook College, Franklin College, Hillsboro College, and Providence University, faded almost from memory. A pair of urban Roman Catholic colleges, Mary Manse and Edgecliff, endured a similar fate. However, Rio Grande has not. The school that once had the motto "The Lamp of the Hills" still glows.

One

A Free Will Baptist Educational Enclave 1876–1917

Rio Grande College began fulfilling its mission on September 13, 1876, with 15 students enrolled, all in the Preparatory Department. With the completion of the Boarding Hall a few weeks afterward, enrollment increased to 75 by the spring term. Tuition was $6 per term, with $2 more for incidentals or $25 for the whole year of four terms, a savings of $7. Since the entire staff and governing board were dominated by Free Will Baptists and many also doubled as ministers in area churches, they provided a network that served as a recruiting tool for the school, increasing its student clientele. These minister-trustee-faculty folk in the early years included such figures as H.J. Carr, Lyman Chase, Clarence Clark, John Merrill Davis, William J. Fulton, James Martin, Thomas Peden, David Powell, and Bradbury Tewksbury.

When Ransom Dunn returned to Hillsdale in 1878, Albanus A. Moulton became the second president. Although he was widely esteemed as a scholar and leader, his precarious health limited his time in the office, and Prof. John Merrill Davis took his place, holding the presidency from 1887 until 1911, still the longest tenure in that position. Women were not ordained as ministers within the Free Will Baptist hierarchy, but they played major roles on the faculty from the beginning. The more significant included Ruth Brockett, Chestora McDonald Carr, Stella Fulton, and Nellie Phillips. By Rio's second year, five students enrolled in the Collegiate Department. Through 1900, the school awarded 53 bachelor's degrees, with the largest number coming in 1892 with a class of eight.

More than preparatory and collegiate, from 1877, the greater number of enrollees were part of the normal or teacher training courses, often in the summer terms. As time passed, this circumstance increased, especially in the presidency of Simeon Bing (1911–1923), who came from a public school background rather than the pulpit. Midway through his tenure, fire destroyed the Boarding Hall, although the inhabitants escaped safely. This tragedy marked the end of one era in Rio Grande's history and the beginning of another.

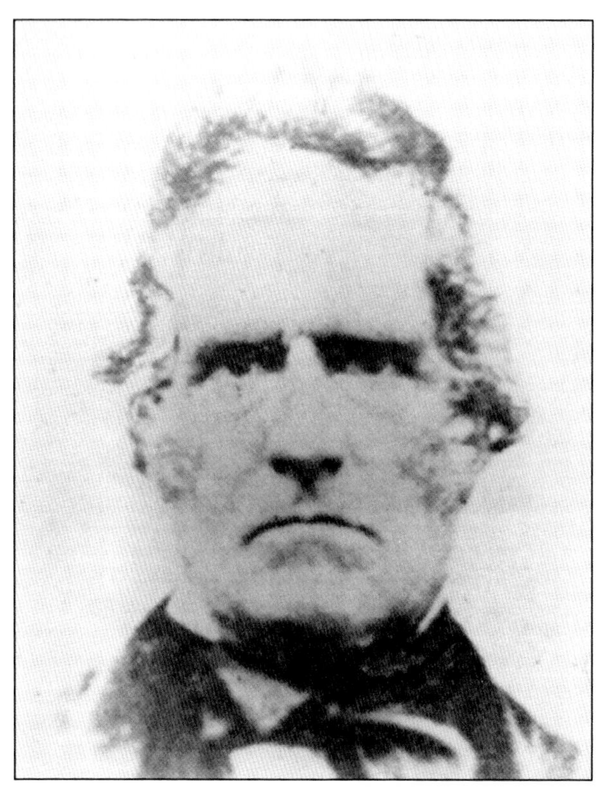

Nehemiah Atwood (1792–1869) and his wife, Permelia (1802–1885), prospered as operators of a wayside inn on the road between Gallipolis and Jackson. After their conversion to the Free Will Baptist Church, they left their modest fortune to initiate and support Rio Grande College. Despite legal efforts by relatives to break Permelia's will, the Ohio Supreme Court supported the college board and upheld Permelia's last wishes.

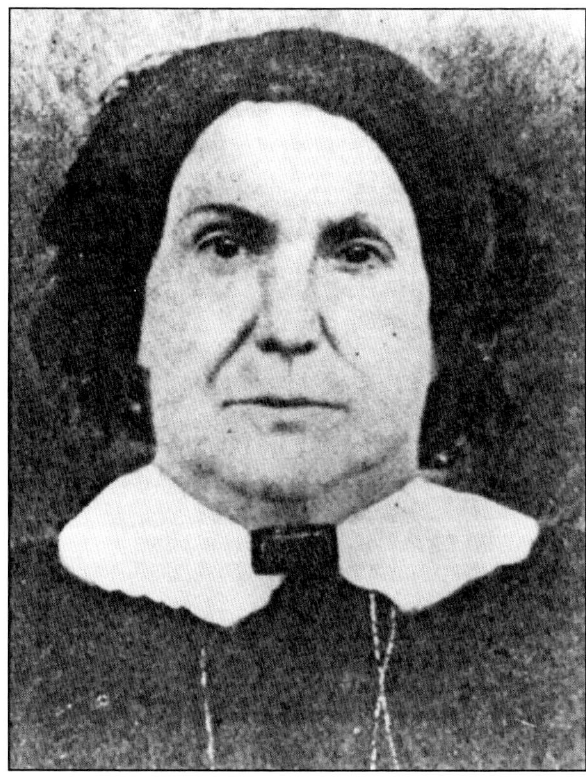

Free Will Baptist minister Ira Z. Haning (1825–1878) founded several churches in southeastern Ohio, including Calvary Baptist. Haning inspired the Atwoods to support and endow Rio Grande College. Two of the first four graduates in 1883 were his daughters. Like the Atwoods, Haning and his wife, Irene, are buried in the Calvary Cemetery near the Rio campus, adjacent to the church he founded.

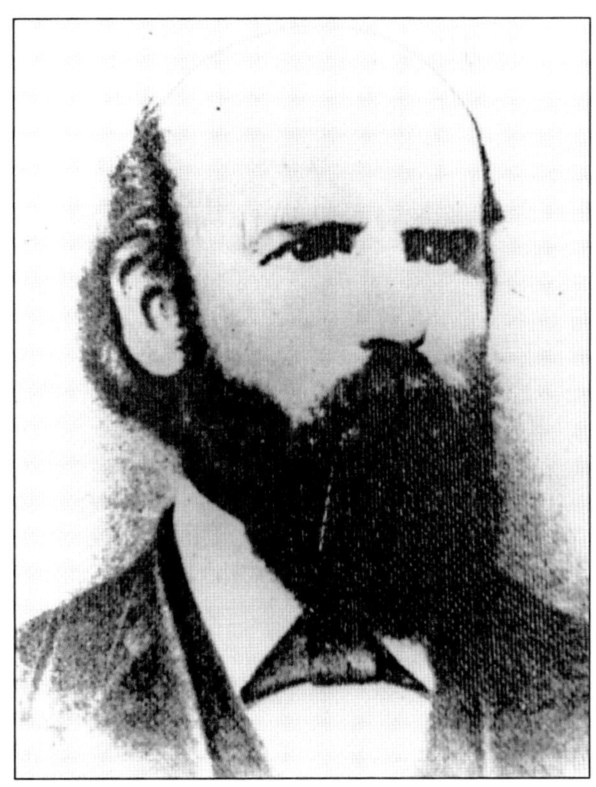

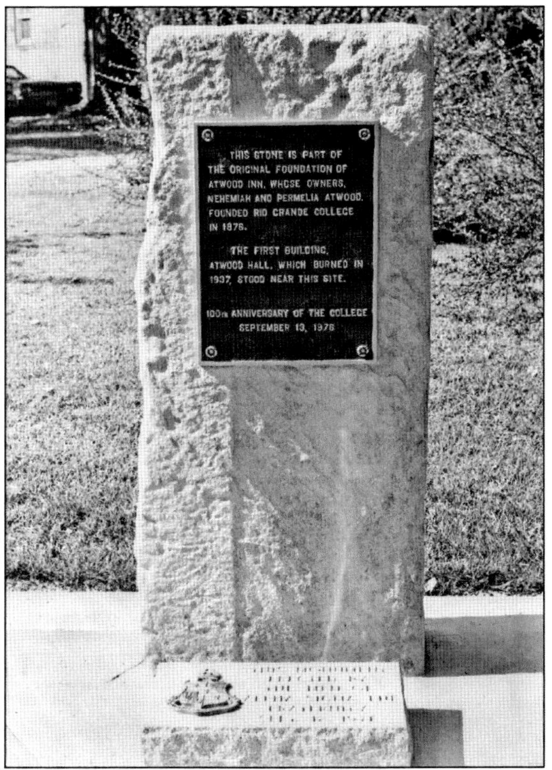

On September 13, 1976, Rio Grande College celebrated its 100th anniversary. A stone from the original Atwood Inn some two miles away was placed on campus near the site of Atwood Hall with a metal plaque attached. The lower flat stone informs that the stone and plaque were so placed as a project of the local chapter of Alpha Sigma Phi fraternity.

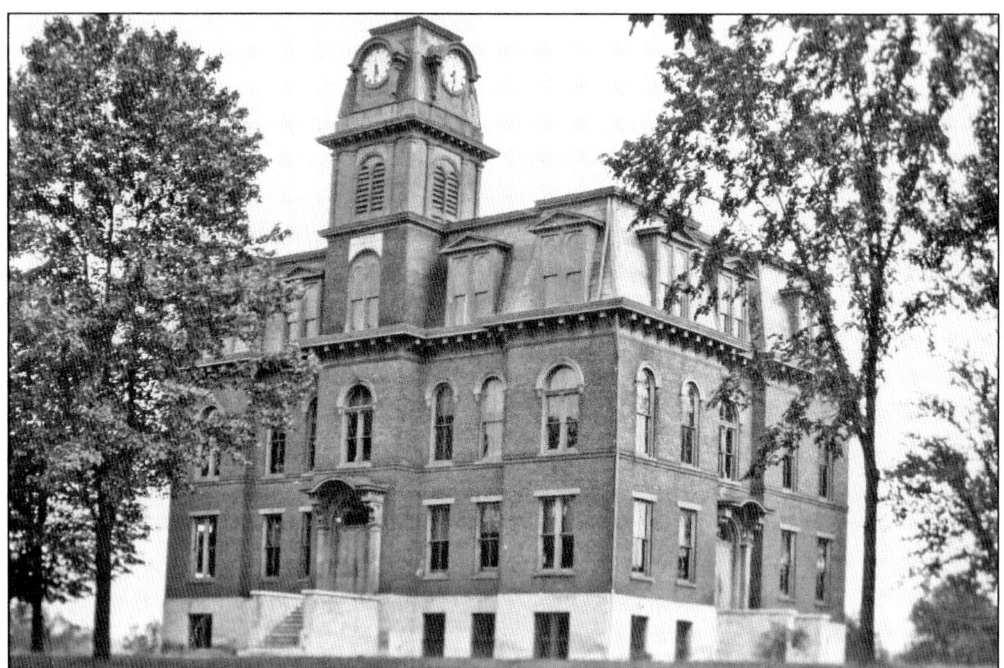

Construction began on what soon became known as Atwood Hall late in 1874, and the building was dedicated on August 30, 1876. Classes commenced two weeks later. It remained the principal building of Rio Grande College until consumed by fire on the early morning of November 19, 1937. Many feared the college would not survive, but like the proverbial phoenix, Rio rose from the ashes.

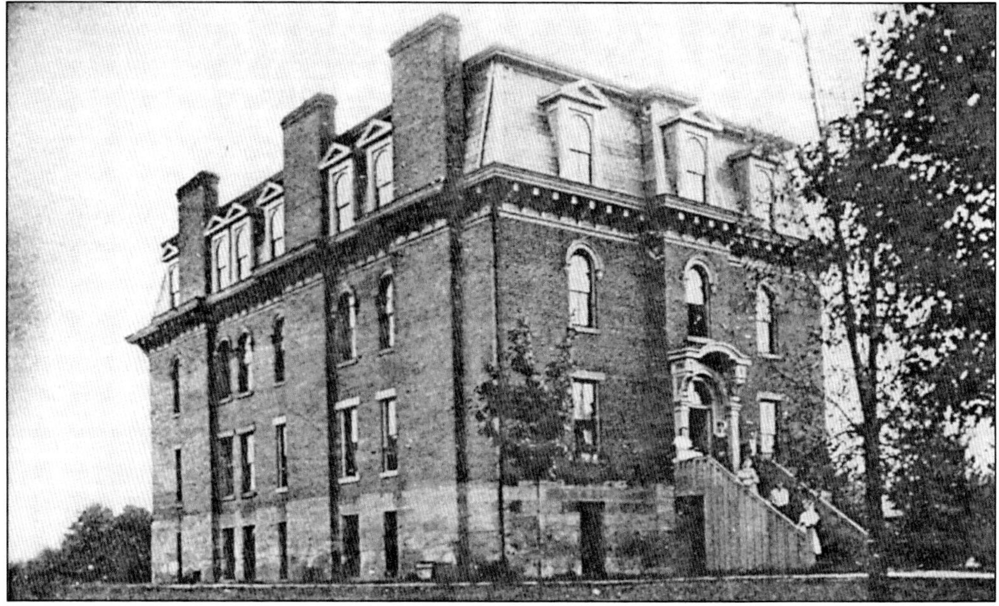

The Boarding Hall was completed a few months after Atwood Hall and could provide housing for 72 students, both male and female, on separate floors. After four decades, it burned down on the morning of February 9, 1917. Forty students escaped safely from the flames. One of the students, Charles Weed, wrote two days later that "we had a hot time last Friday morning."

The first printed announcement of the opening of Rio Grande College was this brochure from September 1876. While not listing individual classes, it does show the scientific and classical courses as well as Preparatory and Normal Departments and fees. Note that it explains how to arrive by stagecoach on the line "between Portland [Oak Hill] and Gallipolis" as Vinton and Gallipolis had no rail connections until 1880.

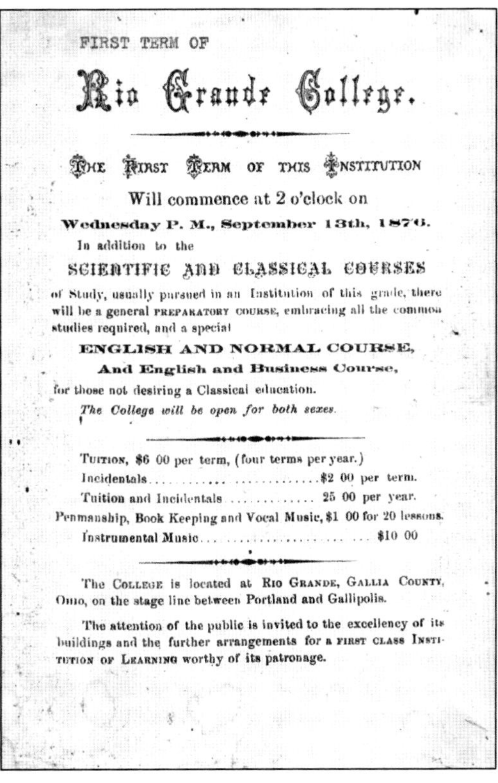

FIRST TERM OF

Rio Grande College.

THE FIRST TERM OF THIS INSTITUTION

Will commence at 2 o'clock on

Wednesday P. M., September 13th, 1876.

In addition to the

SCIENTIFIC AND CLASSICAL COURSES

of Study, usually pursued in an Institution of this grade, there will be a general PREPARATORY COURSE, embracing all the common studies required, and a special

ENGLISH AND NORMAL COURSE,

And English and Business Course,

for those not desiring a Classical education.

The College will be open for both sexes.

TUITION, $6 00 per term, (four terms per year.)

Incidentals .... $2 00 per term.

Tuition and Incidentals .... 25 00 per year.

Penmanship, Book Keeping and Vocal Music, $1 00 for 20 lessons.

Instrumental Music $10 00

The COLLEGE is located at RIO GRANDE, GALLIA COUNTY, OHIO, on the stage line between Portland and Gallipolis.

The attention of the public is invited to the excellency of its buildings and the further arrangements for a FIRST CLASS INSTITUTION OF LEARNING worthy of its patronage.

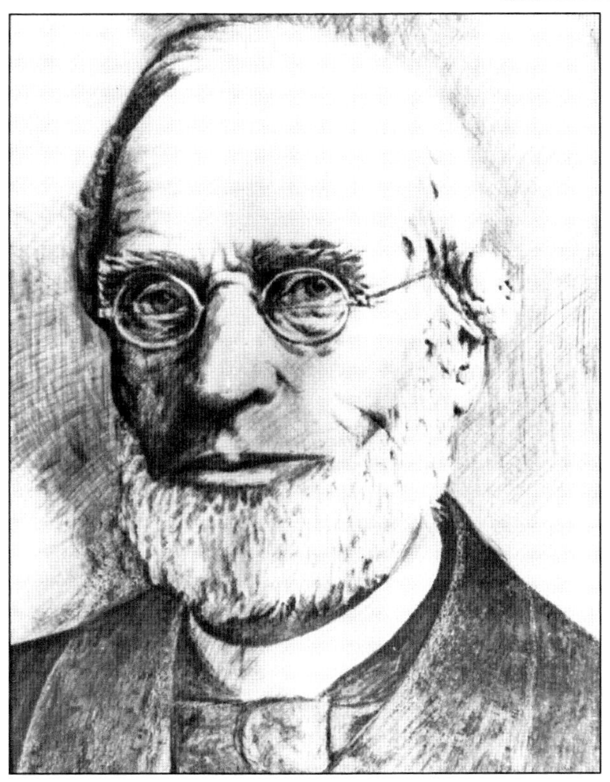

Ransom Dunn (1818–1900), another Free Will Baptist minister, served as Rio Grande's first president for two years while on an extended leave from Hillsdale College in Michigan, a school that served as a model for Rio Grande College in its early years. In a twist of fate, Hillsdale in 1953 was Rio's basketball opponent when Bevo Francis set his 113-point scoring record.

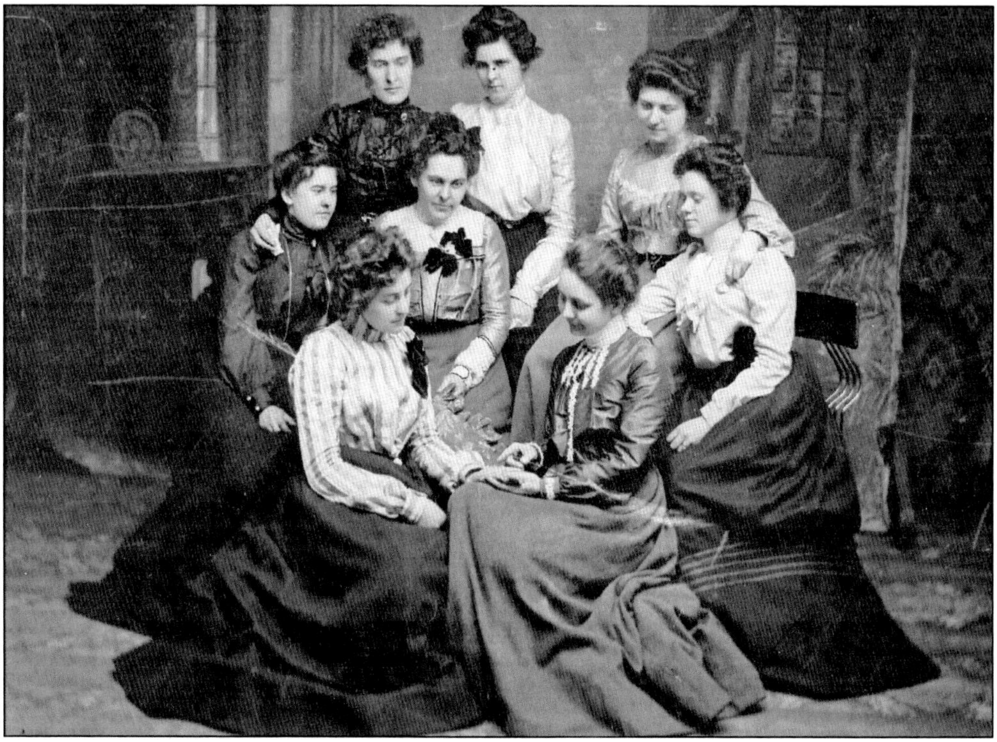

Nellie Phillips (1853–1906) served Rio Grande College as its first preceptress from 1876 to 1878 and also taught English. Born in India to Free Will Baptist missionaries, she later earned a doctorate and returned to India as a medical missionary. Phillips is pictured at far left in the top row with a group either of students or church ladies. This photograph may be the oldest actual previously unpublished image in this volume.

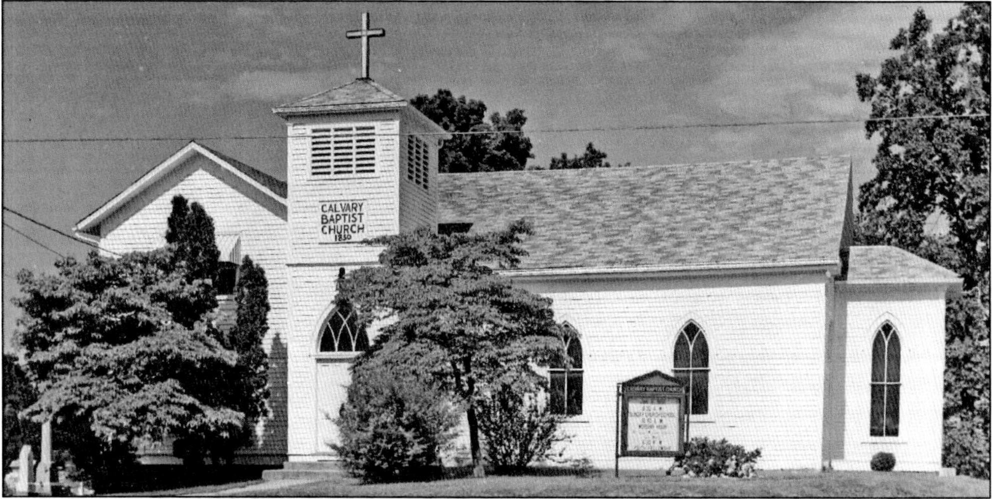

For two decades before Rio Grande was anything other than a rural post office (let alone a townsite, village, or college), the Calvary Free Will Baptist Church, founded by Rev. Ira Z. Haning, thrived as a center of rural community life. Since 1876, a faculty member, president, or trustee has often served as minister. Furthermore, the founders and many other college folk are buried in the adjacent cemetery.

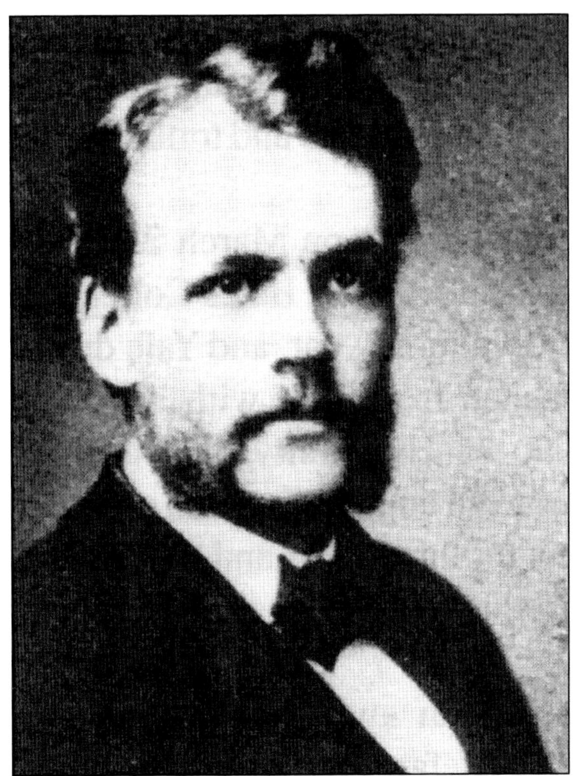

Albanus Avery Moulton (1848–1888), a Massachusetts native with a Yale degree, came to Rio Grande to teach Latin and Greek in 1876 and later became the school's second president. He wrote a book titled *Mathematical Geography* but suffered from consumption and took a health leave to Colorado in 1885. Moulton died there three years later, and his remains were returned to Ohio; he is buried in Calvary Cemetery.

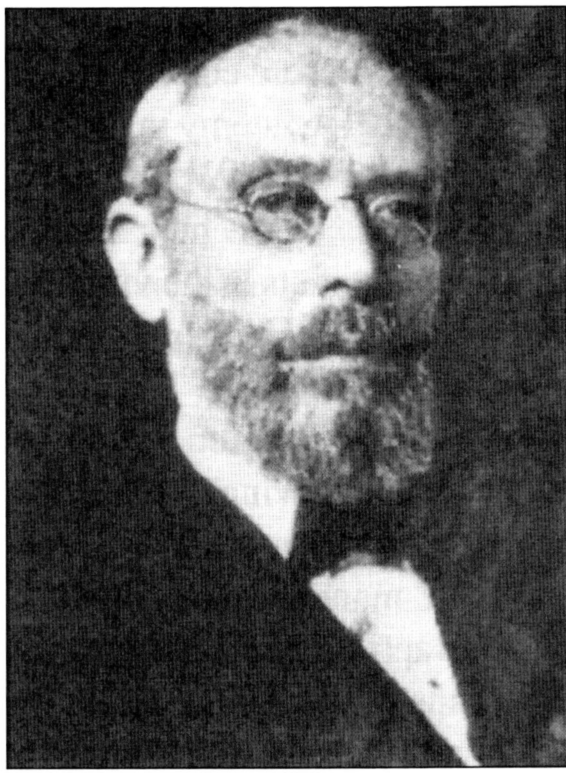

Meigs County native John Merrill Davis (1846–1920) served Rio as president longer than any other. He also served on the faculty both before and after his presidential term. Both of his sons, W. Merrill and J. Boyd, also had long Rio Grande College connections. Davis also ministered at Calvary Baptist. After his death, his former home became Davis Cottage (1921–1957).

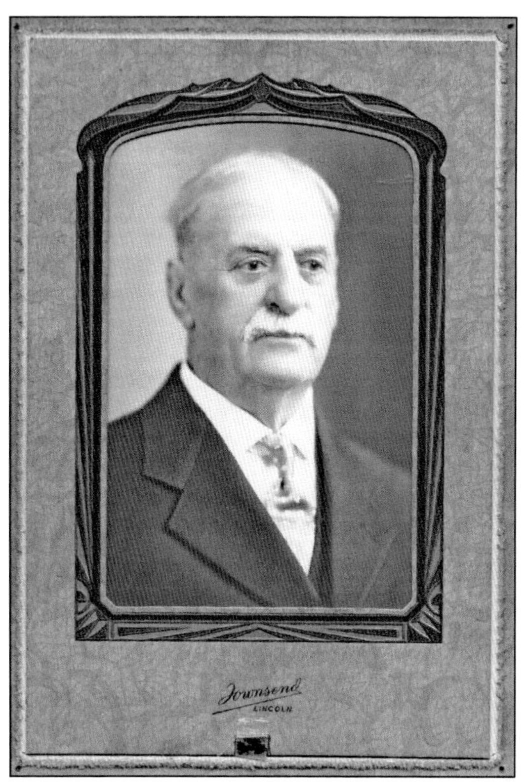

The oldest and longest-lived of the initial 1883 graduates, Thomas D. Davis (1854–1942) was born in Cora Mill and was the first of numerous Welsh Americans to earn a degree at Rio Grande. He became a Congregational minister; moved to Nebraska, where he ministered at several churches; and twice served as chaplain of the Nebraska Legislature. Davis lived in Casper, Wyoming, at the time of his death.

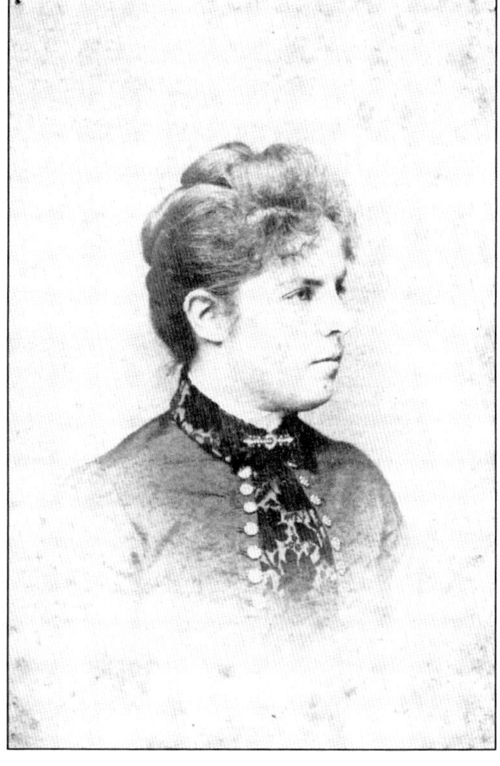

Gertrude Rebecca Haning (1862–1937) gave her graduation oration on the subject of uncrowned sovereigns. Like her sister, she taught music briefly at Rio. She subsequently married H.G. Bowles and lived in Huntington, West Virginia. She became a member of the board of trustees, as did her daughter, Irene Bowles Caldwell.

All of Rio Grande's first four graduates made names for themselves. After teaching music and German at the school for two years, Ida Belle Haning (1860–1904) married Dr. Henry Brandeberry, who became mayor of Huntington, West Virginia. Unfortunately, she contracted consumption (tuberculosis) and died shortly before her 44th birthday. Her graduation speech was titled "Our Inheritance."

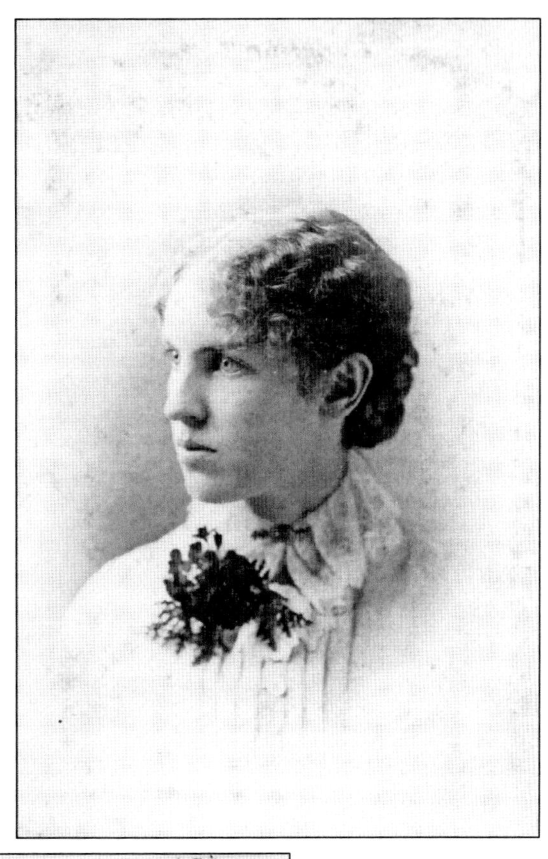

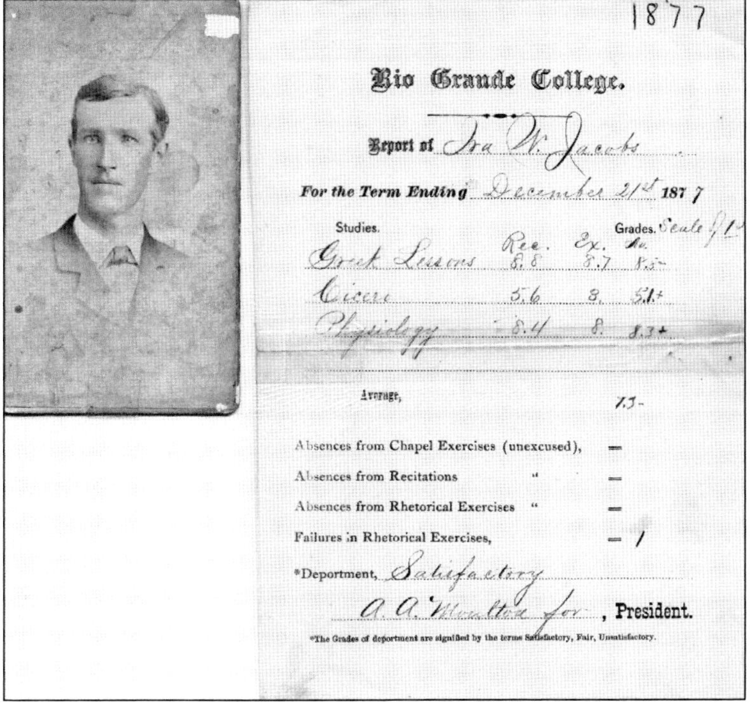

1877

Rio Grande College.

Report of Ira W. Jacobs

For the Term Ending December 21st 1877

Studies.	Rec.	Ex.	Av.
Greek Lessons	8.8	8.7	8.5
Cicero	5.6	8.	5.1+
Physiology	8.4	8.	8.3+
Average,			7.3-

Grades. Scale of 10

Absences from Chapel Exercises (unexcused), —

Absences from Recitations " —

Absences from Rhetorical Exercises " —

Failures in Rhetorical Exercises, — 1

*Deportment, Satisfactory

A. A. Moulton for, President.

*The Grades of deportment are signified by the terms Satisfactory, Fair, Unsatisfactory.

Ira Jacobs (1860–1937) was the only one of Rio's initial graduates to remain in Gallia County. He taught at one-room schools for a couple of years before becoming county surveyor and later a merchant in his hometown of Vinton. Jacobs spoke on the timely topic of energy. A rare copy of an 1877 grade report for Jacobs accompanies his photograph.

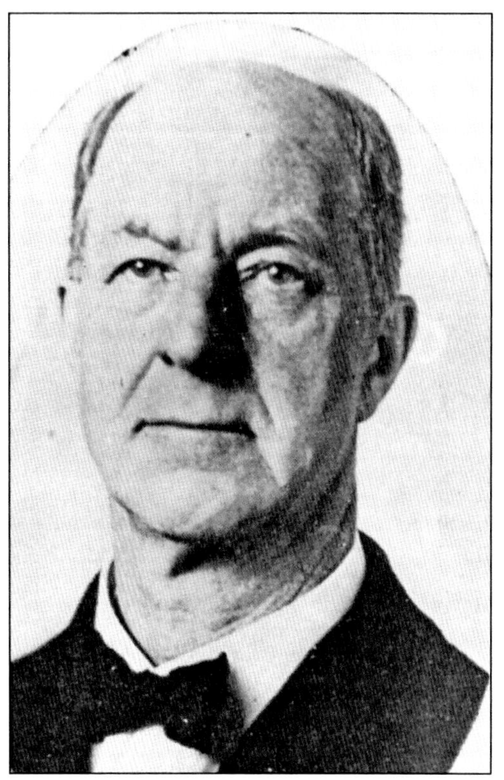

Clarence Clark (1855–1943) was a Rio Grande fixture for over 50 years. A native of Upstate New York, he came to Rio Grande College in 1887 after three years teaching at Atwood Institute in Albany. Clark headed the Science Department until he retired in 1924. He also preached at the Harrisburg Free Will Baptist Church, served as college treasurer, operated a service station, and bore with good humor comments about being "hair-challenged."

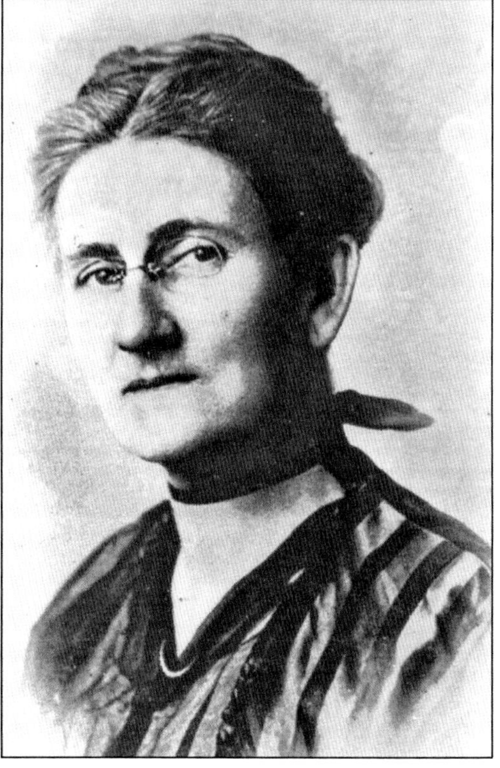

Like her father, William, Stella May Fulton (1871–1960) gave Rio Grande College long years of faithful service that included teaching English and Latin (1893–1931); heading the Preparatory Department (1893–1911); and serving as high school principal (1911–1930). Never married, she occupied her father's house, which as college property became known as the Fulton House.

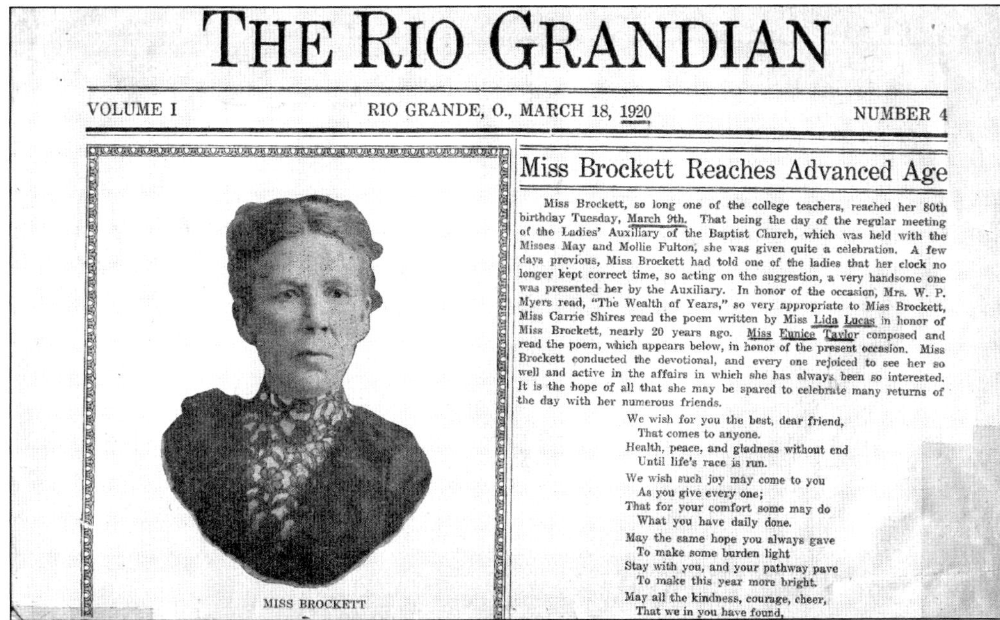

THE RIO GRANDIAN

VOLUME I — RIO GRANDE, O., MARCH 18, 1920 — NUMBER 4

MISS BROCKETT

Miss Brockett Reaches Advanced Age

Miss Brockett, so long one of the college teachers, reached her 80th birthday Tuesday, March 9th. That being the day of the regular meeting of the Ladies' Auxiliary of the Baptist Church, which was held with the Misses May and Mollie Fulton, she was given quite a celebration. A few days previous, Miss Brockett had told one of the ladies that her clock no longer kept correct time, so acting on the suggestion, a very handsome one was presented her by the Auxiliary. In honor of the occasion, Mrs. W. P. Myers read, "The Wealth of Years," so very appropriate to Miss Brockett, Miss Carrie Shires read the poem written by Miss Lida Lucas in honor of Miss Brockett, nearly 20 years ago. Miss Eunice Taylor composed and read the poem, which appears below, in honor of the present occasion. Miss Brockett conducted the devotional, and every one rejoiced to see her so well and active in the affairs in which she has always been so interested. It is the hope of all that she may be spared to celebrate many returns of the day with her numerous friends.

We wish for you the best, dear friend,
That comes to anyone.
Health, peace, and gladness without end
Until life's race is run.

We wish such joy may come to you
As you give every one;
That for your comfort some may do
What you have daily done.

May the same hope you always gave
To make some burden light
Stay with you, and your pathway pave
To make this year more bright.

May all the kindness, courage, cheer,
That we in you have found,

Ruth Brockett (1840–1923) exemplified the Victorian career woman in academe. A native of Trumbull County, she graduated from Hillsdale. She arrived at Rio in 1887 for a $450 annual salary and retired in 1911, teaching English, German, rhetoric, and especially botany. After retirement, she spent the rest of her life in Rio Grande and tended her botanical garden.

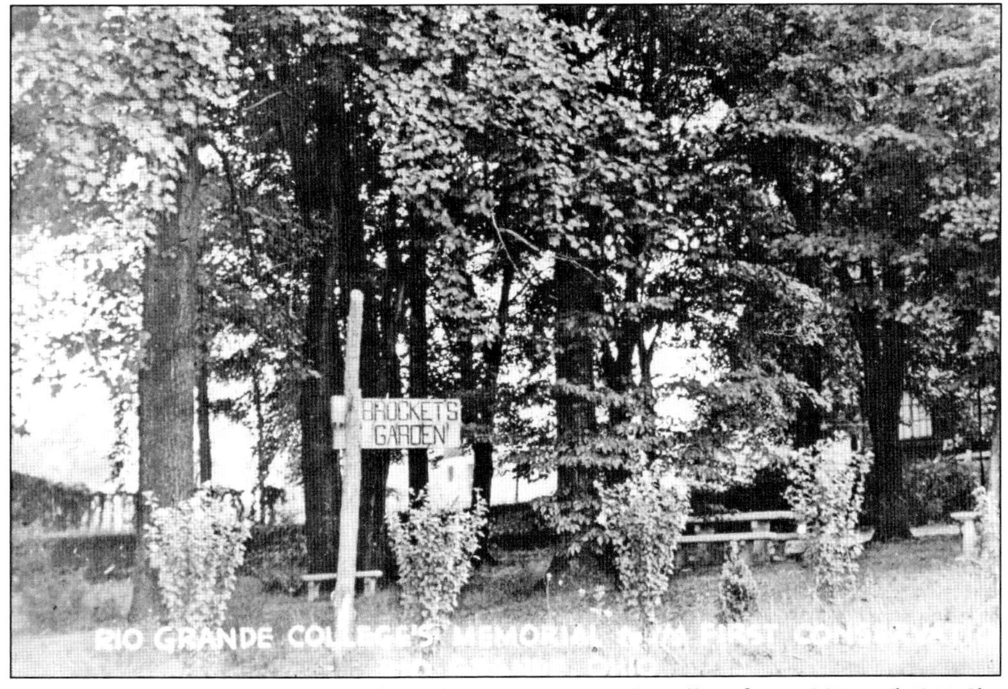

Ruth Brockett taught botany and other subjects at Rio Grande College from 1887 until 1911. She also established a botanical garden near the northeast corner of the campus block that became known as Brockett Garden. By 1947, the local garden club was responsible for its upkeep. With construction beginning on Davis Hall in 1955, Brockett Garden passed into extinction.

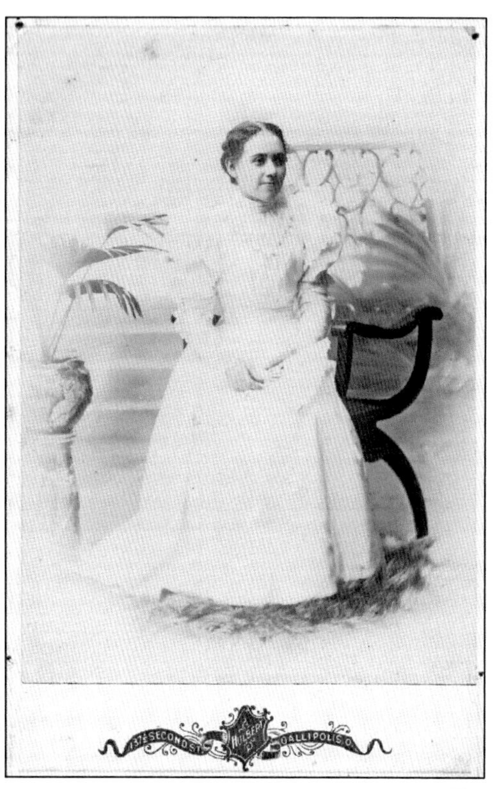

Edith Clare Corn graduated with a music diploma in 1897. Between 1896 and 1928, Rio Grande awarded 38 nondegree music diplomas. Recipients were certified to give private music lessons and work as church accompanists (probably on piano and/or pump organ). In 1956, Corn was buried in the same dress she had worn at her graduation.

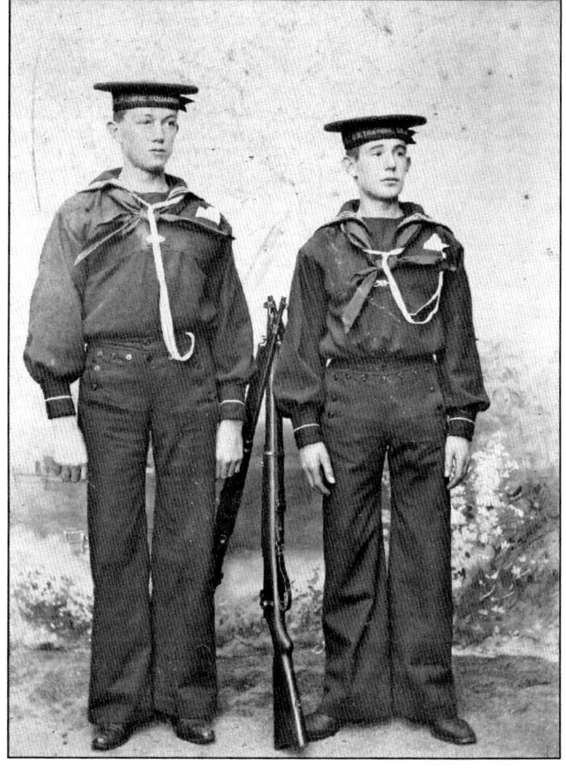

In 1898, Joseph Houlsworth (right), in his mid-teens, was a student in the English and Normal Department at Rio Grande College. He joined the US Navy in December 1900 (pictured here with a buddy) but five months later died of pneumonia, leaving a promising career unfulfilled. His younger brother Addison also joined the Navy and died but of meningitis.

Chestora McDonald Carr taught elocution and drama at Rio Grande but only in the spring term from 1901 to 1929 and in 1932. She also directed programs, plays, and pageants ranging from *The Merchant of Venice* to *Rio Grande College: The First Fifty Years*. She spent the remainder of her time touring on the Chautauqua circuit, where she became known for her mimicry of various birds, winter winds, and frontier preachers.

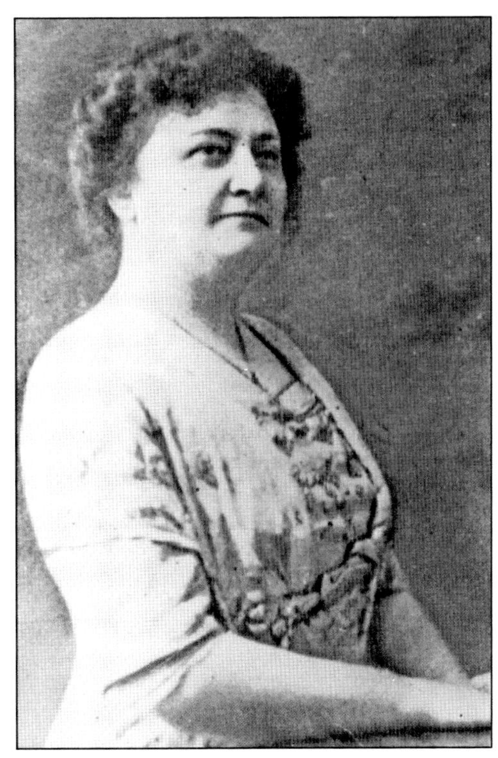

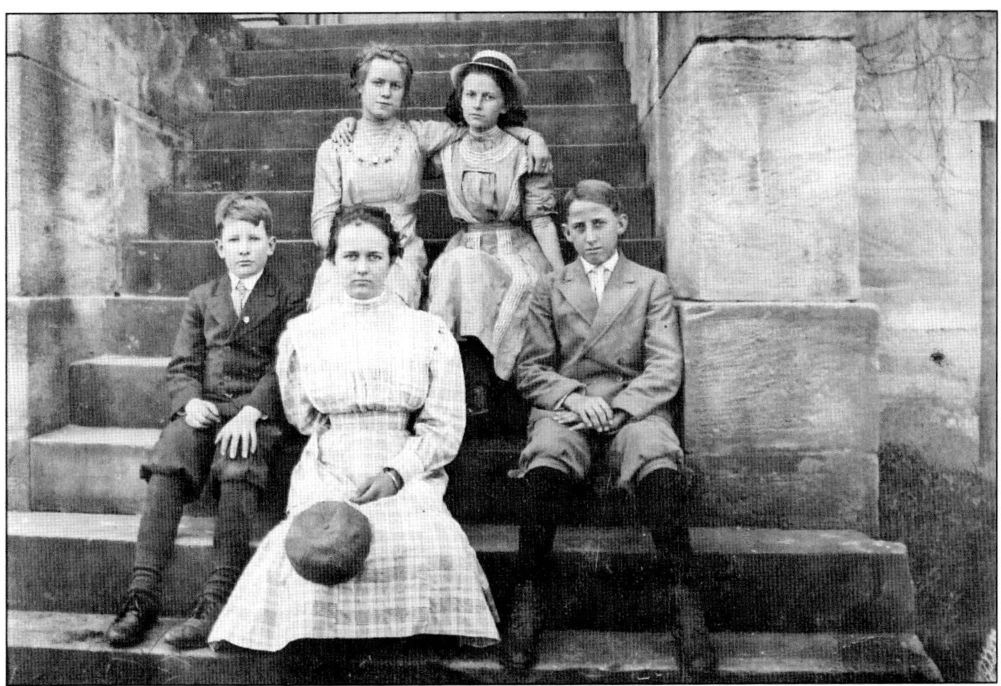

Students from the college and the local public schools frequently posed for pictures on the steps, in the front, or by the side of Atwood Hall. This image from 1908 or 1909 shows, from left to right, (first row) Harper Vanden, Nellie Clark, and unidentified; (second row) Helen Martin and Faye Clark.

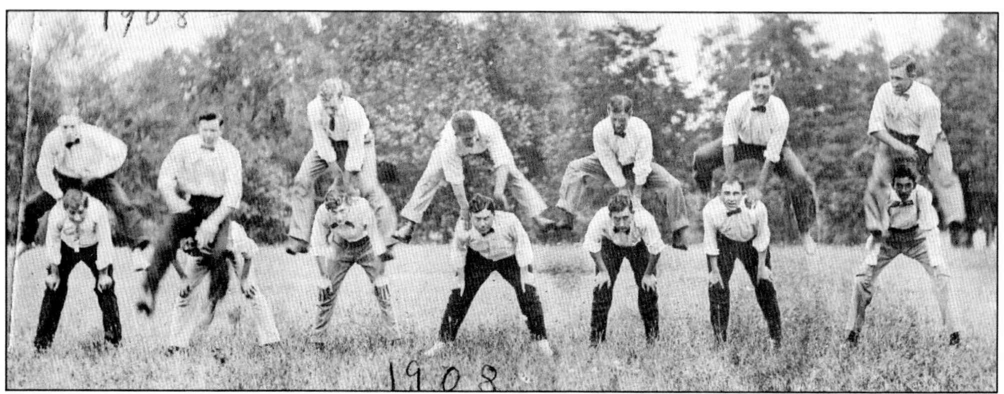

The members of what appears to be the Rio Grande Men's Glee Club pose for a photograph while playing the old children's game of leapfrog. Sadly, neither identifications nor correct date has been provided, but the photograph probably dates from about a century ago. It does illustrate that even in those olden times, fun was more than possible.

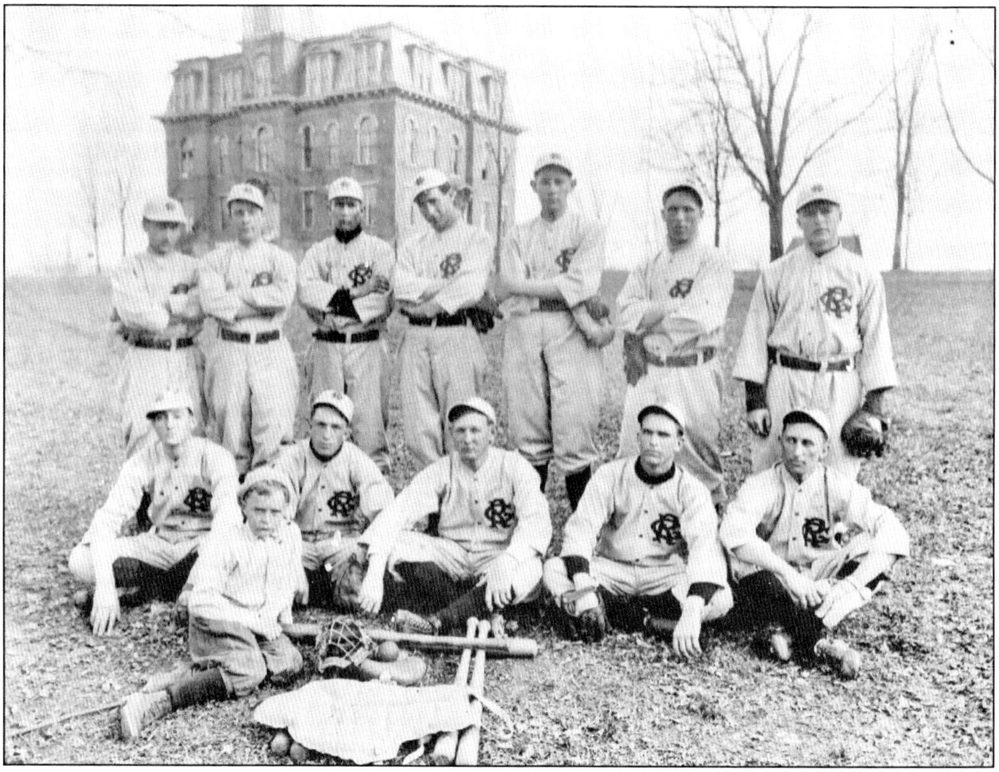

The Rio baseball team of 1912–1913 consists of, from left to right (first row) Elmer Fitzpatrick, Clarence Watson, Arthur Sisler, Alfred Berridge, and Edwin Ross; (second row) Henry McCown, Rothbe Kirkendall, Asa Stevens, Harley "Lefty" Dillinger, Clarence Myers, Neal Berridge, and Lester Berridge. Grayum Bing, the president's son, is the batboy. Dillinger later pitched briefly for Cleveland.

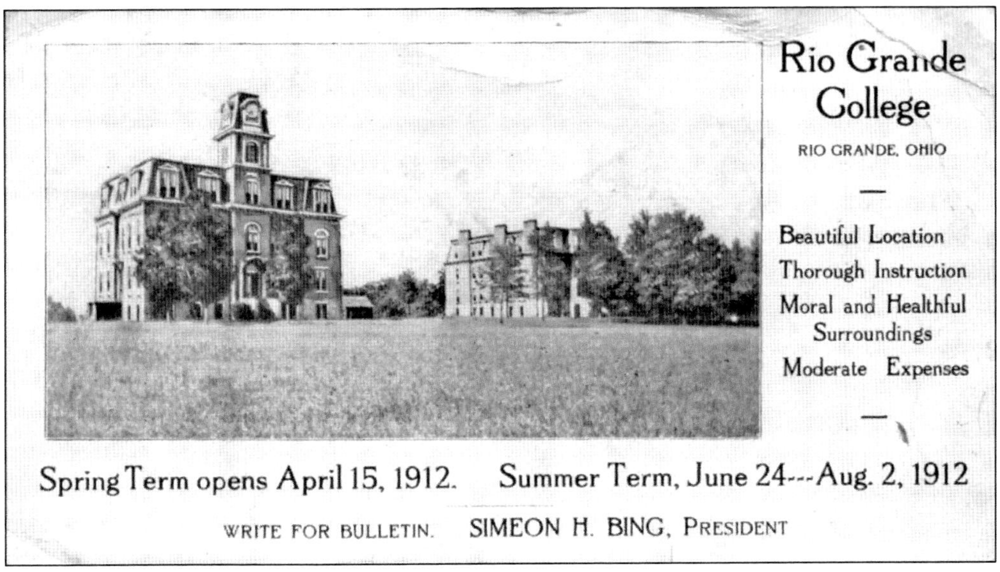

This postcard advertisement for Rio Grande College's 1912 spring and summer terms emphasizes the modest costs and rural atmosphere. In those days, enrollments increased dramatically in those terms because many students were teachers in the area's many one-room schools taking courses to maintain their certificates. In 1912, enrollment for summer jumped from 19 to 61. Tighter laws by the 1920s saw the summer numbers often surpass 300.

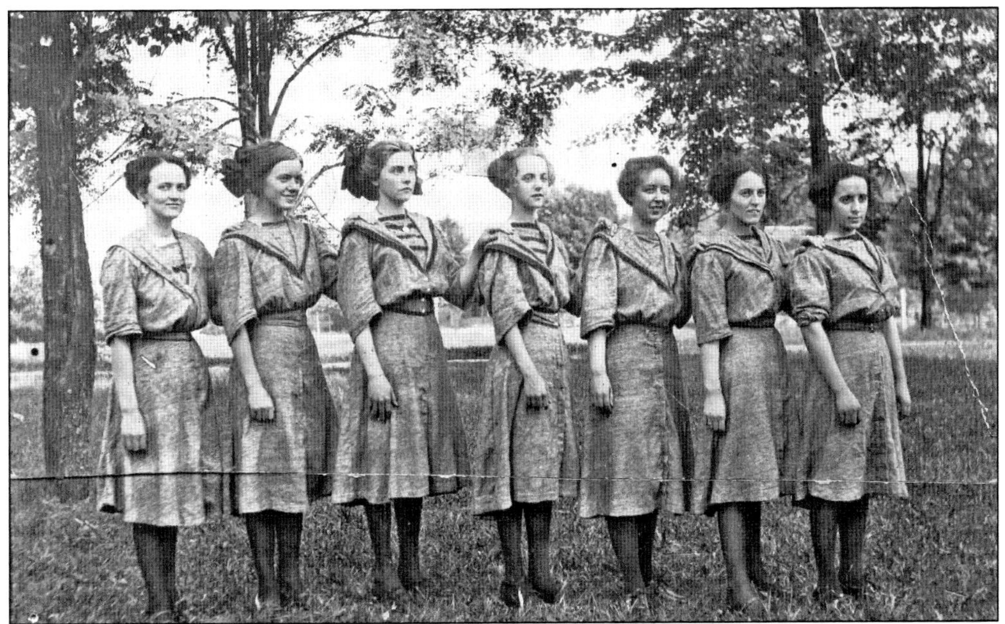

In 1911–1912, Rio Grande fielded its first women's basketball team with girls from both the high school and college on the squad. From left to right are Faye Clark, Helen Martin, Cecile Halley, Beryl Halley, Florence Weed, Lyrl Clark, and Freda Koontz. In the early years, students from area high schools made up the opposing teams.

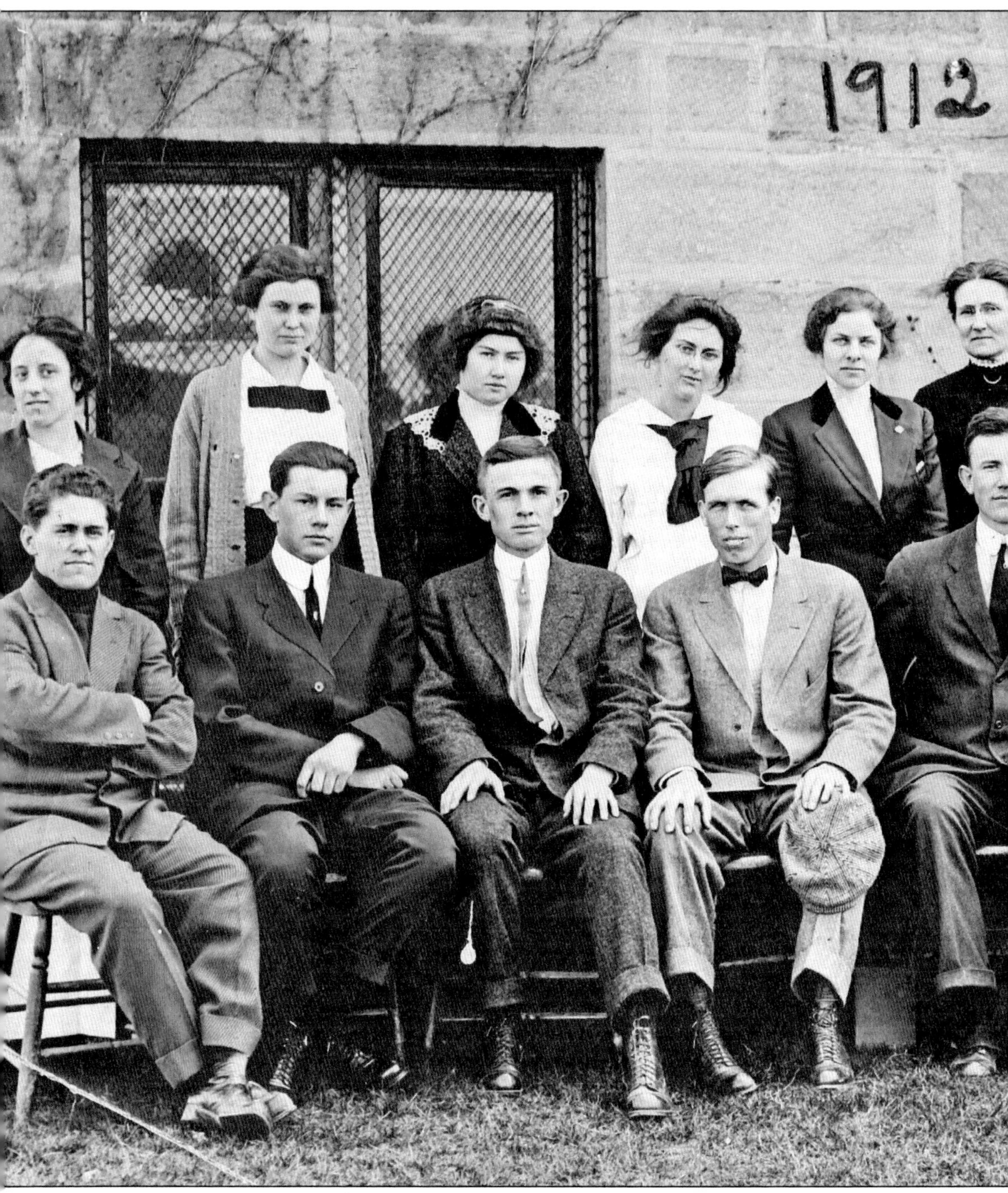

This group of Rio Grande staff (some of whom are also students) is pictured in 1912. From left to right are (first row) Charles Corbin, Clarence Myers, Harold Davis, Neil "Kate" Berridge, Stanley Lewis, Clovis McKibben, Rothbe Kirkendall, William Lewis, and Narsa Morgan;

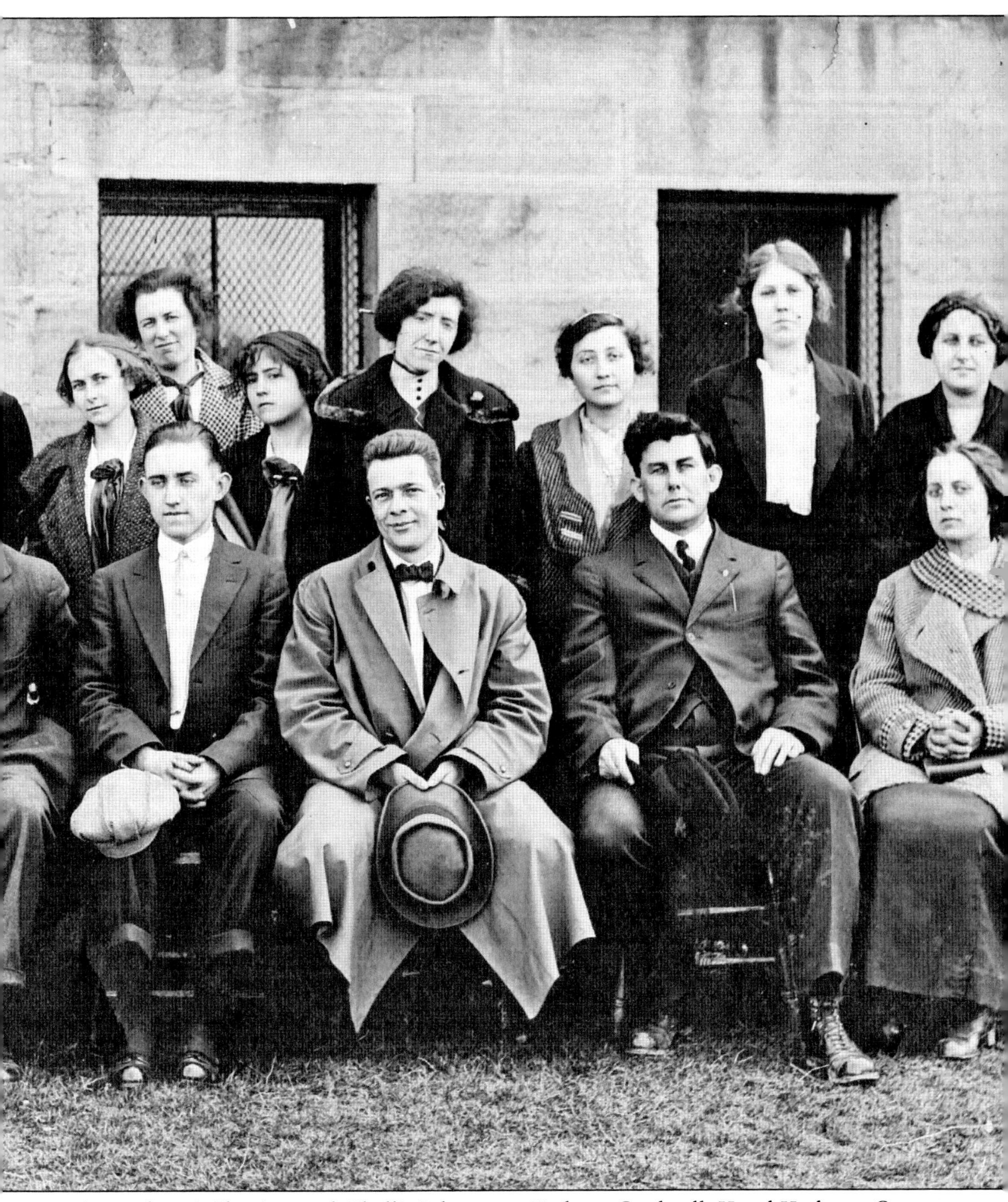

(second row) Elva Anstead, Phyllis Johnstone, Kathryn Cardwell, Hazel Harbour, Garnet Hamm, Stella May Fulton, Nellie Clark, Gertrude Corbin, Hazel Moomaw, Ethel Campbell, Mame Griffith, Carrie Cofer, and Helen Lewis.

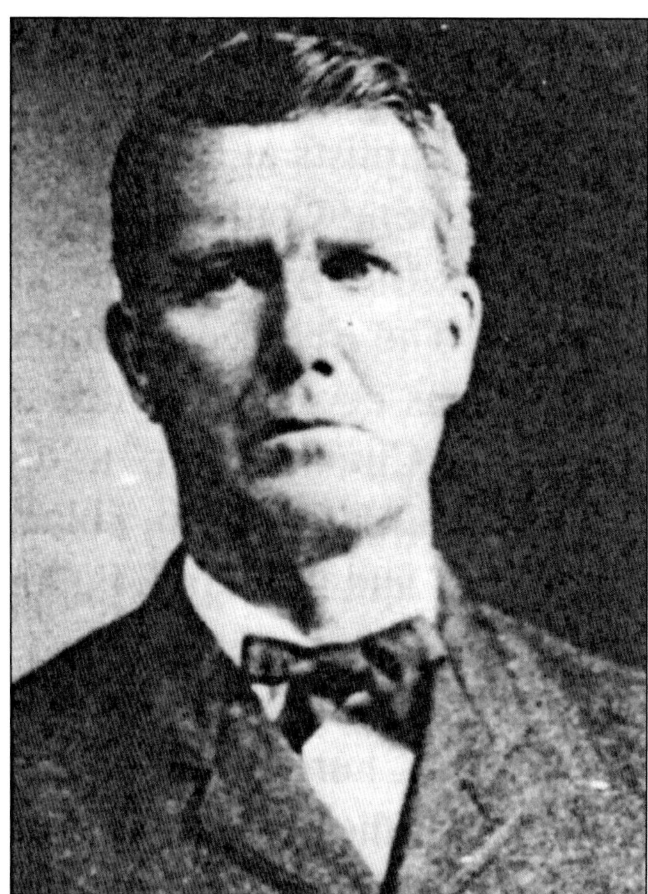

Of the Free Will Baptist ministers with Rio Grande College connections almost back to the beginning, none had longer service than William J. Fulton (1847–1927), who served as a trustee for 50 years, 23 of them as president of the board. He also served many years as pastor of Calvary Baptist Church and other neighboring Free Will Baptist congregations. He also was president of the Vinton Banking Company.

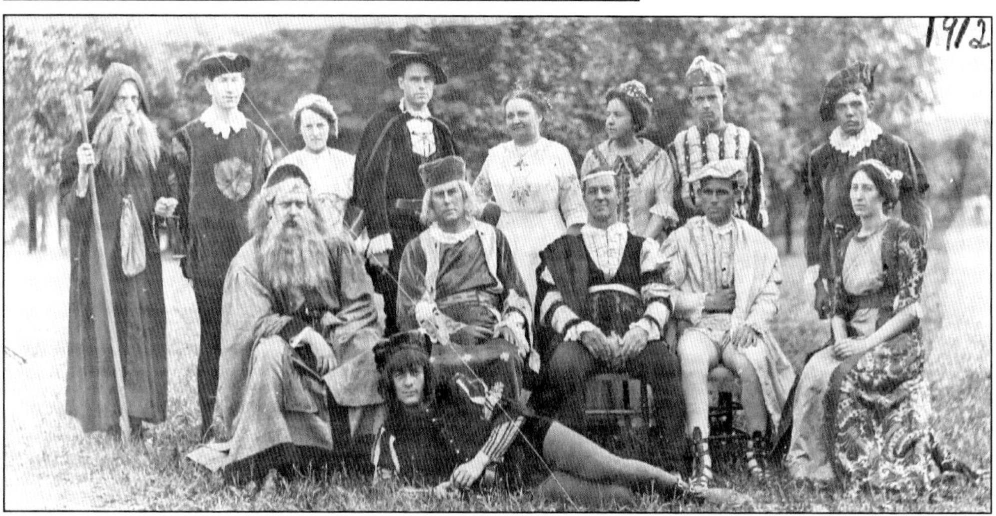

Chestora McDonald Carr directed dramas that were a highlight of the spring term for some 30 years. The June 20, 1912, cast of *The Merchant of Venice* consists of, from left to right, (lying down in front) Rothbe Kirkendall; (first row) Pres. Simeon Bing, William Lewis, Clarence Clark, Oyer Saunders, and Martha Ward; (second row) Merrill Davis, Herman Lewis, Lyrl Clark, Wilber Scarberry, Chestora Carr, Melba Kirkendall, James Collier, and Boyd Davis.

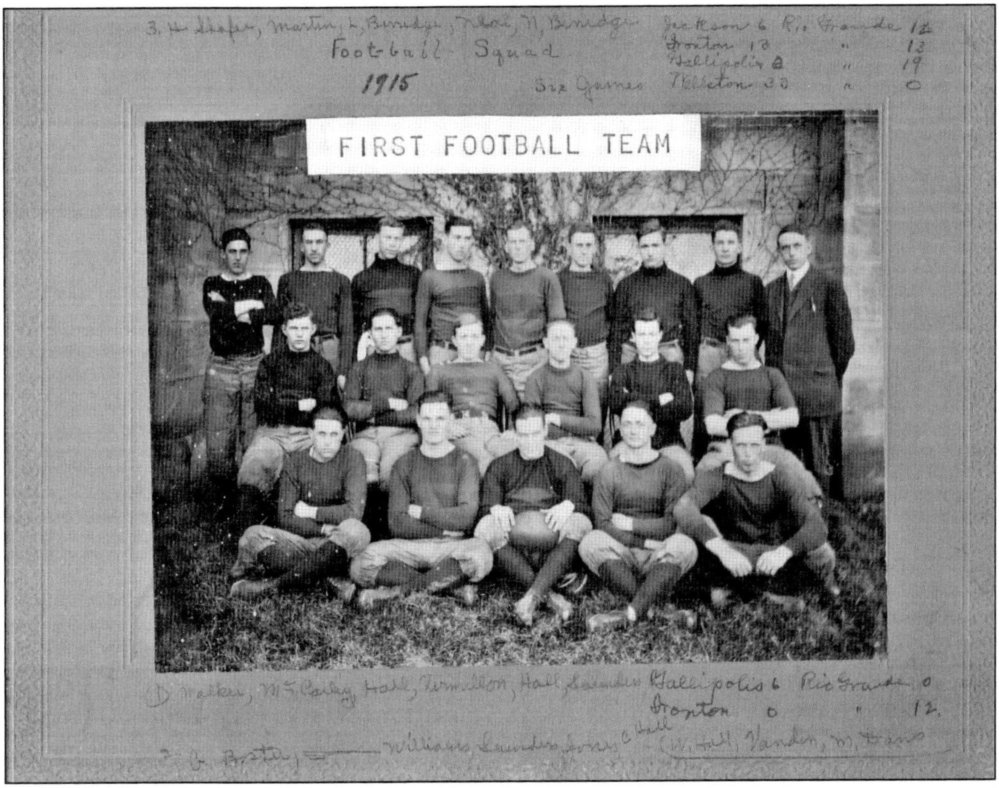

In the fall of 1915, Rio Grande fielded its first football team, compiling a 3-2-1 record. None of the games were with other colleges; Rio Grande played high schools and teams representing their home communities. Rio defeated Jackson, Ironton, and Gallipolis, but lost to Wellston and a second game with Gallipolis. A second Ironton contest ended in a tie.

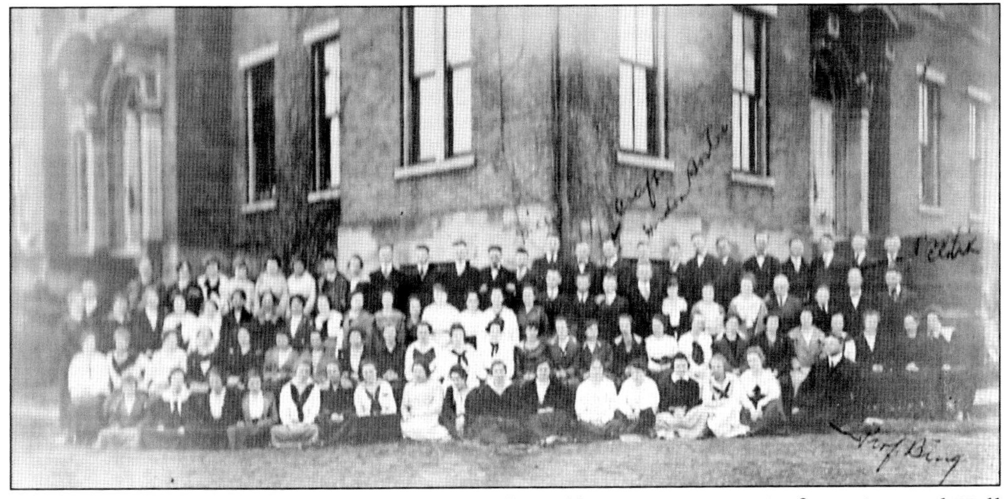

Group photographs of the entire Rio Grande College community in front Atwood Hall were taken frequently in the 1910s, but this one from 1916–1917 is unique in that it displays Atwood Hall at an angle.

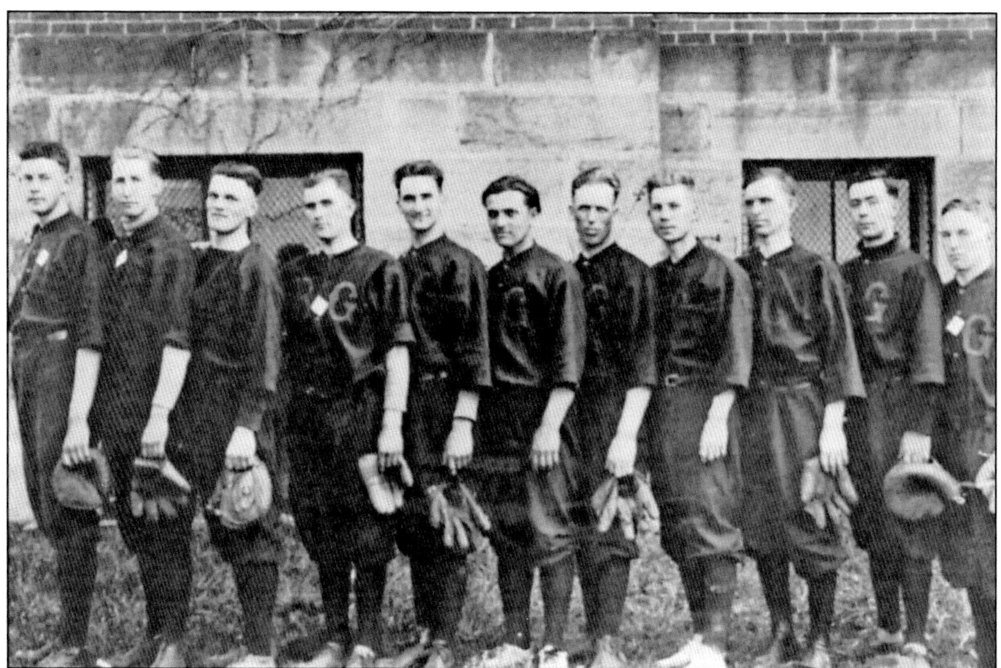

In 1916, eleven players of the "Rio Nine" lined up for this photograph. Clyde Fisher, the star pitcher (far right), later played 15 years as a professional, winning 154 games (21-10 at Buffalo in the International League in 1922), including briefly with the Washington Senators. Other key players included "Kate" Berridge, Ken Vermillion, ? Matthews, and ? Myres.

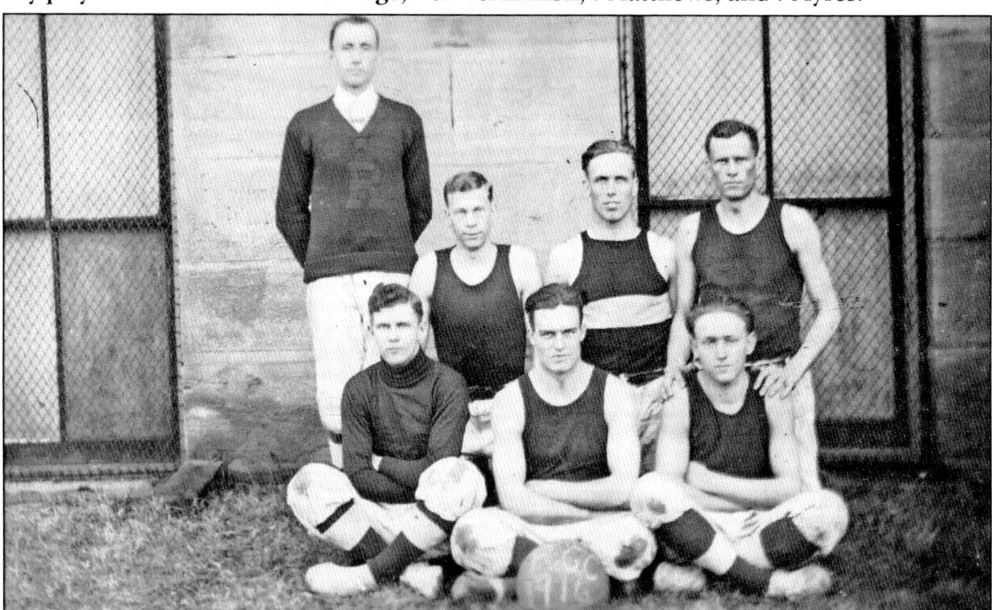

One of the earlier men's basketball teams (1916) is pictured here. From left to right are (first row) Gordon Boster, Lester Berridge, and Clarence Myers; (second row) Earl Craft, Sherman Hall, Cornelius "Kate" Berridge, and Stanley Hall. Opponents tended to be the larger high schools, such as Jackson, Gallia Academy, and Ironton. Compared to recent years, scores were often quite low.

Two

Rio Grande between Fires 1917–1937

Student and president's son Grayum Bing recalled that when the Boarding Hall burned, "there were . . . many people who thought that would be the end of Rio Grande College." Trustees planned two new buildings, but with the United States entering World War I, they scaled back their goal to one structure containing a combined gymnasium/auditorium. Community Hall was dedicated on May 5, 1918. This edifice endured for 60 years. In 1926, classroom building Anniversary Hall (still in use) went up in commemoration of the school's 50th year. In addition, Rio Grande trustees acquired adjacent homes and businesses near the campus green to house students, such as Davis Cottage in 1921 and Varney House in 1935.

While classroom work and academics remained paramount, student activities broadened. Earlier student groups were confined to religious and literary societies, such as the Shakespearian and the Ciceronian, but new ones, such as English, German, and glee clubs, flourished. Baseball and football appeared in 1913, but most opposition tended toward area pickup teams or larger high schools. Rio's first known intercollegiate gridiron contest came in 1916 with a loss to Marshall, but from 1922, it competed with other small colleges. When Paul Lyne became coach, he made Rio Grande football respectable if hardly spectacular. Both men and women had basketball teams, although most opponents were area high schools, with some contests played on outdoor courts.

Horace Houf, a Baptist preacher born in Missouri, became president from 1923 until 1928, during which time the road between Gallipolis and Jackson was paved. A few commuters came to Rio from those locales, as well as from Oak Hill and Vinton. When Houf departed, Eugene Bartlett became president for three years, during which time the school became a de facto junior college, awarding no four-year degrees but only two-year diplomas. Most of the 666 diplomas during the Depression were in elementary education. Bartlett seemed too out of touch for local tastes, and in 1931, Prof. William Lewis became president, serving until 1940. On November 19, 1937, another fire destroyed the venerable Atwood Hall. However, the perennially financially strapped college moved ahead with a newly named "Forward Movement."

RIO GRANDE COLLEGE

REPORT OF TEACHER TO REGISTRAR

Lola M. King (TEACHER) Dec - 21 1916

NAME	Days in Term	Days Present	Days Absent Unexcused	SUBJECT Pub. Sc. M. Hours	Grade	Days in Term	Days Present	Days Absent Unexcused	SUBJECT Hours	Grade	REMARKS
Donnelly - Helen	29	29	0	3	D-						
Gillis, Willard	"	27	1	3	C						
Halley Beryl	"	28	1	3	C+						
Jones Francis	"	29	0	3	D-						
" Lewis	"	20	0	3	B						
" Marie	"	27	1	3	B-						
" Viola	"	29	0	3	a						
Morgan, Mary	"	28	1	3	B+						
Waddell, Ermie	"	24	2	3	a						
				Harmony					History		
Bing, Grayum	29	29	0	3	C-				✓		
Davis Hazel	"	26	1	3	B-	15	15	0	1½	a-	
Kirkendall Melba	"	27	0	3	B+	15	14	0	1½	B+	
Wiseman Flo	"	29	0	3	C+	15	15	0	1½	C+	

Faculty grade reports in 1916 were submitted to the registrar on this type of form. In addition to several students with Welsh surnames, two others are notable: Beryl Halley, who later performed on Broadway with the *Ziegfeld Follies*, and Grayum Bing, son of Pres. Simeon Bing. No grade inflation or favoritism is apparent.

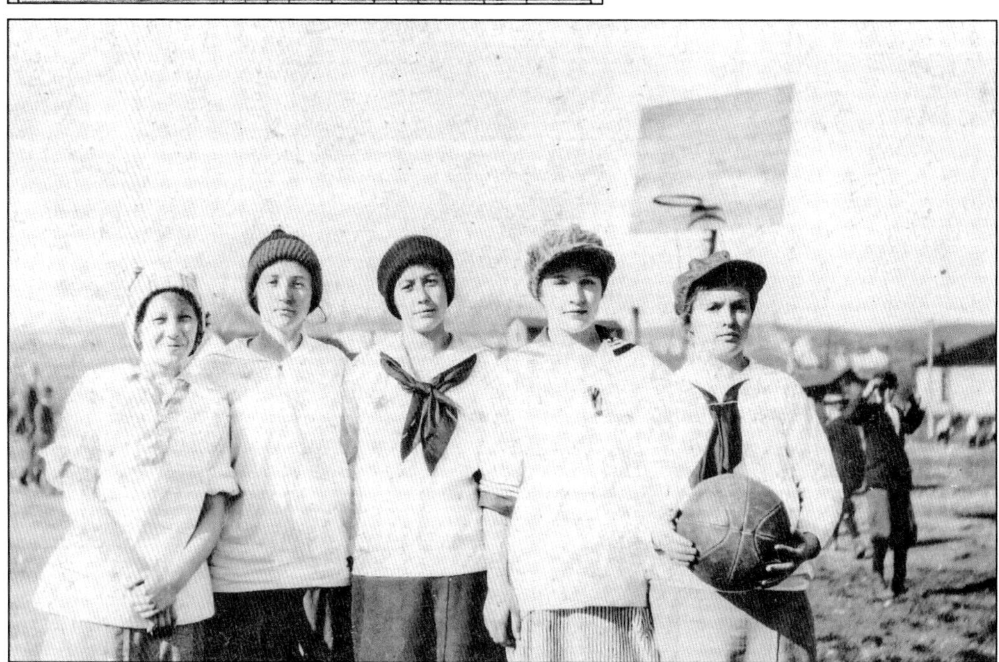

Prior to the building of Community Hall, Rio Grande College basketball teams of both sexes played many of their games on outdoor courts. This image of five female players shows the backboard and hoop in the upper right background. Only when indoor hard floors became common did dribbling become a necessary skill.

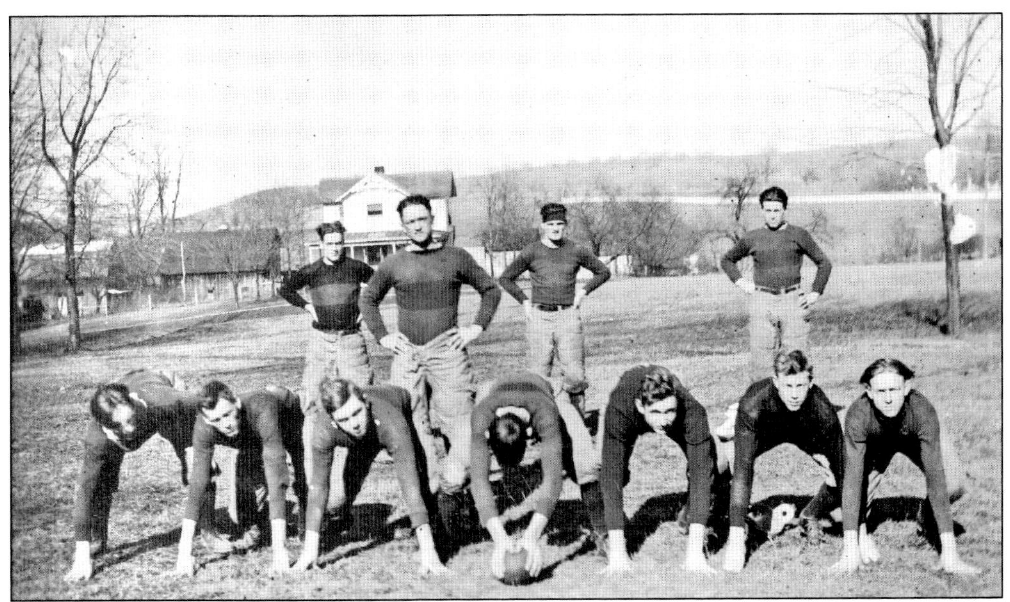

In the fall of 1916, the Rio Grande College gridiron squad lines up in formation for practice. The center is ready to hike the ball to one of the foursome in the backfield. The guards, tackles, and ends are in position ready to move forward. In the upper right, the Calvary Baptist Church and adjoining cemetery can be seen in the distance.

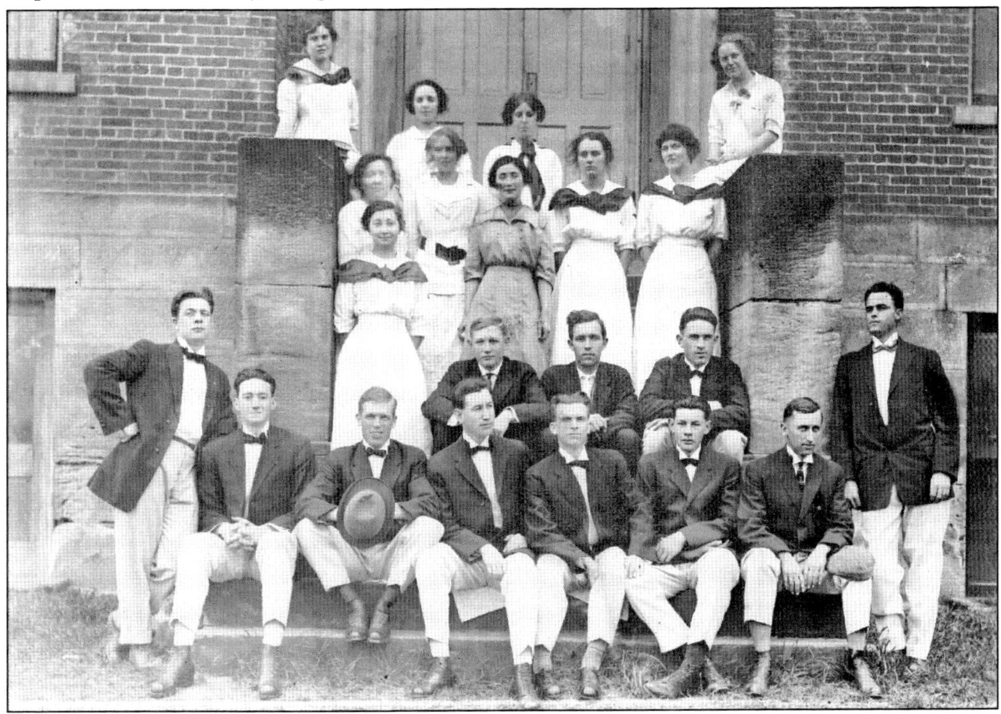

The women's glee club would sometimes join with the men's chorus for performances. Classic selections, college glees, solos, comic stunts, and quartets were performed. Sometimes, a reel of a moving picture might be shown. Admission would be a dime or 20¢. This photograph is rare in that it shows both groups together.

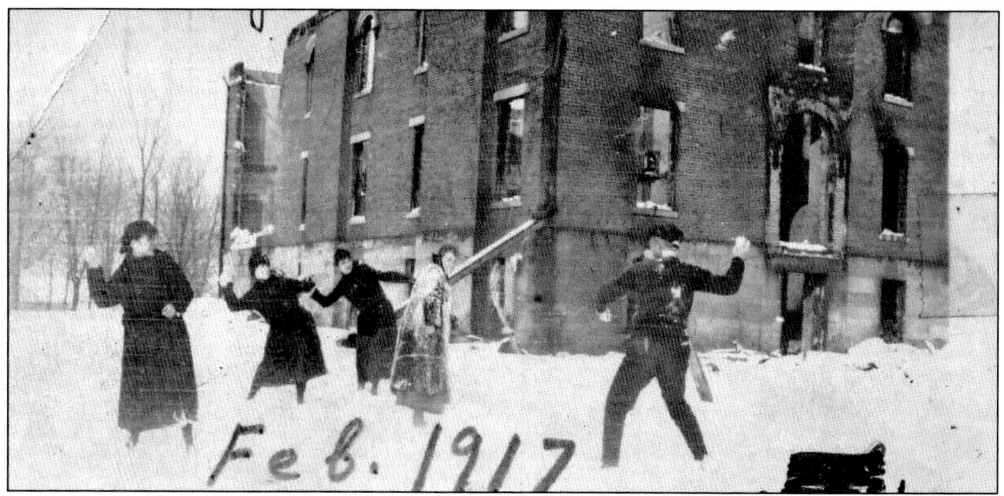

Despite the disastrous fire that destroyed the Boarding Hall in February 1917, Rio Grande College students could still engage in an old-fashioned snowball fight. This one appears to feature a battle of the sexes. The stark still-standing walls of the burned-out Boarding Hall can be seen in the background.

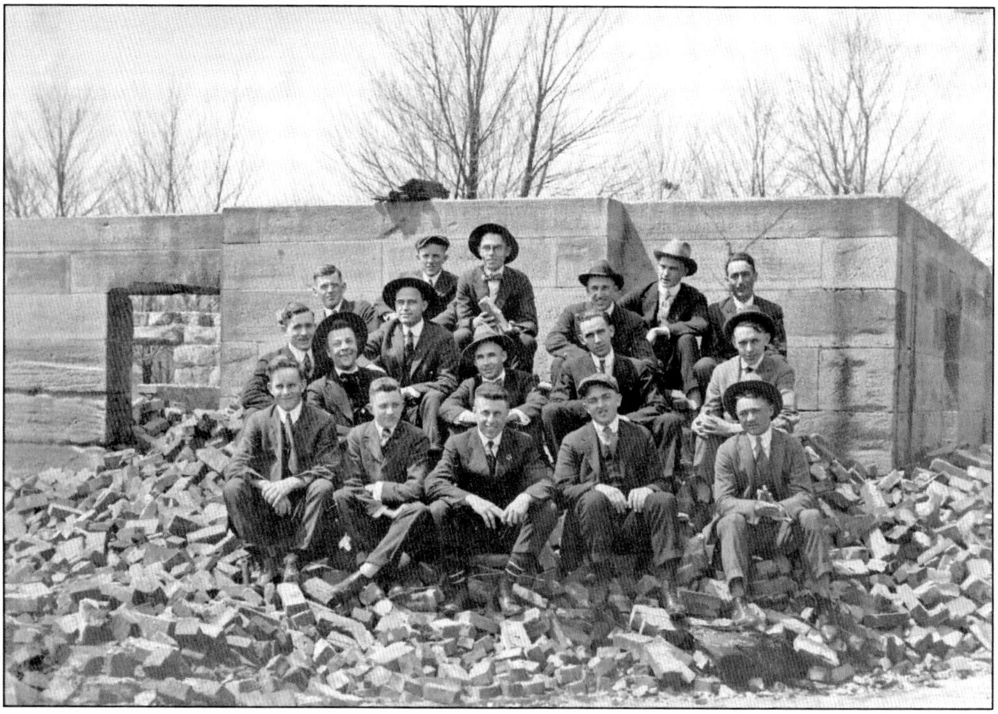

The Rio Grande College Men's Glee Club poses for this picture on the ruins of the burned Boarding Hall after the snow melted. Pictured are (not in order) Gus Boster, Ira Topping, Irvin McCarley, Stephen Darby, Elmer Mossbarger, William Hal, Rothbe Kirkendall, Wilbur Scarberry, Phil Wagner, Charles Weed, Merrill Davis, Orin Davis, Phil Evans, Don Allen, Hayden Shaffer, Knox Williams, and Stanley Neal.

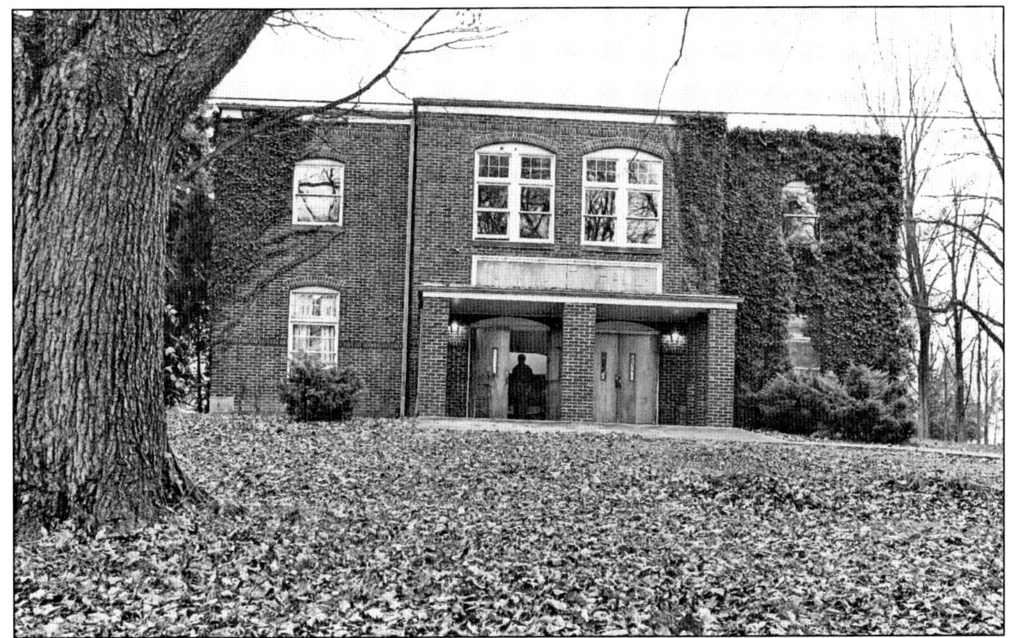

Community Hall was completed and dedicated on May 5, 1918, on the former site of the recently burned Boarding Hall (with some bricks from the original recycled). It served a useful purpose for 60 years as the scene of many community celebrations, plays, musicals, and basketball games. The latter included Bevo Francis's 116-point scoring marathon against Ashland Junior College from Kentucky.

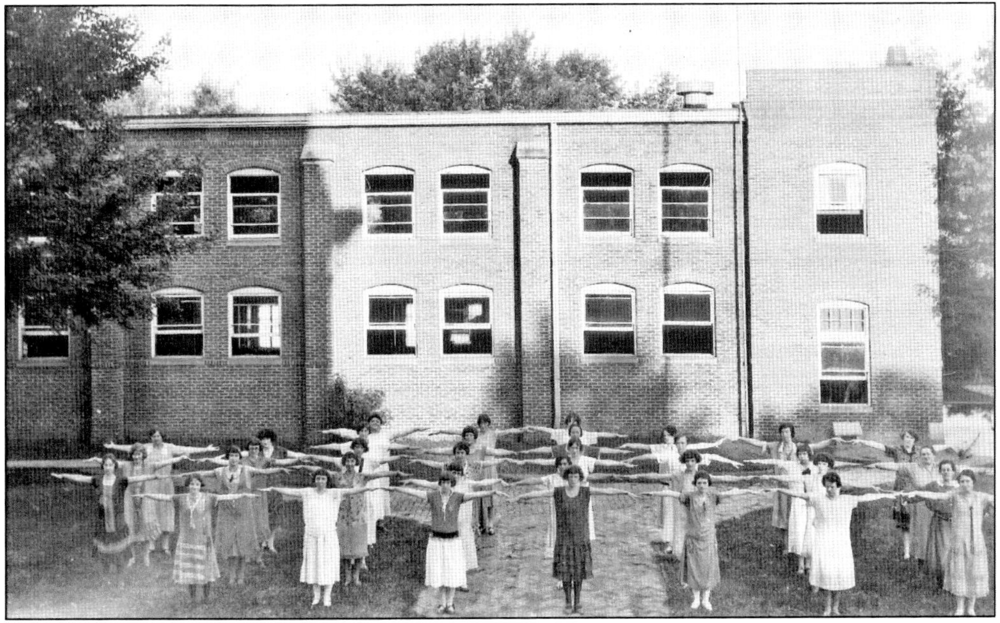

Physical education classes for girls eventually became commonplace at numerous colleges and universities in the early 20th century. This 1919 exercise class picture shows a number of young ladies on the college green with the side of the newly completed Community Hall in the background.

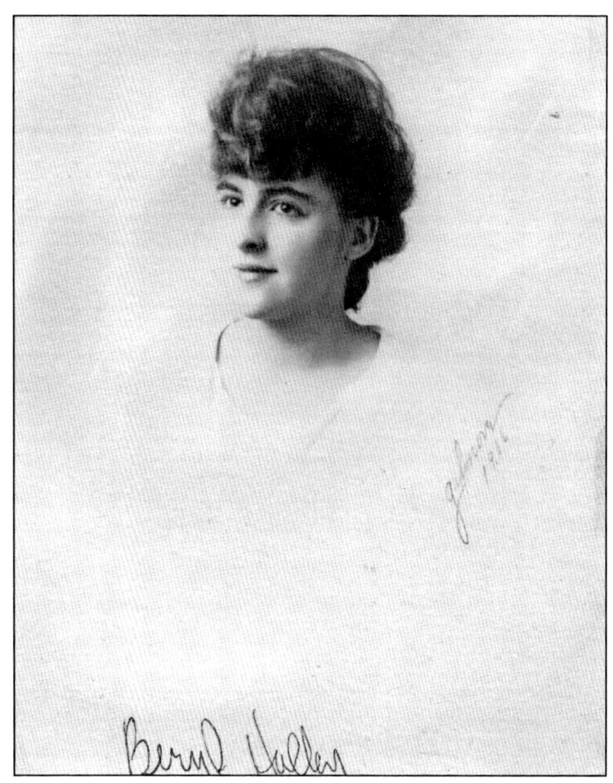

Beryl Halley (1897–1988), a Rio Grande College student in 1916, later became one of the first women to enlist in the US Navy and appeared in the *Ziegfeld Follies* for three seasons (1923–1925), *Earl Carroll's Vanities* (1926), the musicals *Half a Widow* (1927) and *Tangerine* (1921–1922), and the silent motion picture *The Broadway Boob* (1926). *Tangerine* was a hit that starred Jackson County native Frank Crumit and his future wife, Julia Sanderson.

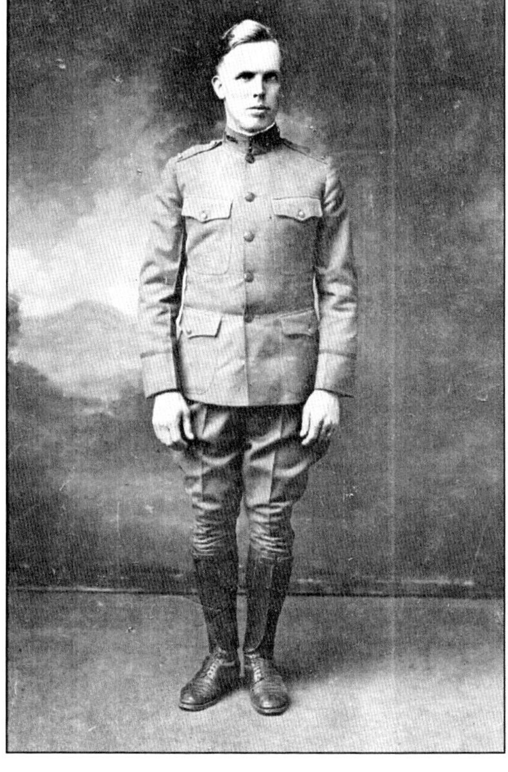

Cornelius Kinder "Kate" Berridge (class of 1916) ranked as a highly significant figure during his student days. As an athlete, he played on the baseball, basketball, and football teams, and he held a part-time position as librarian and served a term as class president. Following graduation, Berridge entered the Army in World War I, rising to the rank of captain.

In 1923, William K. Wilson (1888–1964, right) of the class of 1920 composed "The Red and White," which became the Rio Grande College alma mater. At the time, Wilson served the Rutland, Ohio, school system as superintendent. In recent years, only the chorus is played at commencement exercises at the University of Rio Grande.

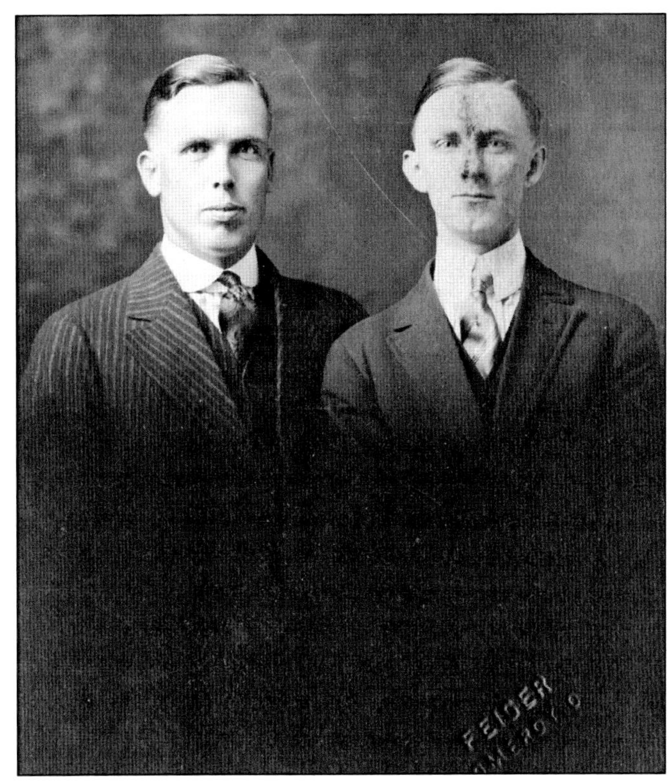

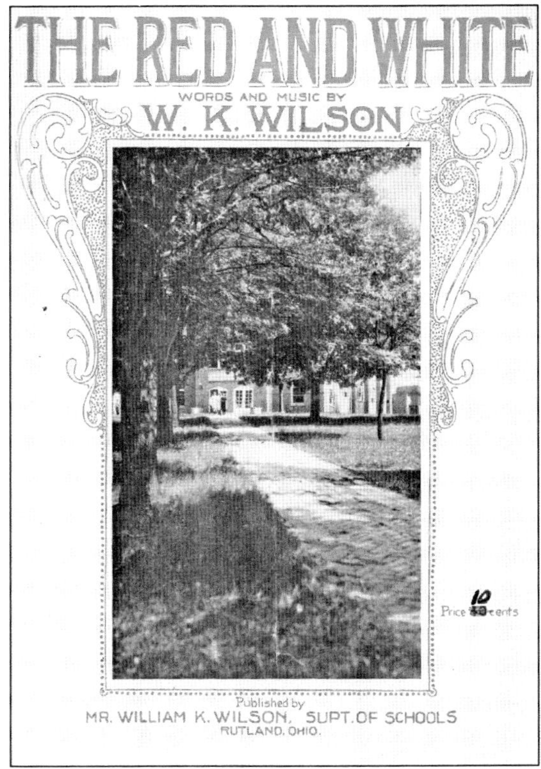

The chorus of "The Red and White" goes: "Then here's to Old Rio, the Red and the White / Stand up and cheer, boys, she stands for all that's right / Long may she prosper, and guide us on our way / Oh! Let us cherish her forever and for aye / Rio, Rio, Rio Grande, to thee we pledge our heart, our hand / And pray that we may understand, and to our pledge be true."

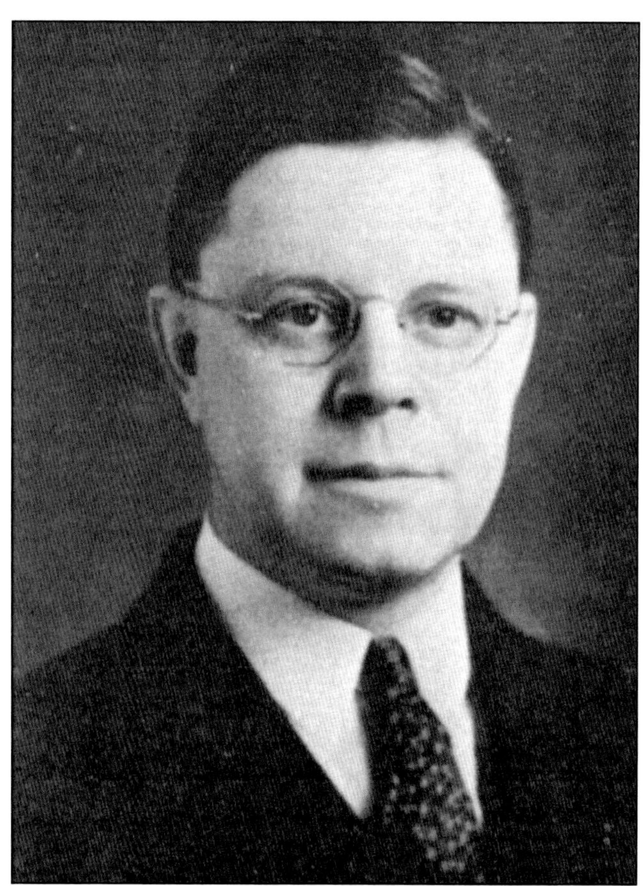

Horace Houf (1889–1959), a native of Missouri and an ordained Baptist minister, served as president of Rio Grande from 1923 to 1928. Paved roads finally reached Rio Grande in his first year at the helm. After leaving, Houf taught philosophy and religion at Ohio University for many years and authored a popular textbook entitled *What Religion Is and Does*.

In 1921, the Rio Grande Board of Trustees purchased the large home of the late president and professor John Merrill Davis and turned it into a small dorm for about 25 girls. Those who lived there often formed lasting friendships. After 1957, the completion of Davis Hall ended its use as a dorm, and it became faculty and staff apartments until it was razed to build a new presidential home.

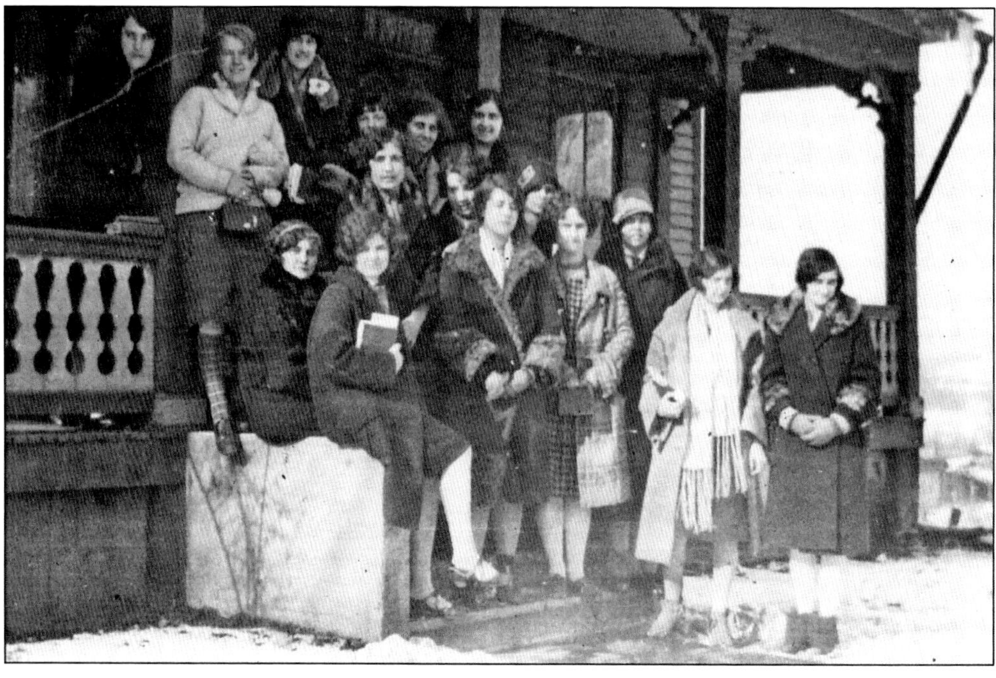

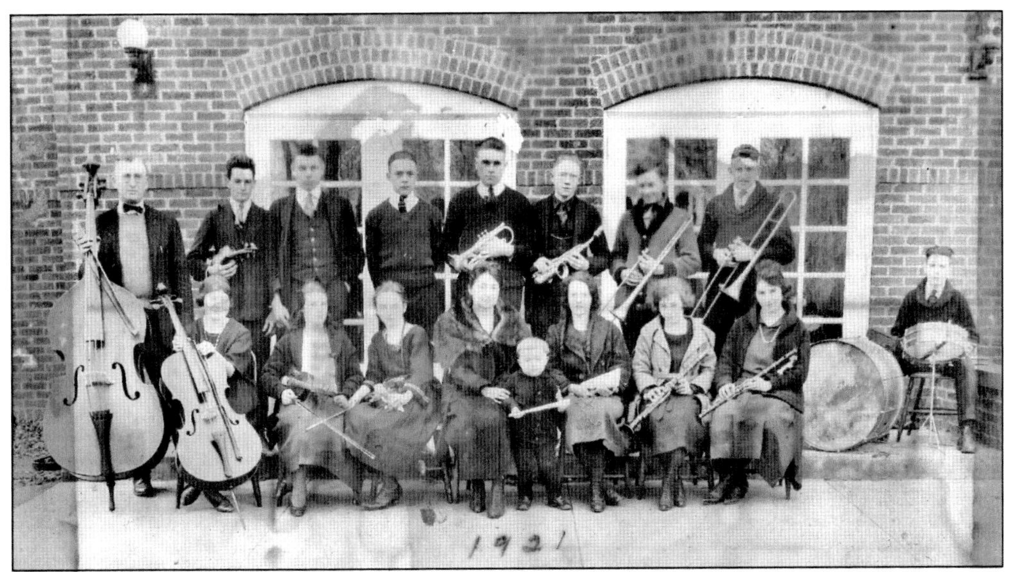

The Rio Grande College Band in 1921 consists of, from left to right, (first row) Amy Griffith, Corin Clark, Mae Bethel, Mrs. Cooperrider, infant Cooperrider, Lola King Cooperrider, Marsha Bing, and Carrie Hutchinson Dale; (second row) Luke Cooperrider, John Miles Evans, R.P. Ewing, Grayum Bing, Hollis Ewing, John Howell, Willard Lewis, Oyer Donovan Allen, and Earl Rosser (on drums).

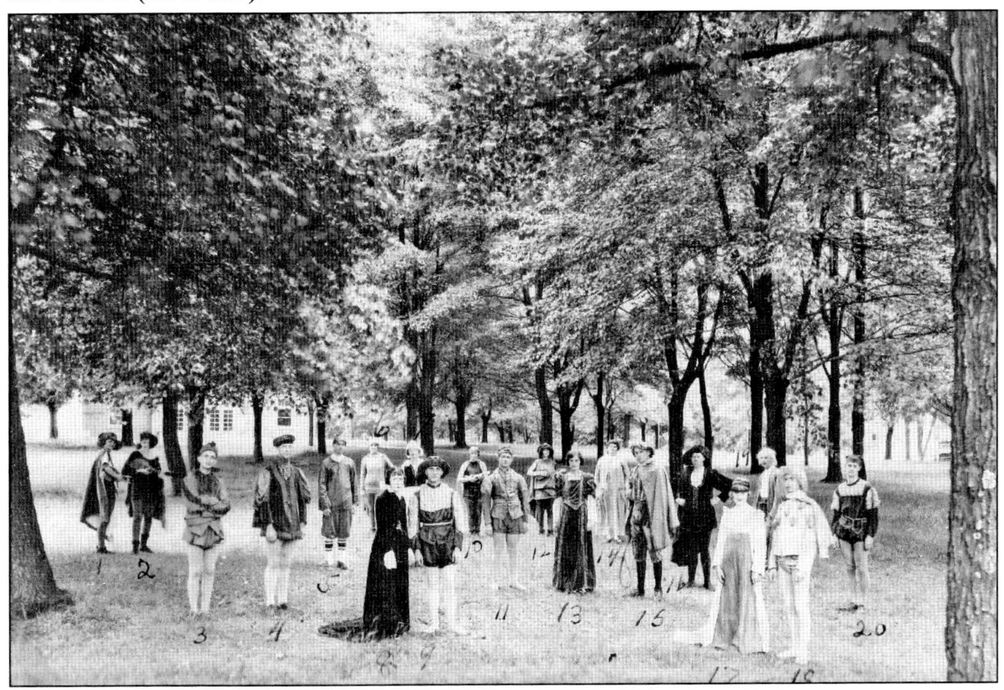

Chestora Carr's 1922 *Taming of the Shrew* cast includes, from left to right, 1. Claire Dwyer, 2. Ruth Warren, 3. unidentified, 4. Elder Warren, 5. unidentified, 6. Chloe Davidson (in rear), 7. Dorothy ? (in rear), 8. Thelma Lewis, 9–13. unidentified, 14. director Carr, 15. Hollis Ewing, 16. Cecil Hankins, 17. Maridel Davidson, 18. Roland Will, 19. Charles Mossman, and 20. unidentified.

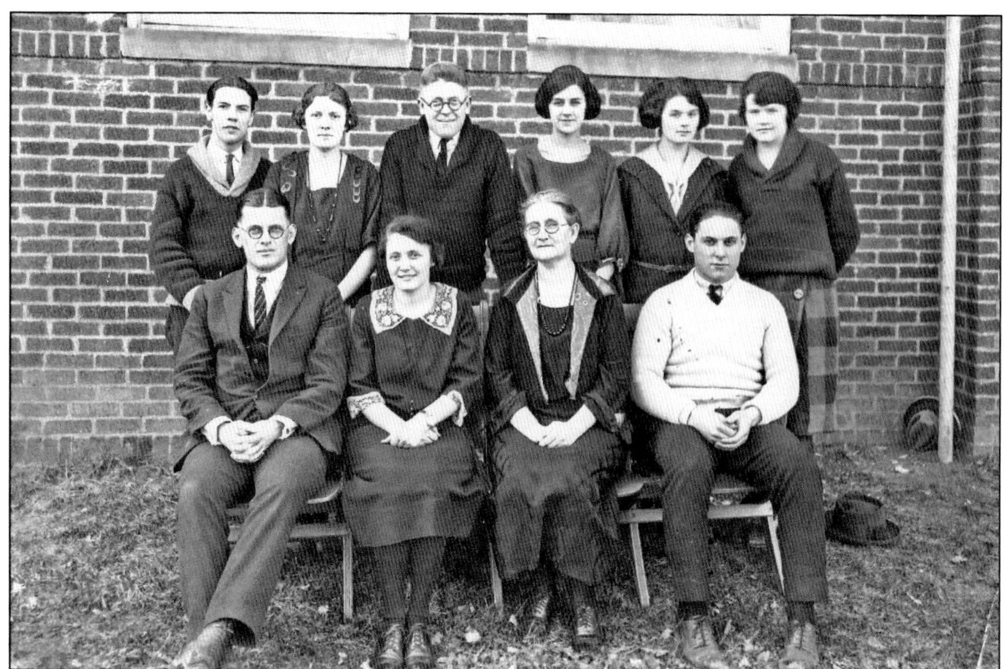

The *Grandion* yearbook first came out in 1915 and has become an important source for students of the institution's history. In 1923, the staff consists of, from left to right, (first row) Orin Davis, Helen Knight, Stella May Fulton (faculty advisor), and Raymond Allison; (second row) Earl Rosser, Elta Hall, David Crow, Thelma Lewis, Dolly Waugh, and Marianna Bing.

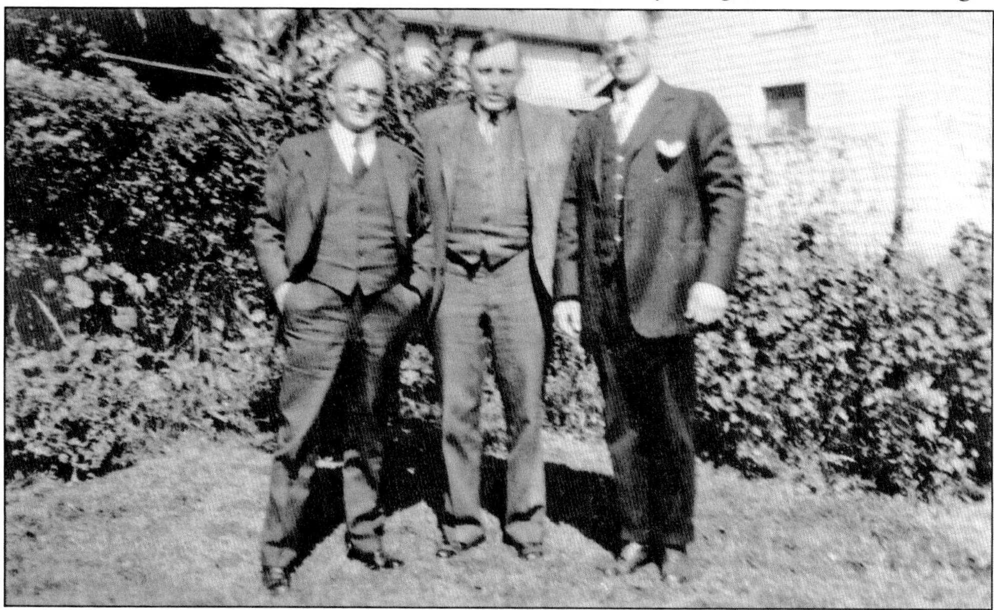

The offspring of Rio Grande College presidents were often treated with special respect, almost like royalty. This image shows, from left to right, Hugh Moulton, J. Boyd Davis, and Hal Moulton. Other presidential children who visited Rio Grande in later years included Gertrude Moulton (who held a faculty position at one time), the oft-quoted Ernest Grayum Bing, and W. Merrill Davis.

The earliest known photograph of Rio Grande cheerleaders is from the 1922–1923 season; the team consists of Maxine "Maxie" Fowler (class of 1927) and Earle Rosser. The latter also served as athletic editor of the *Grandion* that year but is not known to have completed a degree. The photograph is also a good image of the long-vanished water fountain situated between Atwood Hall and Community Hall.

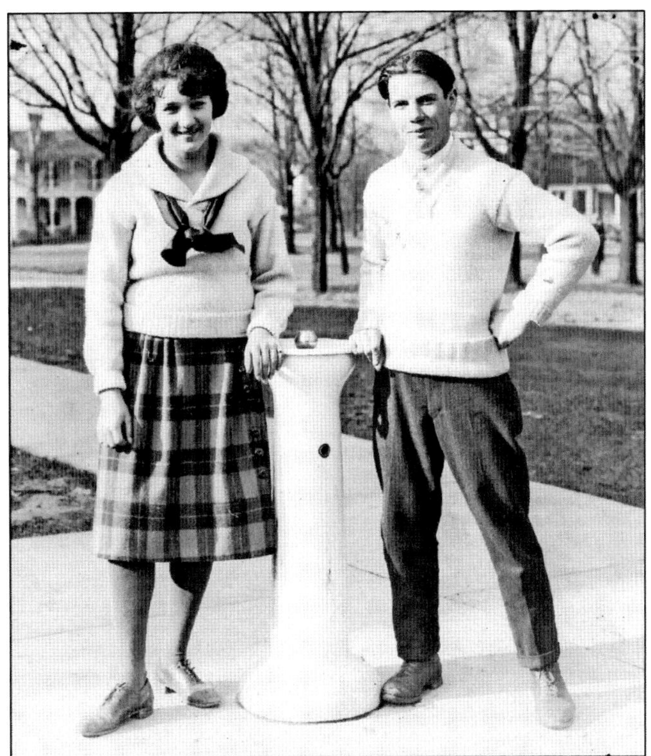

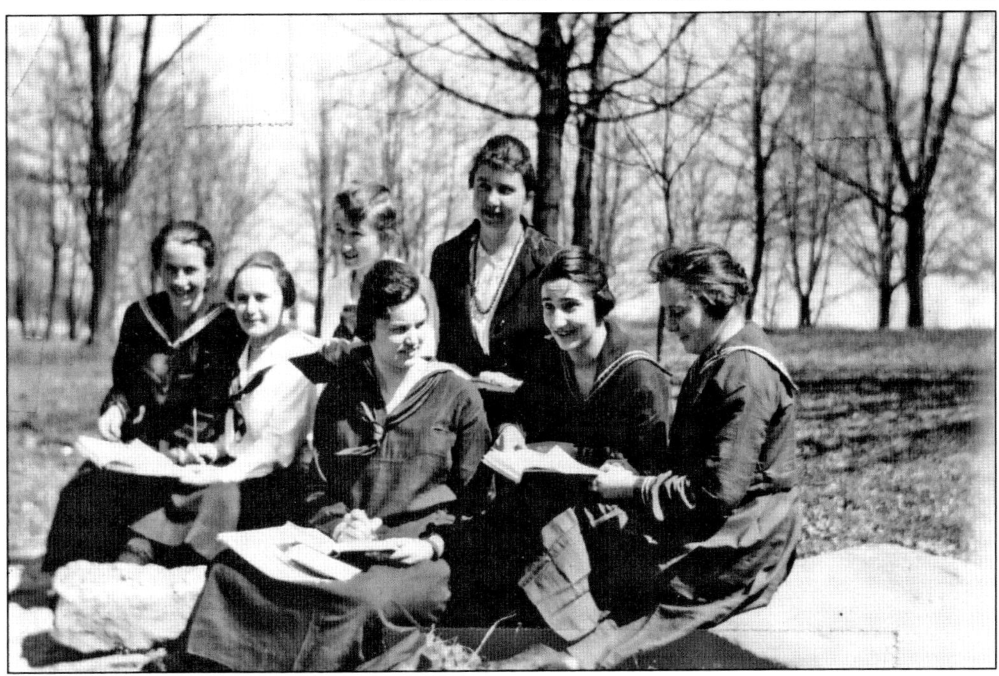

These students appear to be engaging in an outdoor study session in the early 1920s. From left to right are Margaret Noel, Bessie Rees, Mamie Allen, Fleeta Fulks (class of 1923), Pearl Carter (class of 1924), and Genevieve Williams (class of 1925). The subject of their intense study is unidentified. Outdoor sessions of this type continue as long as the weather cooperates.

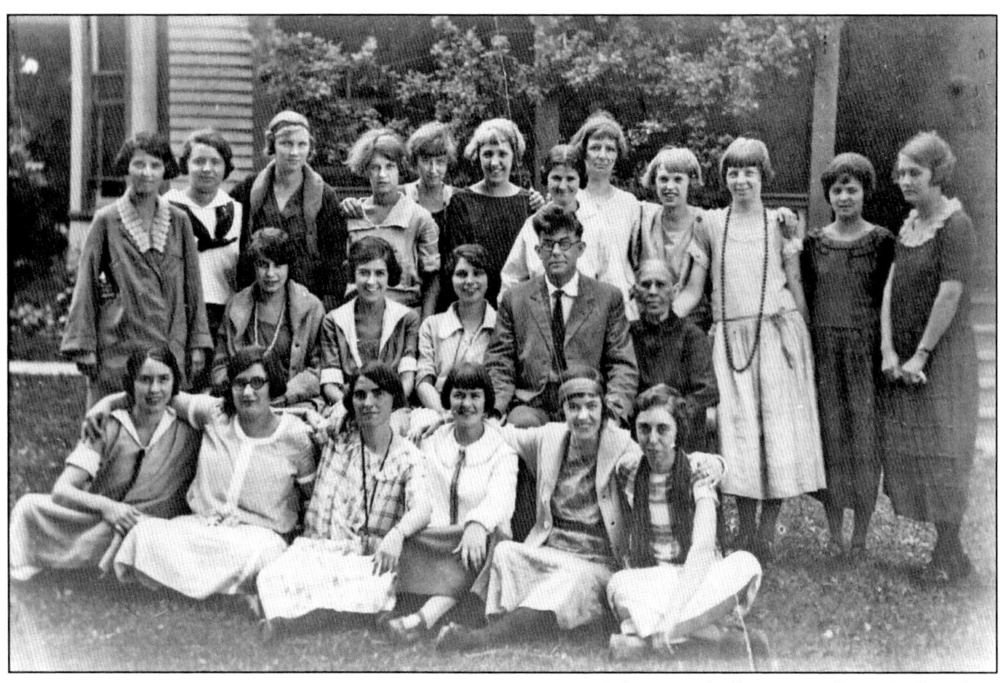

This 1924 photograph includes the residents of Davis Cottage—which had served as a dorm for three years—on the top and bottom rows. Seated in the middle row are unidentified, Thelma Lewis (class of 1923, daughter of William A. Lewis), Mary Lewis (second wife of William A. Lewis), Dean William A. Lewis, and Rachel Scarberry Lewis.

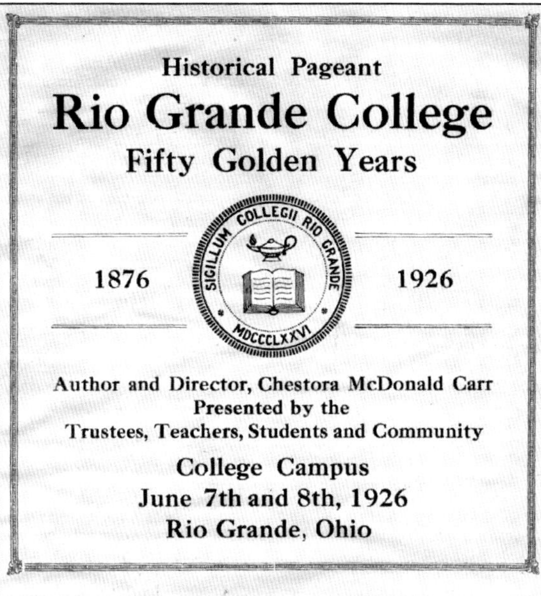

Historical Pageant

Rio Grande College

Fifty Golden Years

1876 1926

Author and Director, Chestora McDonald Carr
Presented by the
Trustees, Teachers, Students and Community

College Campus
June 7th and 8th, 1926
Rio Grande, Ohio

"The Pageant stands for the living picture which unfolds the history of a community."

PURPOSE

To celebrate the Golden Anniversary of our College, in recognition of her service and influence in the community.

To pay tribute to the memory of the men and women who built their lives and sterling virtues into an institution of learning that is one of the educational and spiritual power plants of our state.

PAGEANT OFFICERS

General Chairman—Horace T. Houf.
Business—Perry D. Woods.
Lighting and Grounds—David Wickline, Francis Goetting.
Music—Miss Helen C. Bowles.
Band—James T. Lewis.
Publicity—A. G. Albin, R. C. McMillan, H. T. Houf.
Costumer—Mrs. W. A. Lewis.
Prologue—Paul Hayman.
Heralds—Everett Lewis, Earl Stapf, Lucille Higgins.
Flower Girls—Dorothy Davis, leader; Militia Mae Wickline, Roberta Bullard, Jeane Houf, Jane McMillan, Wilda Jones, Myrtle Wickline.
College Colors—Red and White.

On June 7 and 8, 1926, Chestora McDonald Carr presented a pageant for Rio's 50th anniversary. A series of historic episodes ranged from "The Forest Primeval" to "Dedication of the College." Among noted guests were Ira Jacobs (class of 1883) of Vinton and Nehemiah Atwood Haning (class of 1892) of Wheeling, West Virginia. Carr taught elocution and drama for over 30 years, but only in the spring.

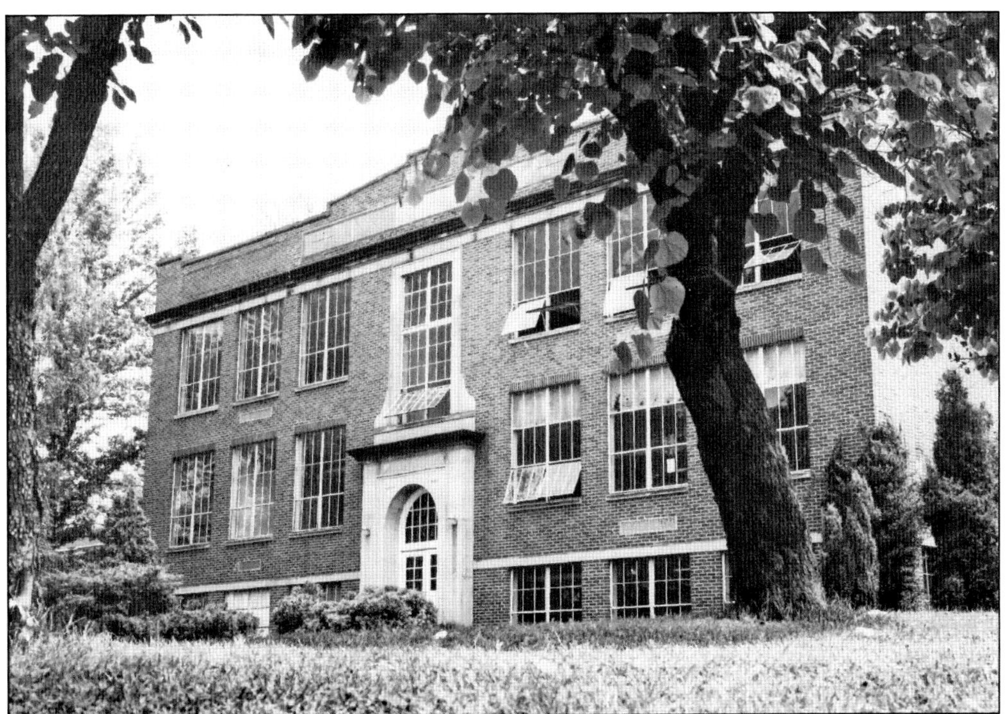

The construction of Anniversary Hall began in 1926 as part of Rio Grande College's 50-year celebration. It gave the college three brick buildings on the college green and has been a key classroom building throughout nine decades. The oldest structure still in use as of 2016, it has all the radiant architectural style of elementary schools built in that era.

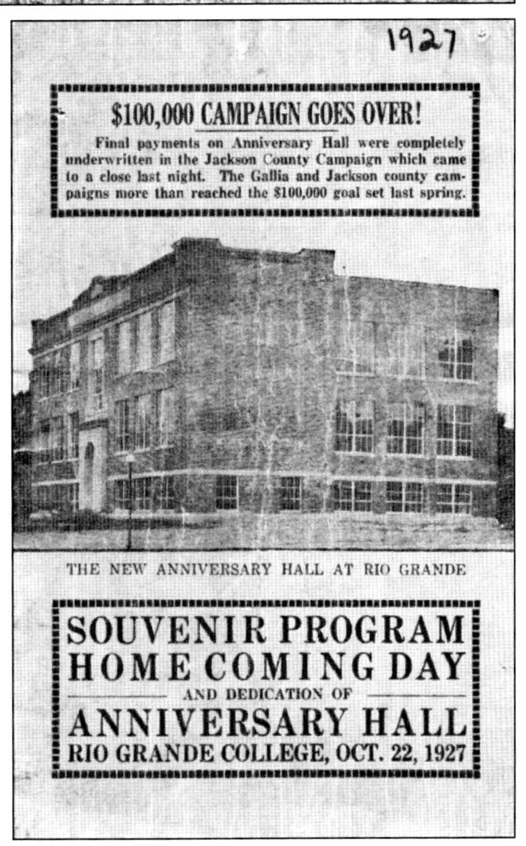

1927

$100,000 CAMPAIGN GOES OVER!

Final payments on Anniversary Hall were completely underwritten in the Jackson County Campaign which came to a close last night. The Gallia and Jackson county campaigns more than reached the $100,000 goal set last spring.

THE NEW ANNIVERSARY HALL AT RIO GRANDE

SOUVENIR PROGRAM
HOME COMING DAY
AND DEDICATION OF
ANNIVERSARY HALL
RIO GRANDE COLLEGE, OCT. 22, 1927

In recent years, colleges and universities regularly hold multi-million-dollar fund drives. But for Rio Grande College in the mid-1920s, $100,000 was a huge, previously unheard-of amount. The goal was used to build Anniversary Hall. The drive succeeded, and the building was begun in 1926 and dedicated on October 22, 1927, as shown on this homecoming program.

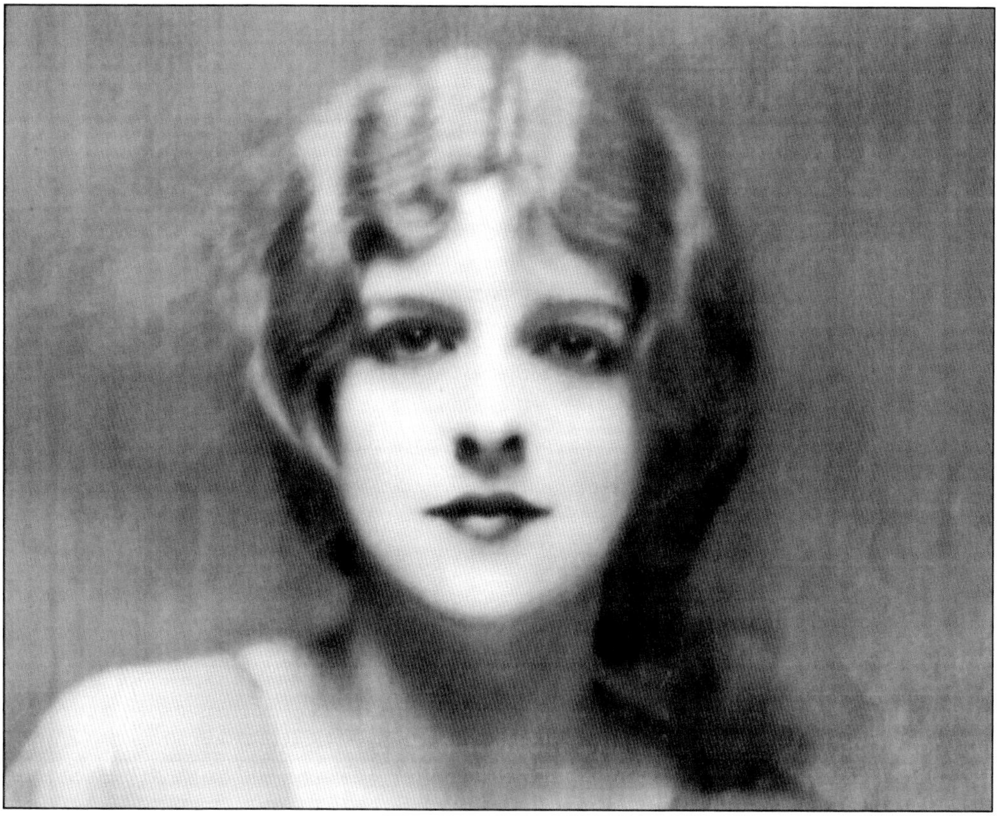

Former Rio Grande College student Beryl Halley, both during and after her Broadway days, was a hot item in New York gossip columns, where she was billed as "the girl with the most perfect figure in the world," portraying Eve in the Garden of Eden in a *Ziegfeld* scene "wearing nothing but a leaf." Though arrested, she established her innocence in court, because she "was not [completely] nude." A headline read "Fig Leaf Wins."

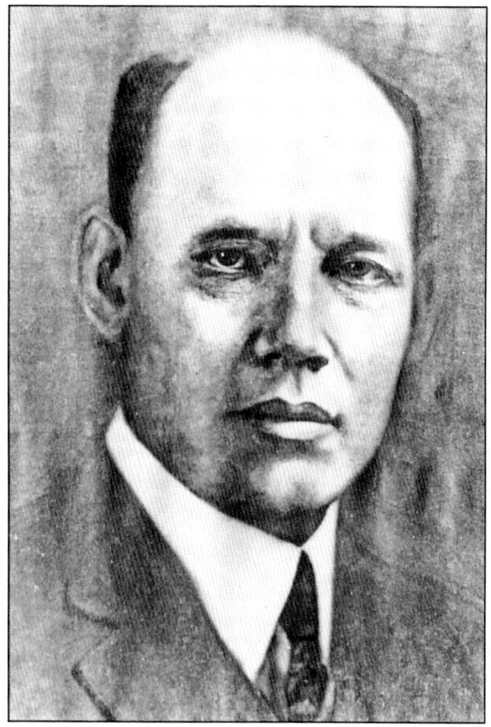

Willard Bartlett (1884–1970) was president of Rio Grande College from 1928 to 1931. At the time, the junior college movement was popular, and Bartlett turned the school into a de facto junior college. Between tendencies to overspend and to modernize too fast, he courted unpopularity in local quarters and resigned. Later, Bartlett had more success as president of Otterbein College in Westerville.

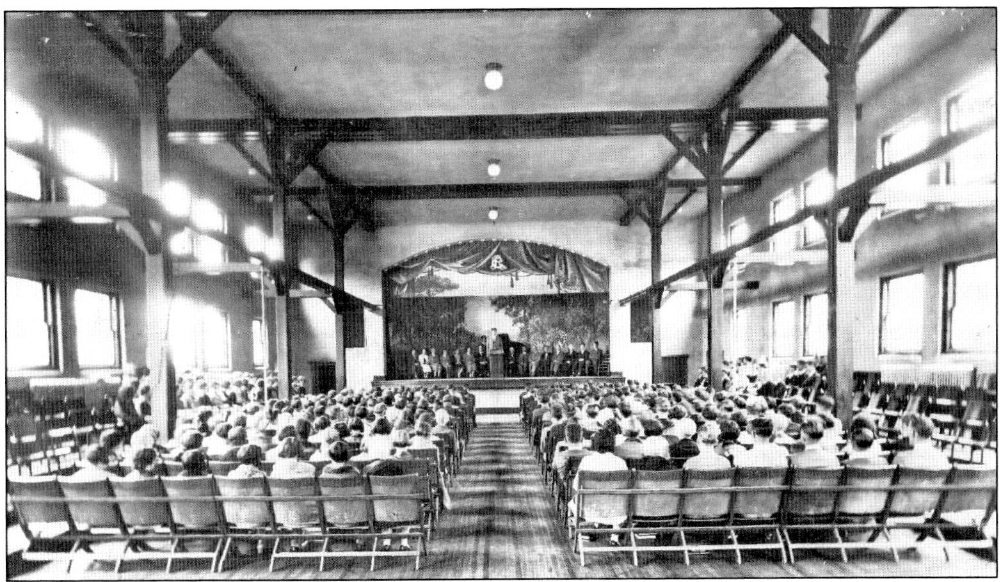

Chapel was a regular occurrence at Rio Grande College for many decades. This image, dated 1925 on the front and 1927–1928 on the reverse, depicts such a service in Community Hall. The students are seated facing the stage, occupied by the faculty and staff. The venerable dean William A. Lewis presides.

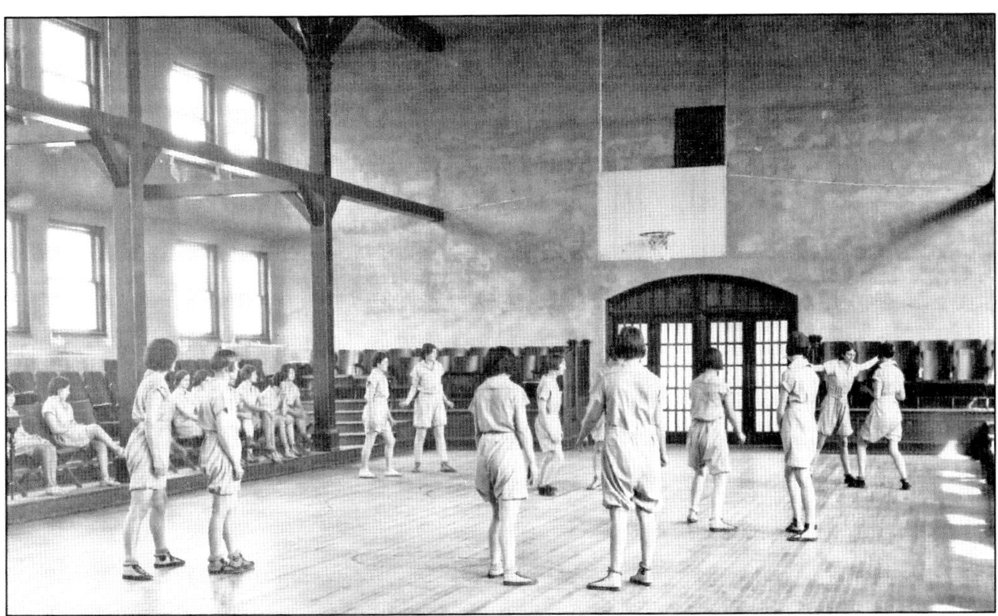

This photograph, taken from the stage in Community Hall in 1929, shows a girls' physical education class where a basketball game is in progress. This shot not only captures the hardwood floor but also offers panoramic view of the gymnasium, which a quarter century later had the less glamorous nickname of "the Hog Pen."

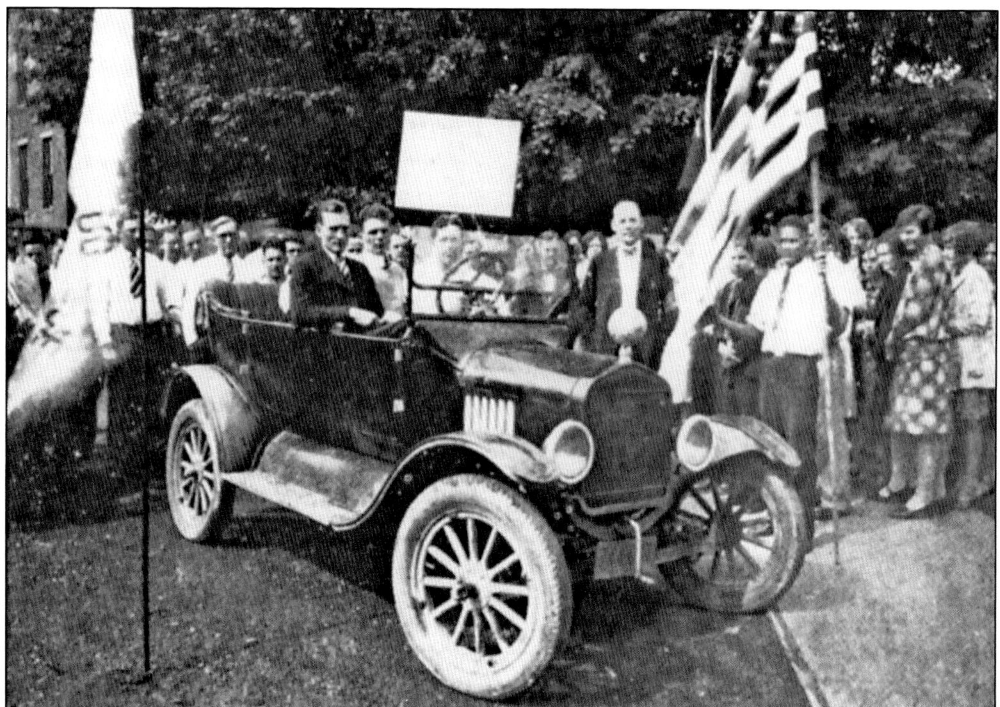

On July 2, 1929, three Rio Grande students, Ralph Brown, Elbert Oder, and Fred Hamrick, embarked on a round-the-world trip. After the three went to San Francisco by car, President Bartlett arranged for them to work as deckhands on the Dollar Lines ship *President Van Buren*. Their trip took them through both the Suez and Panama Canals and back to San Francisco, and they returned to Ohio in November.

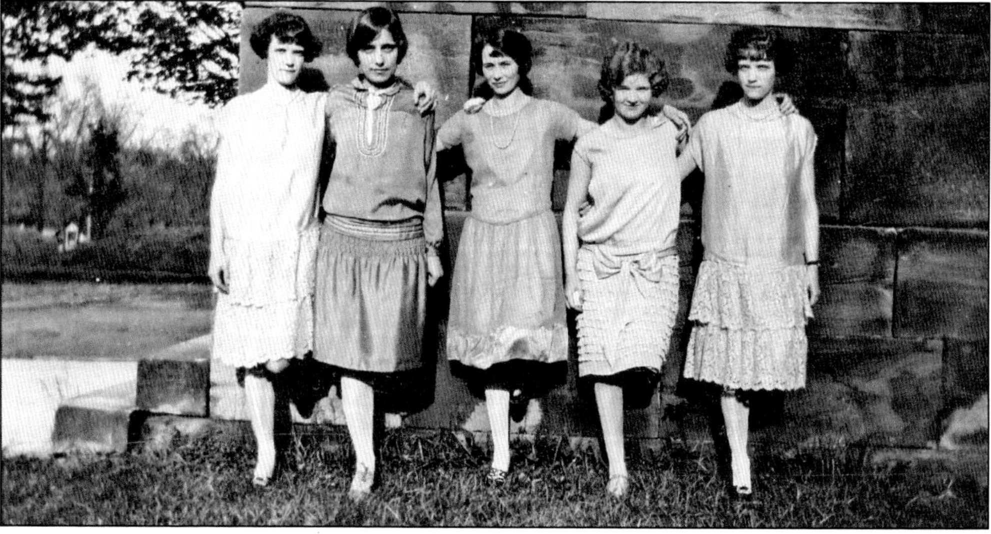

These five Rio girls pose for a photograph in the late 1920s. From left to right are twins Margaret and Marjorie Blazer, Mary Waldron, Marie Hopper, and Gertrude Hannon. Margaret completed her four-year degree in 1929. Incomplete evidence suggests that the others did not graduate and may have been in the high school, which occupied the same buildings until 1930.

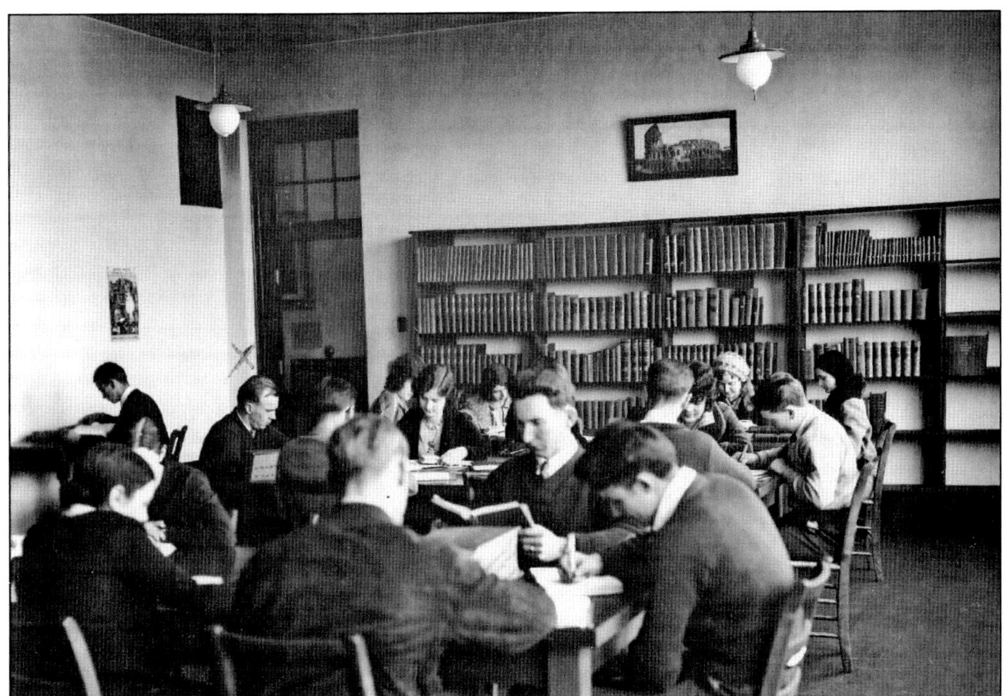

Prior to the construction of the Jeanette Albiez Davis Library in 1965, the small library was often housed in cramped quarters in various locales around campus, including the top floor of Atwood Hall. By the spring of 1930, it was housed in a room in Anniversary Hall. One cannot help but wonder if these students are really studying or if this is a posed picture.

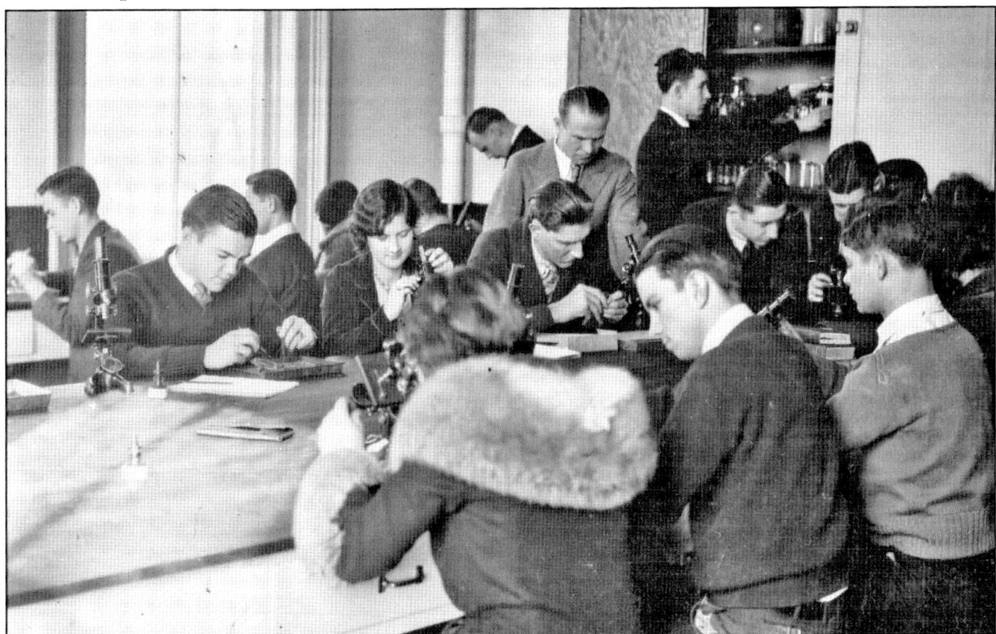

This 1930 biology lab at Rio Grande College, under the charge of instructor J. Dewey Spooner, is seen apparently dissecting specimens, probably frogs. Professor Spooner also taught physical education and coached the football teams in 1930 and 1931.

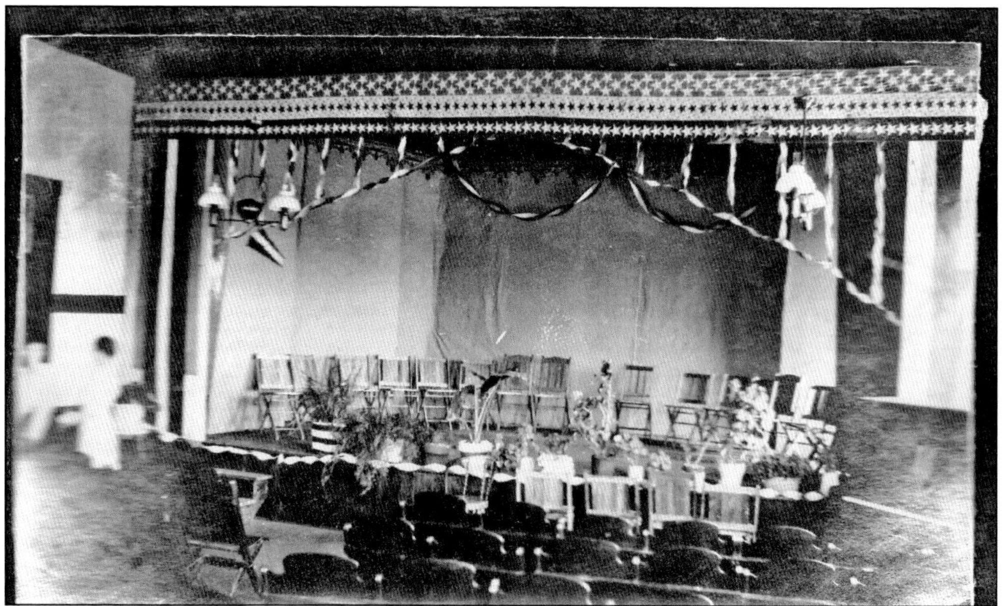

Prior to the building of Community Hall in 1918, the top floor of Atwood Hall served as the Rio Grande College auditorium. Chapel services, dramatic and musical programs, and commencements all took place there, as well as the funerals of Ira Z. Haning and Permelia Atwood. For some years (c. 1918–1927), it also housed the college library. (Courtesy of Michael Thompson.)

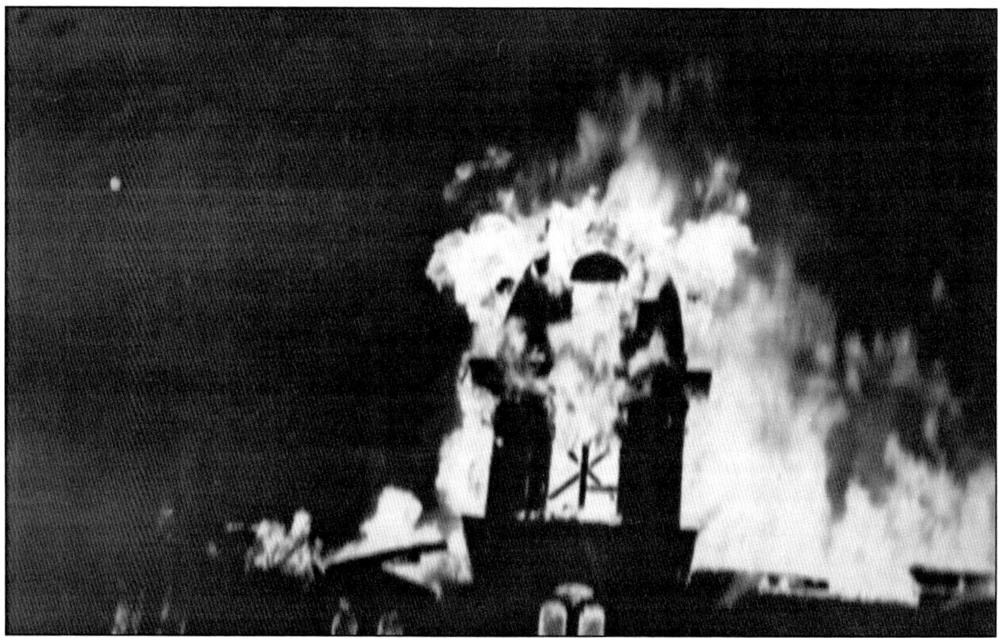

While tragedy and Rio Grande College often go together, no other could equal that of November 19, 1937, when Atwood Hall with its bell tower (pictured here) was consumed by flames. The college's very future at that point was threatened, but trustees, staff, and students pulled together, and "Old Rio" survived to endure further crises.

Three

Struggling to Survive Fire and War 1937–1952

The Rio Grande Board of Trustees adopted the "Forward Movement" just prior to the burning of Atwood Hall. They soon transformed it into the "Self-Help Plan," which had proven useful at Kentucky's Berea College. Haning Hall was built largely by student labor in 1938–1939. The college also operated a farm, a dairy, and a canning operation. How successful this system may have become failed to be realized, because the advent of World War II soon decimated Rio's male student body. An enrollment of 202 in 1940–1941 declined to 33 by 1944–1945, forcing cancellation of the football season because only nine boys were enrolled. On the positive side, the school resumed awarding bachelor's degrees in 1940, many to public school teachers who had toiled in summer school for years.

The end of the war and enactment of the GI Bill brought about an increase in the student body. Numbers jumped to 189 in the fall of 1946 and for the next four semesters passed 200. A second decline saw enrollment drop to 94 in the fall of 1952. After William Lewis returned to the deanship and classroom in 1940, Presidents Lloyd Pobst and Floyd McDermott, aided by a small but dedicated faculty, made the most of the hand fate had dealt them.

Student activities continued to flourish, with homecoming and May celebrations being major campus events. From 1938 through 1942, the Redmen gridiron squad suffered five winless seasons, including a 104-0 loss to Morehead State. Finally, in 1943, the team broke the losing streak with a 7-6 victory over Hiram, and in 1946 managed a rare winning season. Mercifully, the trustees abolished football in March 1950. Basketball teams compiled a mixed record, but some outstanding players, typified by Jack Duncan, Newt Oliver, and George Stephenson, provided the local fan base with moments to cheer about on the tiny hardwood floor in Community Hall. Meanwhile, the American Baptist Convention grew increasingly disenchanted with the struggling college, and after an investigation, abandoned Rio Grande on May 1, 1952, leaving the college to again face an uncertain future.

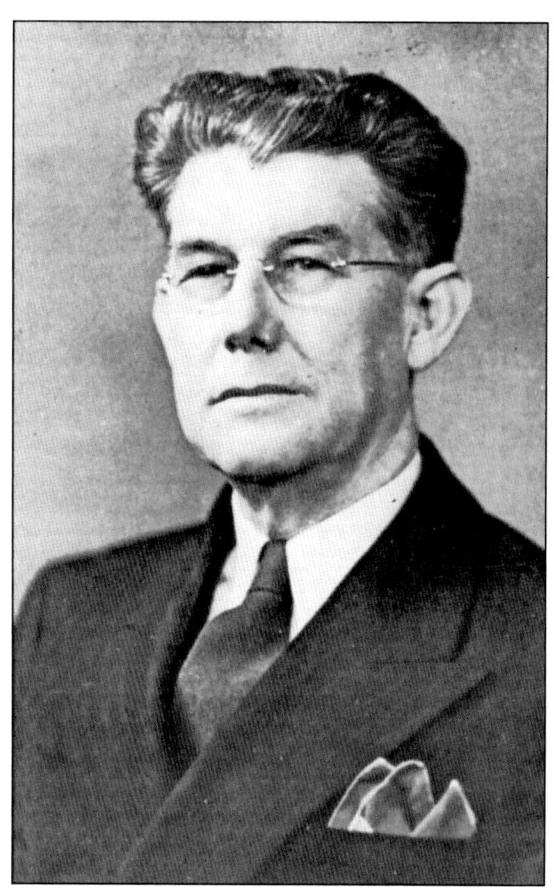

After 10 months as acting president, William Lewis (1877–1956) was elevated to the role of president in June 1932. He was a Rio graduate, had served as a professor of psychology, had been the dean of the normal school, and would serve a total of nine years as president. With the destruction of Atwood Hall, the school teetered on the brink of closure. Under the steady hand of Lewis, the school managed to overcome the odds. A fine example of Lewis's leadership is the amazing fact that not one class was cancelled due to the fire that destroyed Atwood Hall, often called the College Building.

In earlier days, the Frank Allen House had a balcony over the residential portion of the structure. Many male students lived there during their student days in private housing. It was purchased by Rio Grande College in 1964 and converted initially into a bookstore and faculty offices. Today, the third floor contains the archives that house many of the images contained in this volume, while the former store portion is an art gallery.

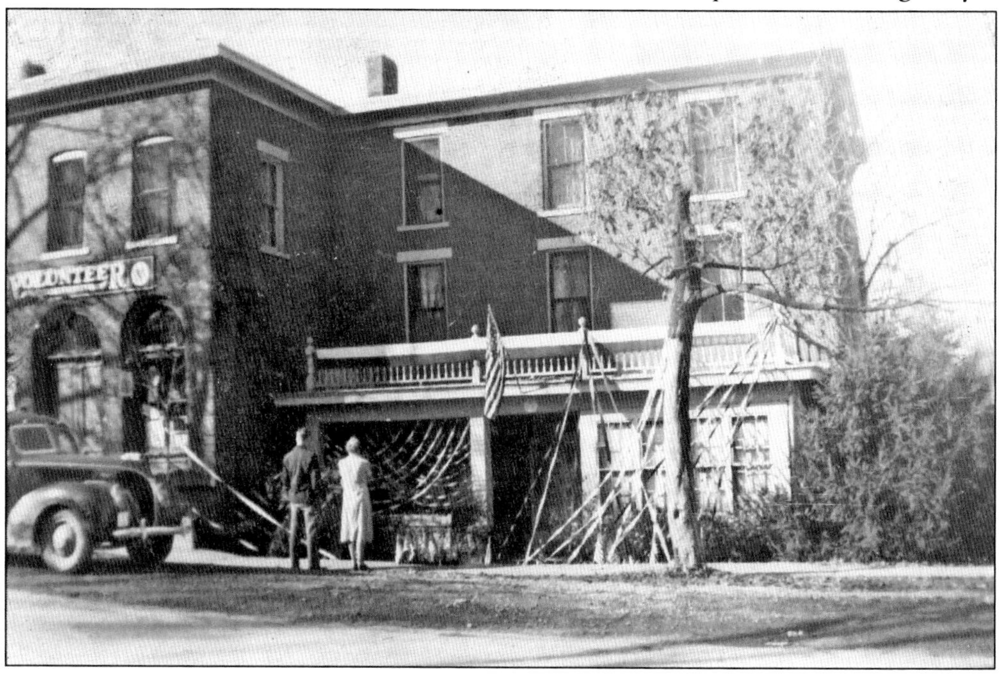

Florence Chubbuck (1888–1940) ranked as one of the most popular faculty members during her eight years at Rio. The Cleveland native also coached the debate team. One of her pupils, the late Luther Tracy, fondly recalled her pleasant persona as he drove her car to debates as far away as Tennessee. Chubbuck died after a short illness and had an Order of the Eastern Star funeral.

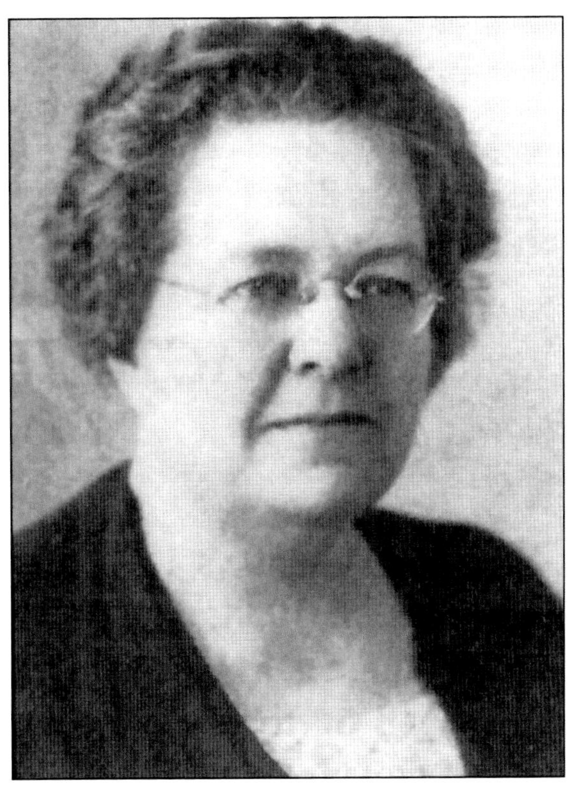

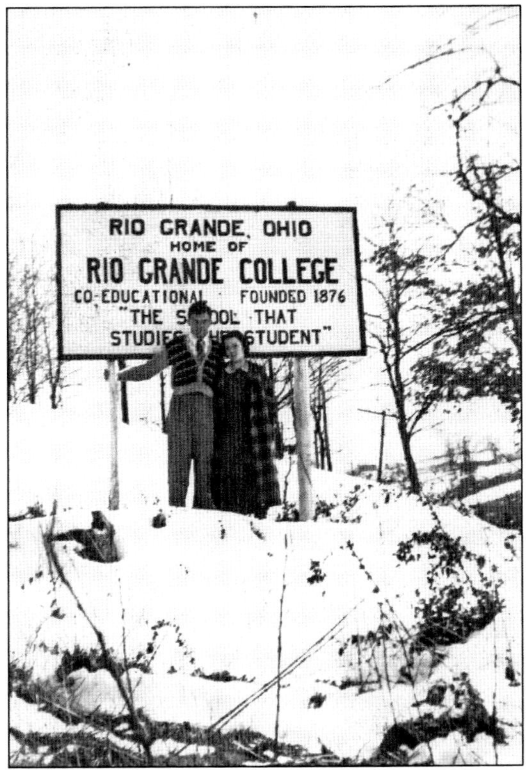

For several years in the 1920s and 1930s, Rio Grande College proudly adopted the phrase "The School that Studies the Student" as a virtual motto and exhibited it on a sign on campus. Whether or not he originated it, the saying was closely identified with the heyday of Dean and Pres. William A. Lewis.

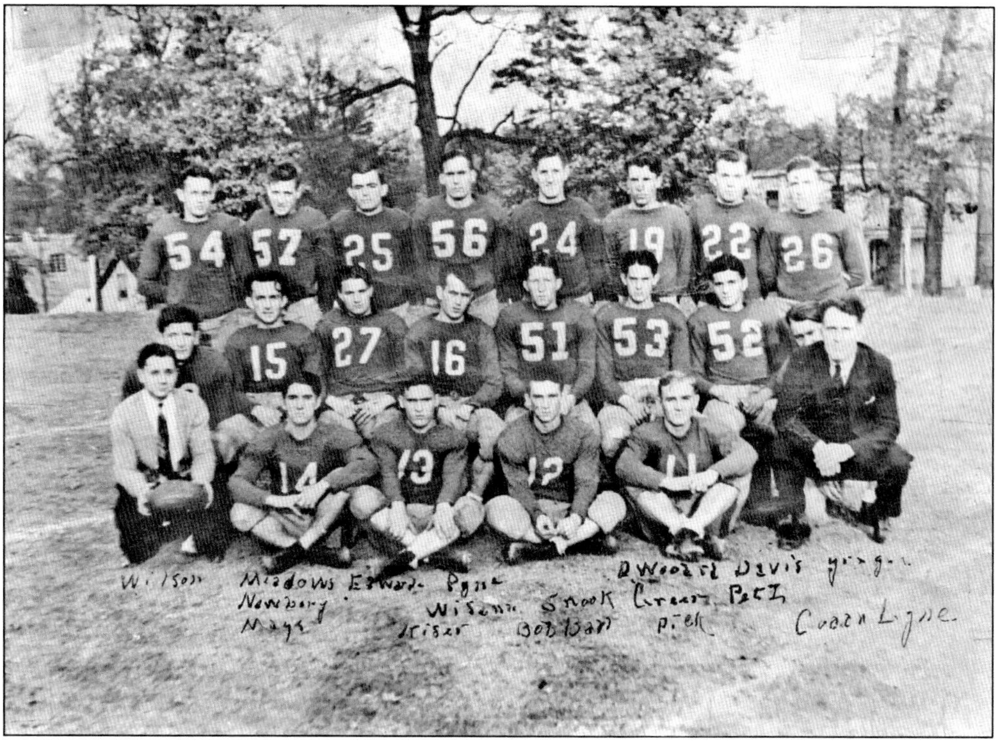

By the mid-1930s, Rio gridiron squads were being referred to as the Redmen. This team photograph from 1937 is illustrative of the more modern uniform with numbers worn at the time under Paul Lyne in his second tenure as coach. It also shows the squad on its normal playing field, which is now occupied by Davis Library and Florence Evans Hall.

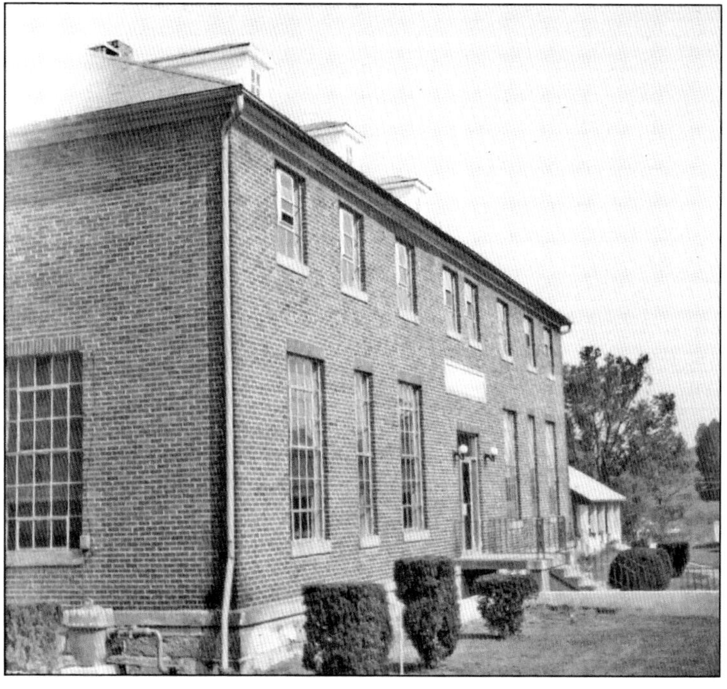

Haning Hall (initially known as Science Hall) became the first of three buildings constructed by student labor under the "Self-Help Plan," which evolved from the "Forward Movement" after the burning of Atwood Hall. Rio science classes were held there from 1939 until 1984, when the oddly designed structure was razed and replaced by a parking lot. For several years, the upper story served as a boys' dorm.

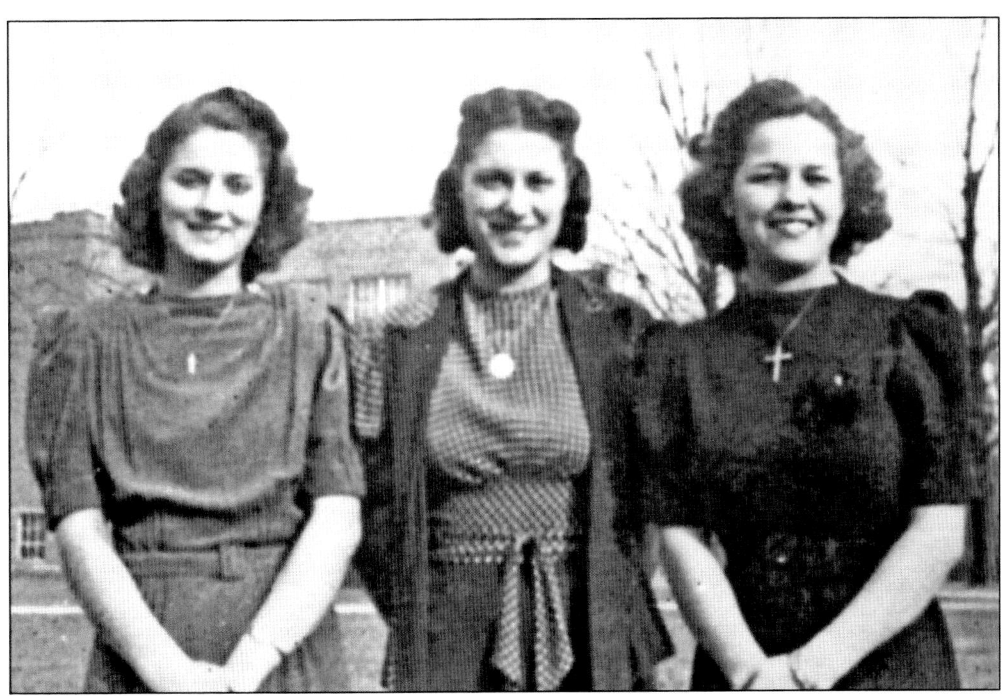

In 1938, Rio Grande College inaugurated a long-standing tradition of homecoming queens when the student body chose freshman Edna Cary for the honor, pictured above flanked by her court, consisting of Ruth Callahan (right) and Pauline Spohn. In later years, as Edna Cary Langdon (right), she served as junior high principal at Dawson-Bryant in Coal Grove, and by 1995, she had retired to Florida.

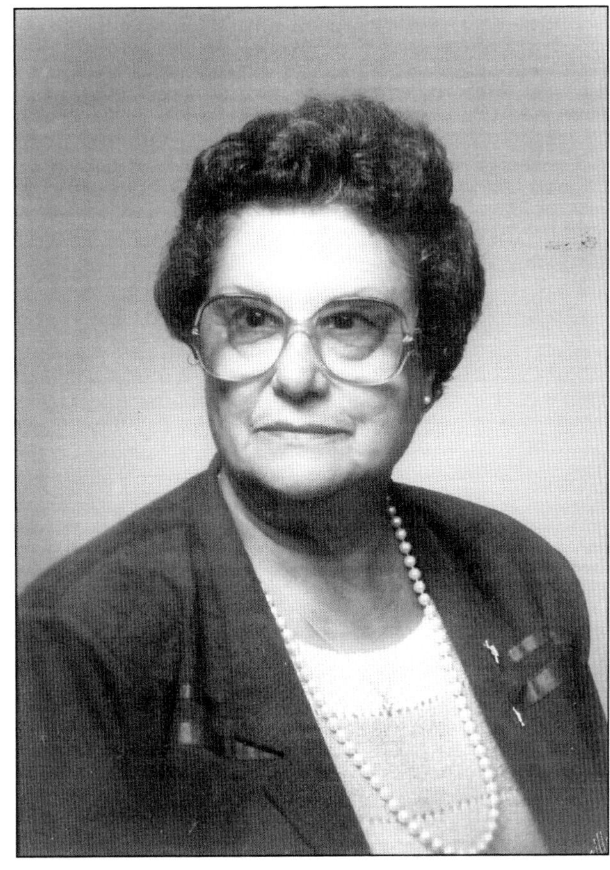

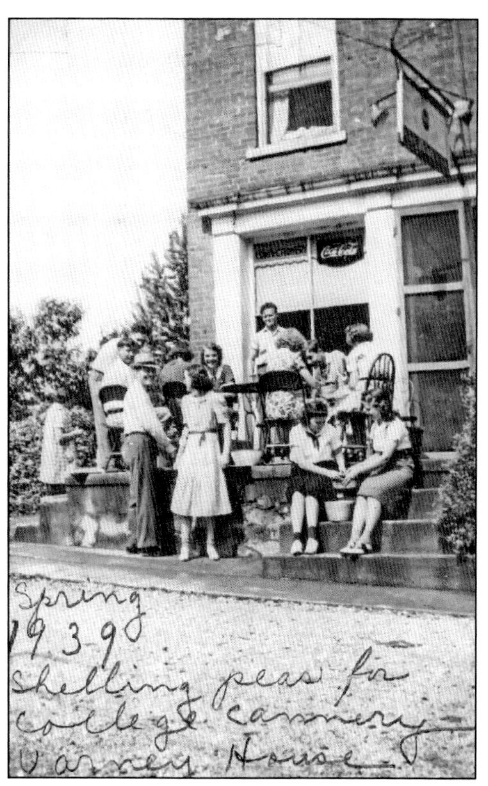

During the years of the Self-Help Plan, Rio Grande College had a farm, operated a dairy, pasteurized and marketed milk, and harvested and canned vegetables. Men worked the farm and milked the cows, while girls prepared and canned. This 1939 photograph depicts girls on the Varney House front porch shelling peas prior to the canning process.

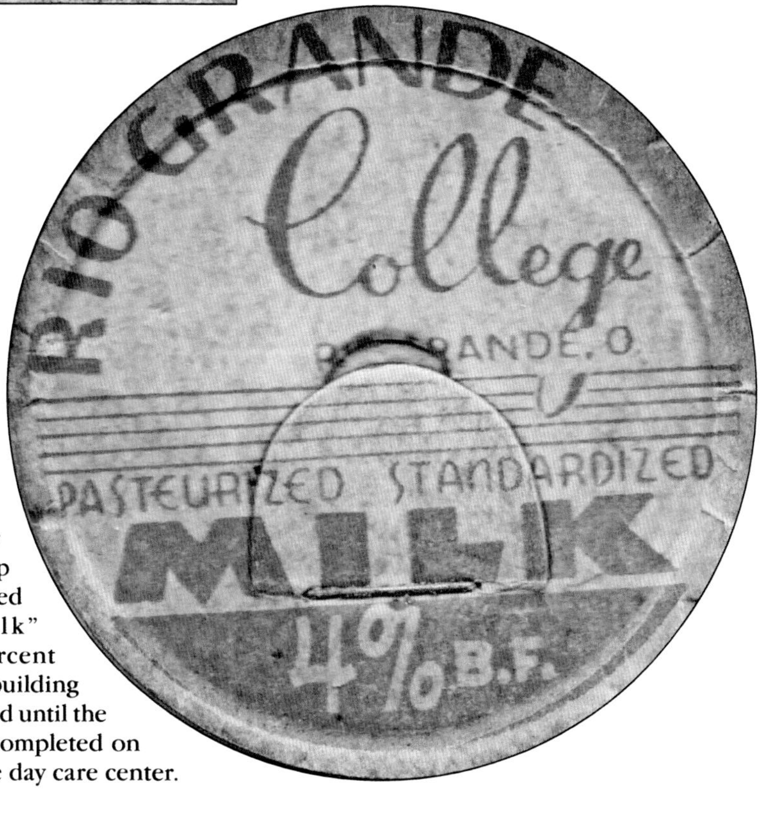

The Self-Help Plan dairy was abandoned about 1951 because losses were quite high. During its heyday, the Rio Grande College Dairy even had printed caps for glass bottles. This cap advertises "pasteurized standardized milk" containing four percent butter fat. Self-Help building construction continued until the third structure was completed on the current site of the day care center.

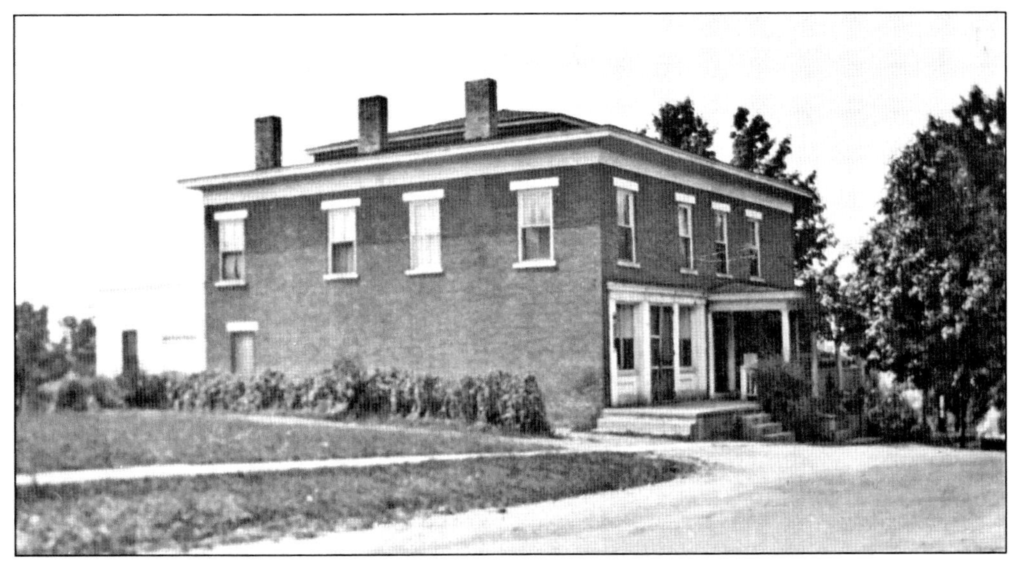

When Rio Grande College was about to open in 1876, John Varney built a general store and hotel across from the campus. In 1935, college trustees bought the building and transformed it into a dorm for 22 girls, with the lower part as a snack bar. In later years, it served a variety of purposes. It was demolished in the late 1970s.

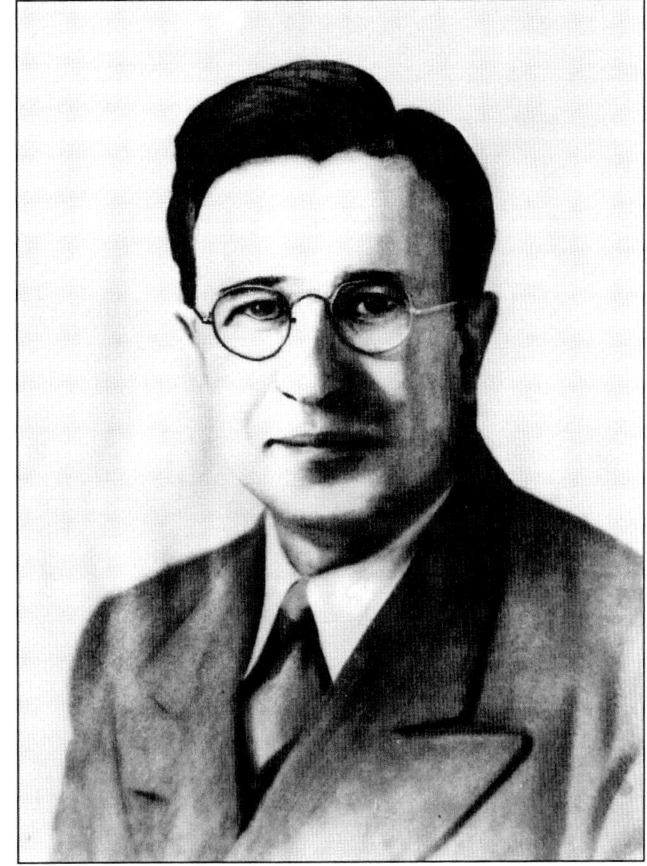

Rev. R. Lloyd Pobst (1904–1966) held the Rio Grande presidency from 1940 to 1944, in a troubled time not of his own making. Rio had reinstituted the granting of four-year degrees and had instituted the Self-Help Plan just before he arrived, continuing it through his term. But with World War II taking the men and defense work for many of the potential women, there were few students. Pobst's initial optimism soon vanished.

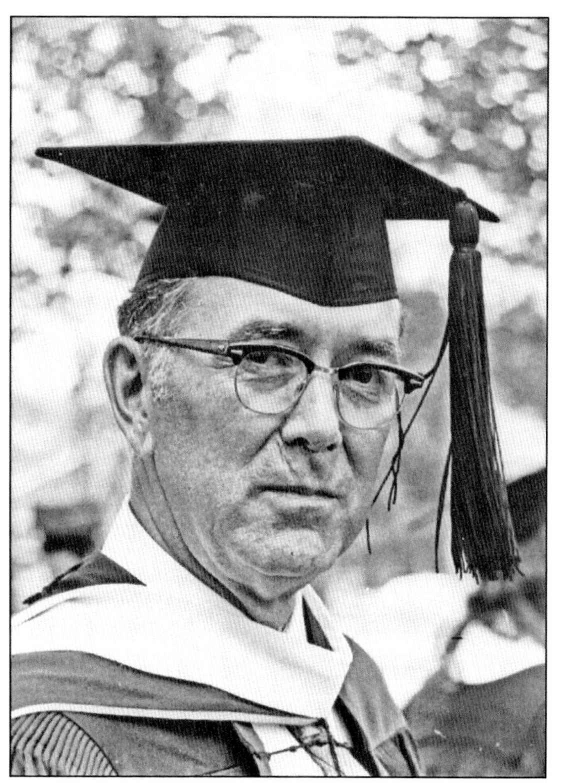

Francis Burdell (1909–2005) served on Rio Grande College's science faculty from 1941 until 1974, having earlier been a student. In addition to his heavy teaching load, he was involved in community activity that was virtually unsurpassed. He was a 4-H advisor, Scoutmaster, member of the Masons and the Grange, and a GOP committeeman. He also farmed to some degree and later helped his son on the farm.

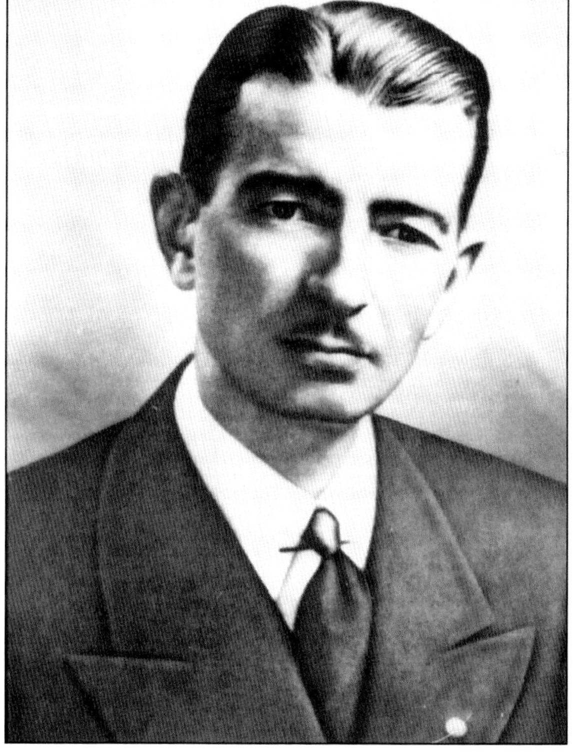

Floyd McDermott (1898–1992), who was Rio Grande's last Baptist minister president (1944–1951), also inherited problems that he had not created. With the war still on in McDermott's first year, student numbers sank to 33. The GI Bill saw enrollment rise to 232 by 1947 and then drop again. The Self-Help Plan gave the campus a new cafeteria in 1948, but losses on the college farm became abysmal.

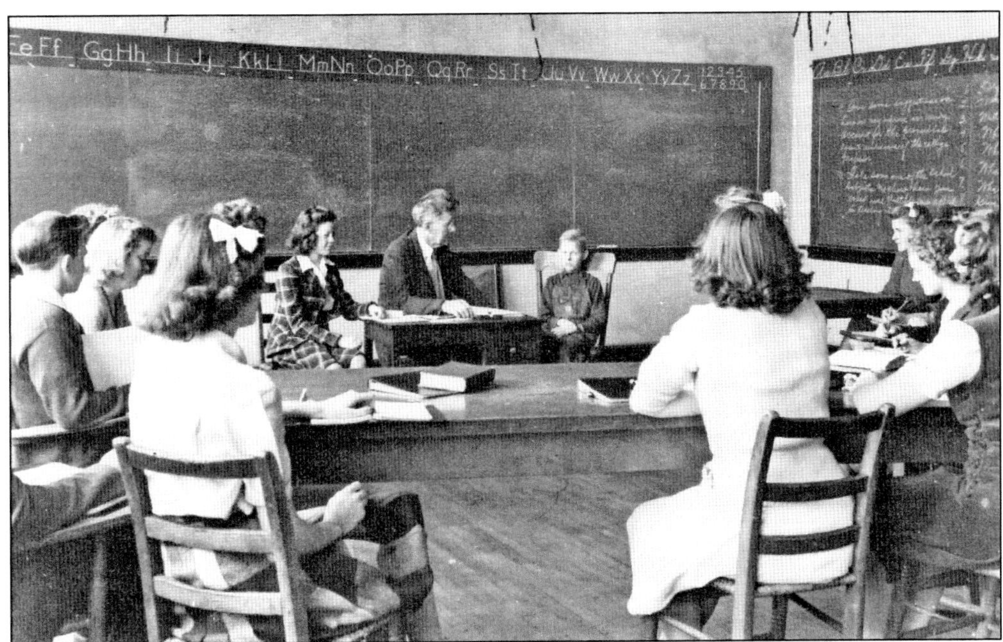

William Lewis became best remembered as a Rio Grande professor for his psychology courses. Not many earlier photographs of a class in action have survived, but this one from 1945, taken in Anniversary Hall, illustrates one by the legendary Lewis in progress. No students are identifiable.

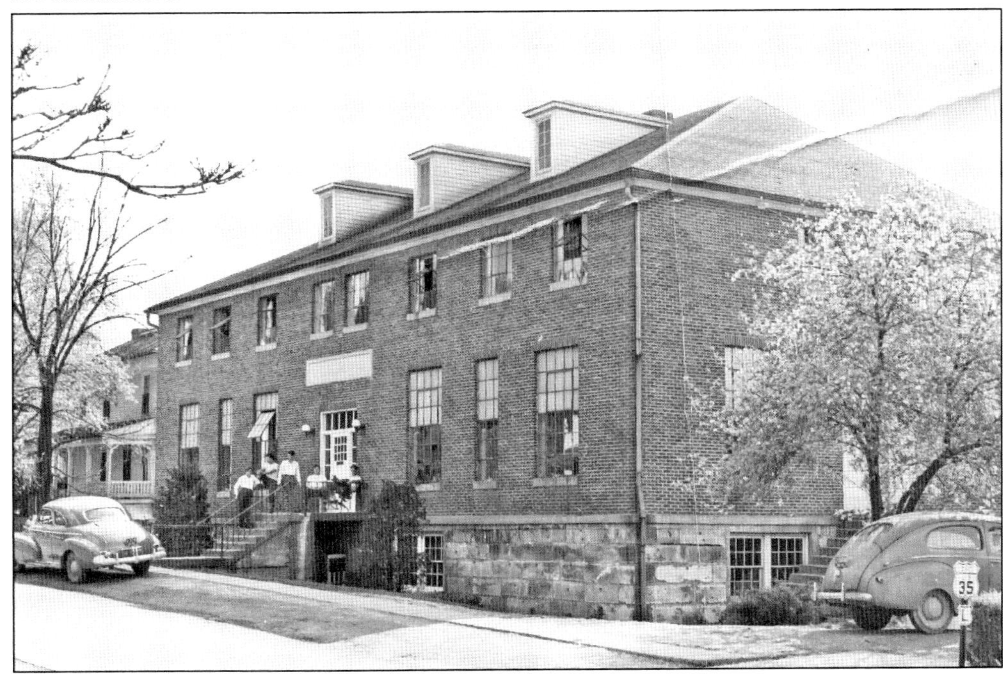

In an earlier day, US Route 35 skirted along West College Avenue, turning right and passing in front of Haning Hall, the top floor of which served as a boys' dorm. This photograph from the late 1940s shows a few students on the steps of their likely residence, with Davis Cottage somewhat more distant.

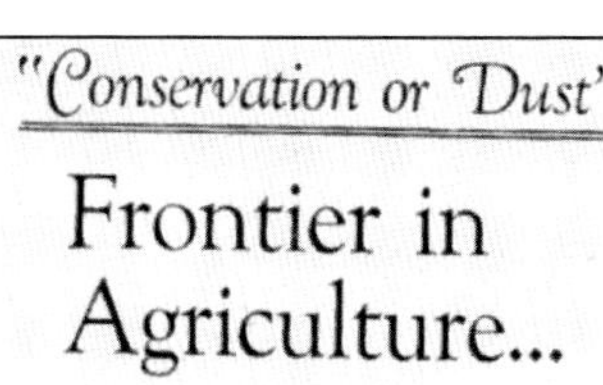

"Conservation or Dust"

Frontier in Agriculture...

AT

Rio Grande College Farm

Rio Grande, Gallia County, Ohio

On Route U. S. 35

September 23-24, 1948

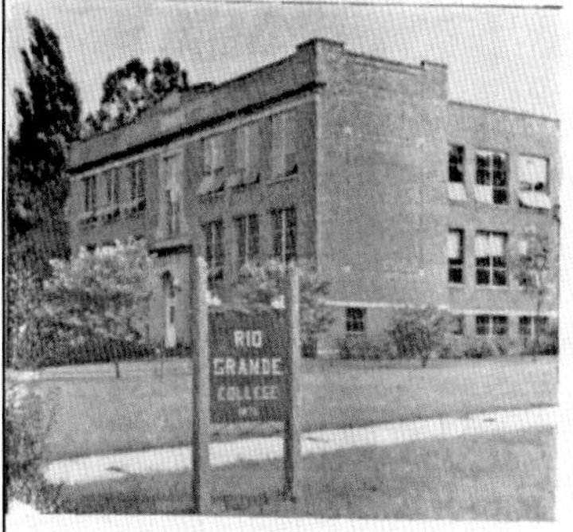

Advances in farm methods will be on parade at the two-day "Second Frontier Days" at Rio Grande College Farm on September 23 and 24. New techniques and improved tools to do the tremendous job of raising food for America and the world will be displayed in practical demonstrations.

In September 1948, the Rio Grande College Farm hosted "Frontier in Agriculture" displays and demonstrations of new agriculture equipment and techniques. Somewhat defensively, a phrase inside the brochure reads, "Contrary to prevailing notions, Rio Grande College is not a couple of ramshackle buildings hidden in a hollow." As events developed, Rio Grande College lost a great deal of money on the otherwise successful venture.

Southeastern Ohio has always had numerous amateur country musicians. This student threesome from about 1950 features, from left to right, Kermit Daugherty Jr., Bob Wion, and Sid Campbell. Daugherty's father wrote the novel *Out of the Red Brush*, Wion became a member of Rio's Athletic Hall of Fame, and Campbell taught school, played in numerous bluegrass bands around Columbus, and composed such classics as "Unfaithful One" and "This Morning at Nine."

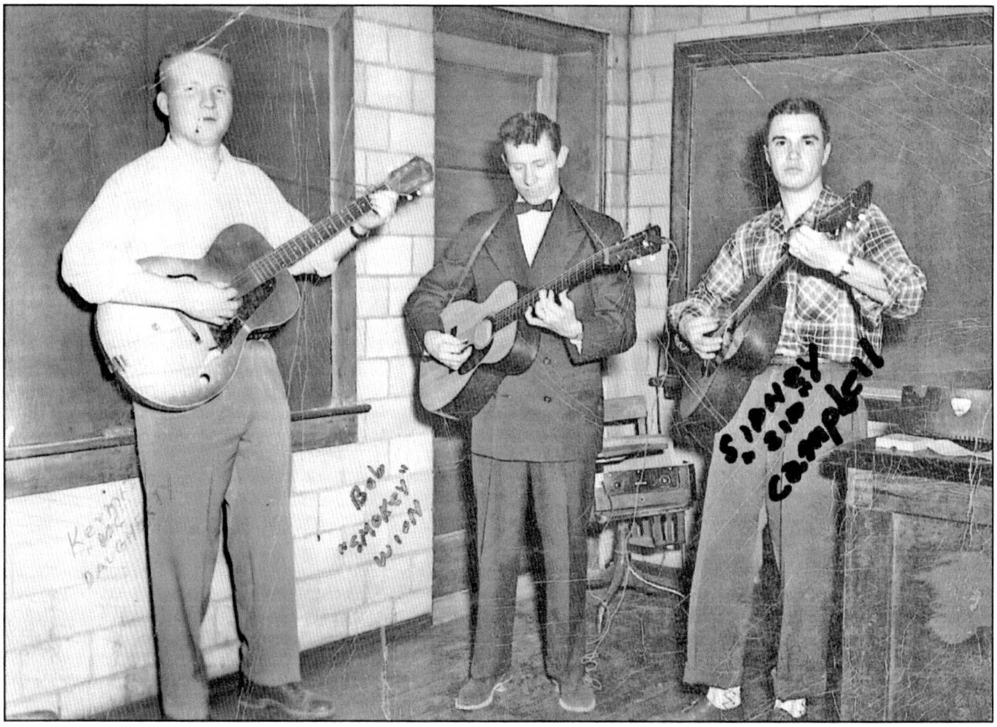

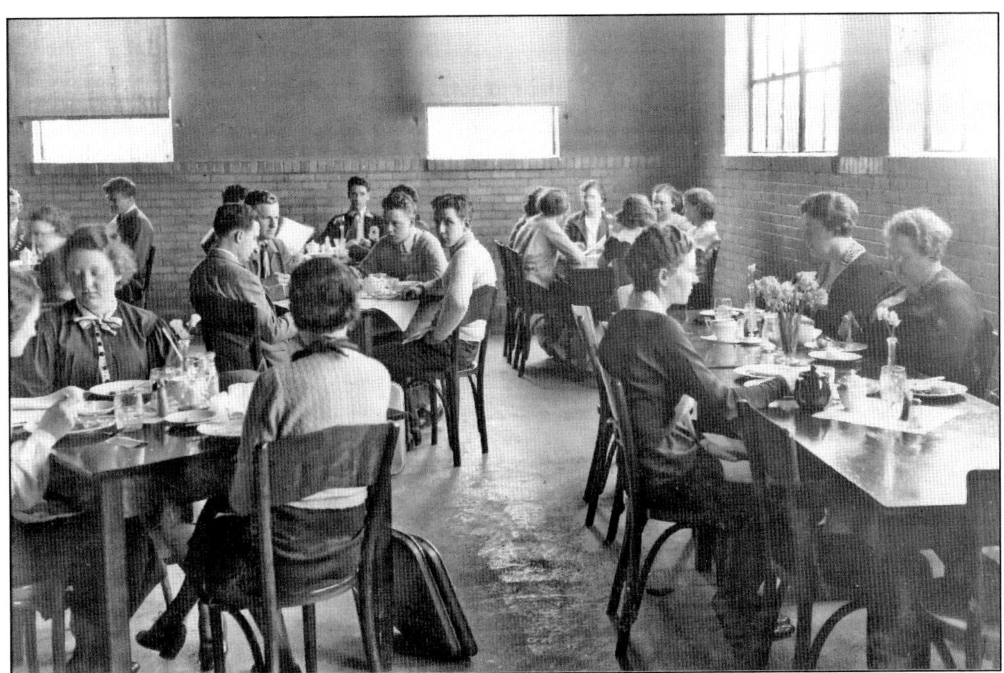

The Rio Grande College cafeteria has seen multiple locations. Prior to 1949, the cafeteria was located in the basement of Anniversary Hall (pictured). It moved from there to what became known as the "old" student center, in 1966 to the new Dining Hall (now Florence Evans Hall), in 1982 to the new Rhodes Center, and finally to its present locale, the Elizabeth and Evan Davis Center.

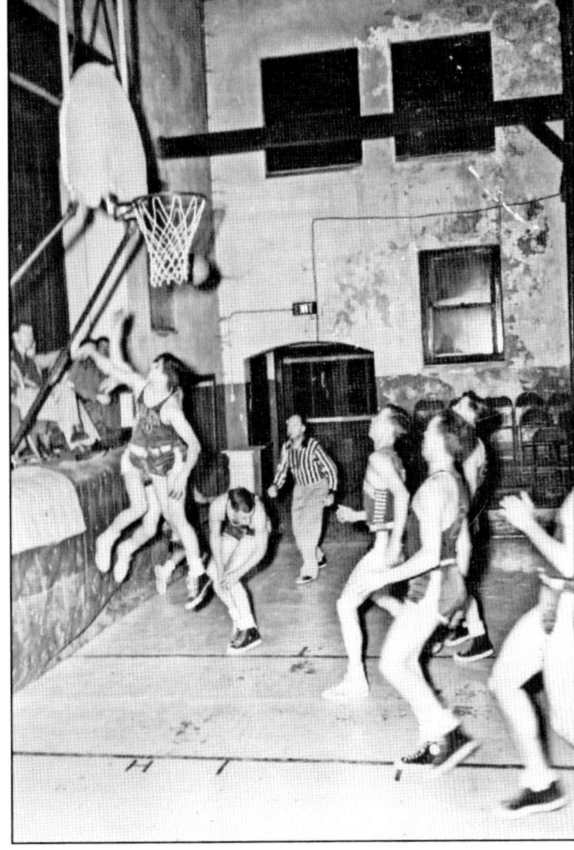

One of America's smallest intercollegiate basketball courts, the one in Community Hall bore the derisive nickname "the Hog Pen." This action photograph from the 1949–1950 season illustrates how it got the name.

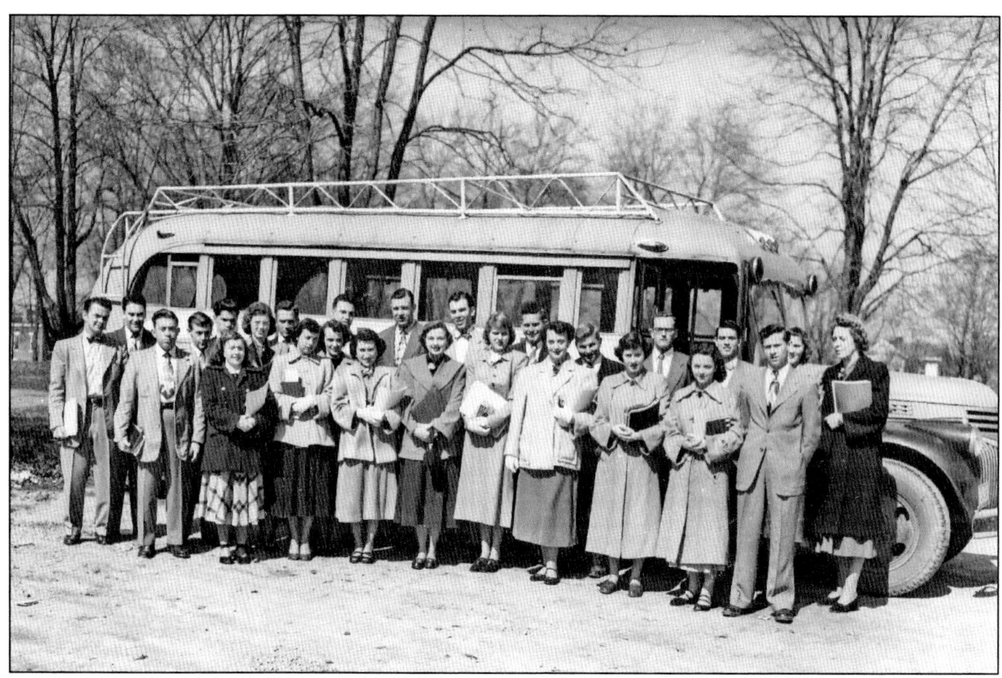

In 1948, the Ohio Department of Education withdrew recognition of Rio Grande College for teacher licensing. So, according to the Rivenburg Report, "alumni, college officials, and trustees, a bus load of students and friends" went to Columbus to appeal and Rio received a three-year reprieve to get its program in line with state requirements, which ultimately succeeded.

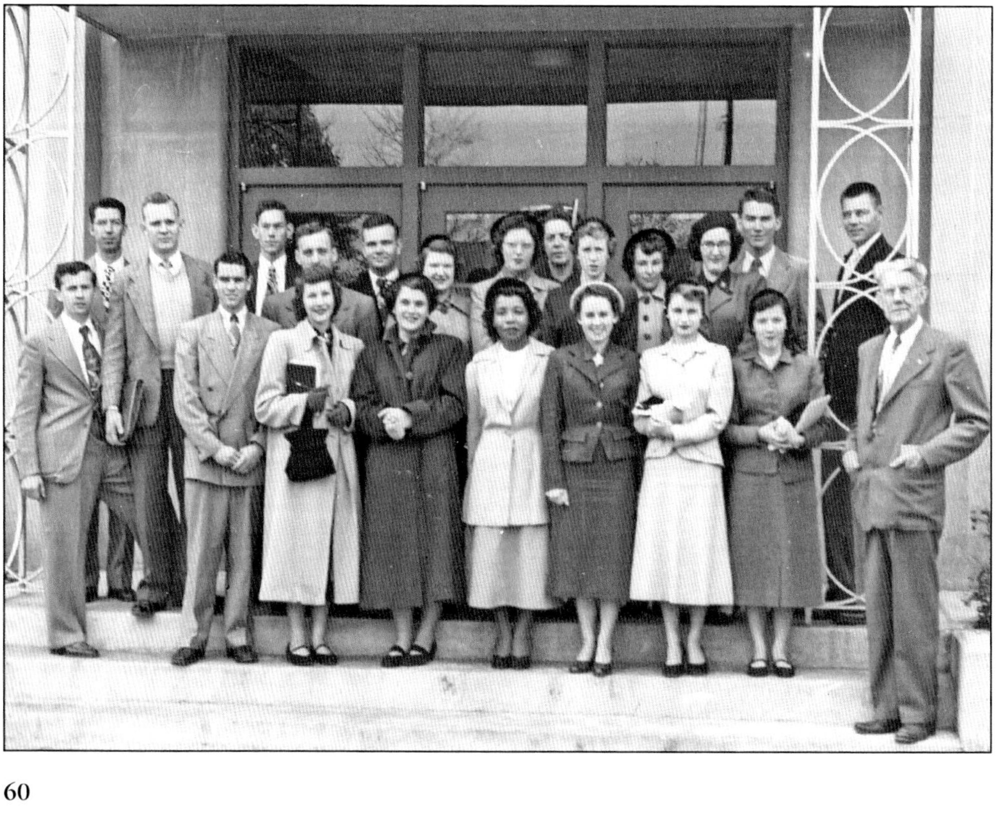

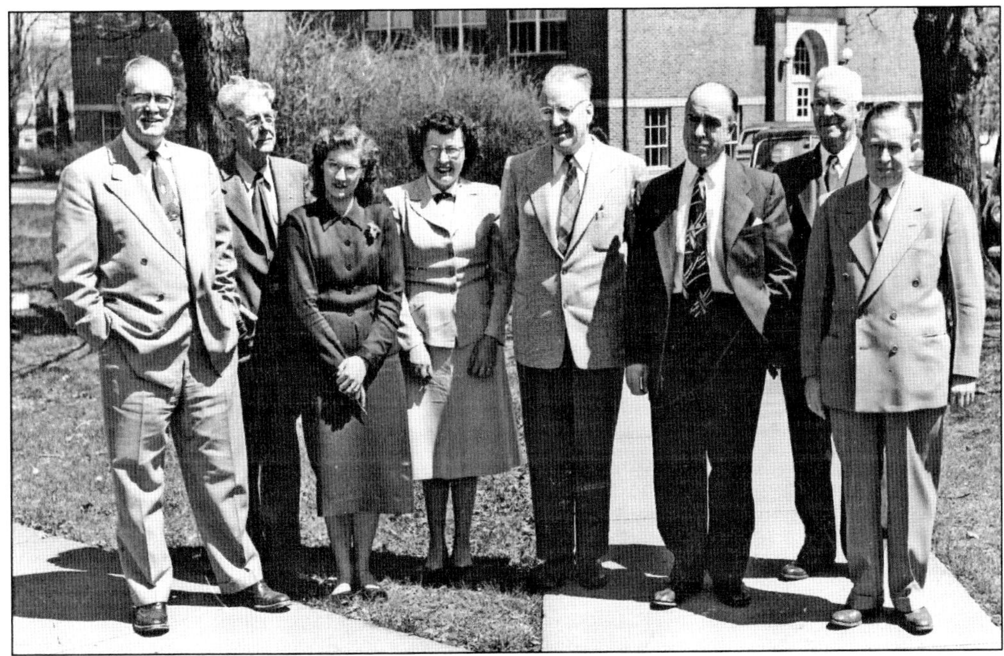

This group attends an Ohio College Association meeting at Rio Grande College about 1951 or 1952; from left to right are Pres. Charles Davis; visibly aging Dean William Lewis; Mildred Harris (president's secretary); Jean Lloyd Cooper (treasurer-comptroller); Dr. Boyd Alexander (Antioch College); Dr. Arnold Thompson (Ohio State University); and Frank Morrow and Jack Stiffler (Rio Grande College trustees). The latest Rio financial crisis was no doubt a discussion topic.

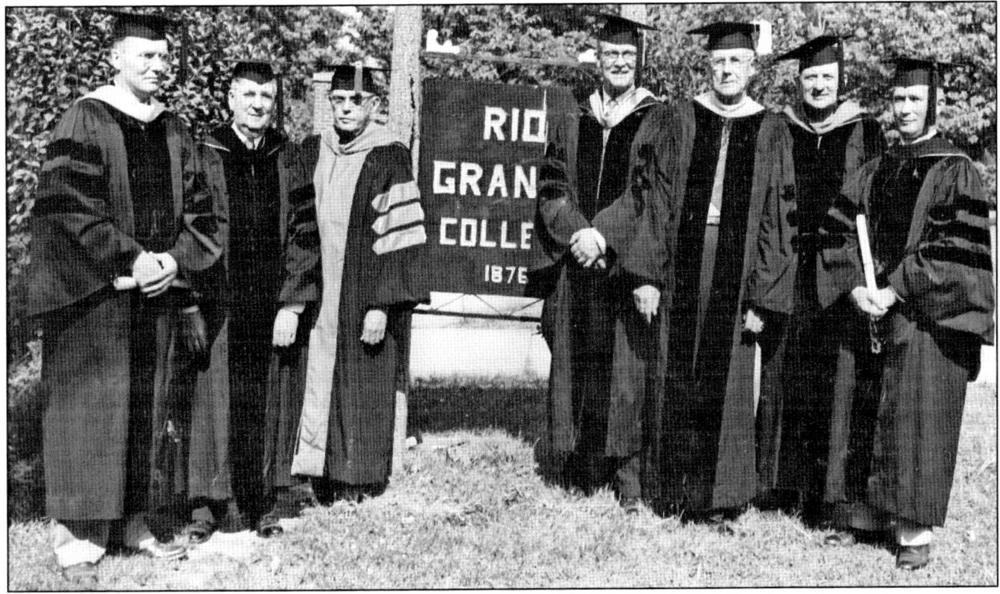

The platform party at the 1952 graduation ceremony includes, from left to right, Kermit Daugherty (soon famous for his novel *Out of the Red Brush*), Thomas Jenkins (17-term member of Congress), Trustee J. Boyd Davis, Pres. Charles Davis, Dean William Lewis, Trustee Don Allen, and Rev. John Yenches.

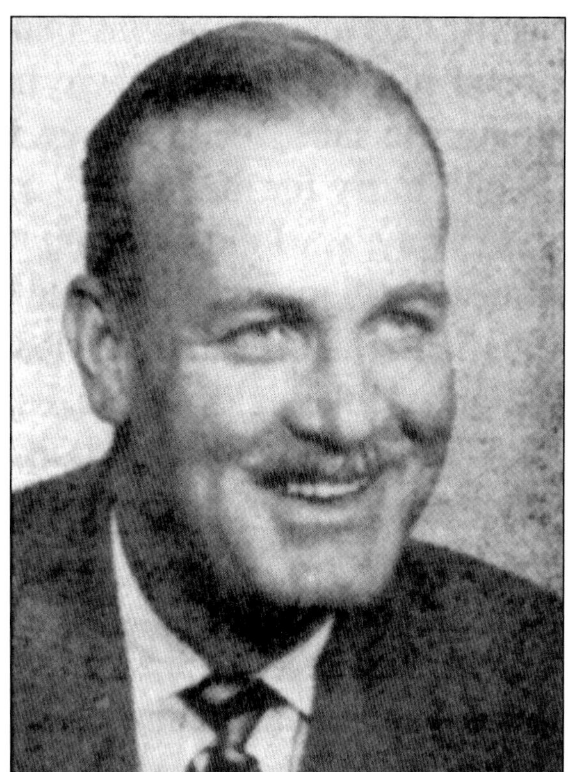

Charles Davis (1881–1961), a 1926 alumnus, served as Rio Grande president for three contentious and controversial years (1951–1954). During that time, the Northern Baptist Convention divested its connection to the college, and the rise and fall of the Newt Oliver–Bevo Francis era took place. Through it all, Rio Grande survived—barely!

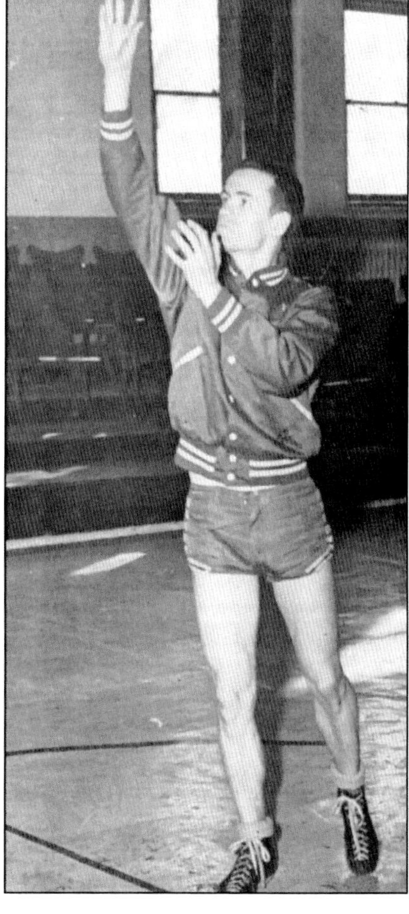

Newton Oliver (class of 1949) first gained basketball renown as a free throw wiz and recipient of the Helms Award. Later, he earned coaching immortality assembling the Bevo Francis team, which brought Rio Grande College national fame and likely saved the school from extinction. Oliver later joined the board of trustees and became the namesake of the arena in Lyne Center.

Four

Saved by a Basketball 1951–1969

When Charles Davis became Rio's 10th president in 1951, he had reason to think that the school's days were numbered. Baptist divestment a few months later gave him further cause for pessimism. Nonetheless, he tried to project optimism the following fall when enrollment dropped to 94 in September 1952 and 88 in the spring. The military stalemate in the Korean War led to a mild decline in the male student ranks.

Then, a flamboyant basketball coach, Newton Oliver, and a tall, lanky freshman player, Clarence "Bevo" Francis, provided the means for survival. Rio Grande victories and Bevo's phenomenal scoring, including 116 points in a single game, attracted national attention, and the away team share of gate receipts provided sufficient cash to pay the bills. The team's 39-0 season and Francis's 1,954 points made the little college more famous than ever before (even though some of the scoring records were disallowed by the NCAA). In the fall of 1953, enrollment jumped to 128 and the Redmen played nearly all four-year schools. Francis did almost as well, totaling 1,319 points in a 21-7 season (113 in a single game) and proving the team competitive against big-name colleges while defeating such teams as Wake Forest and Creighton. After the season, Davis, Francis, and Oliver departed, but Rio Grande endured, slowly increasing enrollment, which reached 295 by 1959.

Former coach Paul Lyne took the helm after Davis, guiding the school through this period. By his last year (1962), enrollment reached 438. Two modern dorms, Davis and Moulton Halls, adorned the campus as did Allen Hall. Alphus Christensen made accreditation with the North Central Association of Colleges and Schools his major goal, achieving it in 1969. More building continued, with Holzer Hall and Boyd Hall dormitories and a new gymnasium, library, and dining hall all completed by 1971, making the campus more viable. Student protests were mild compared to those at most colleges. More than any other leader, Christensen brought Rio Grande into the mainstream. Still, another crisis soon loomed on the horizon.

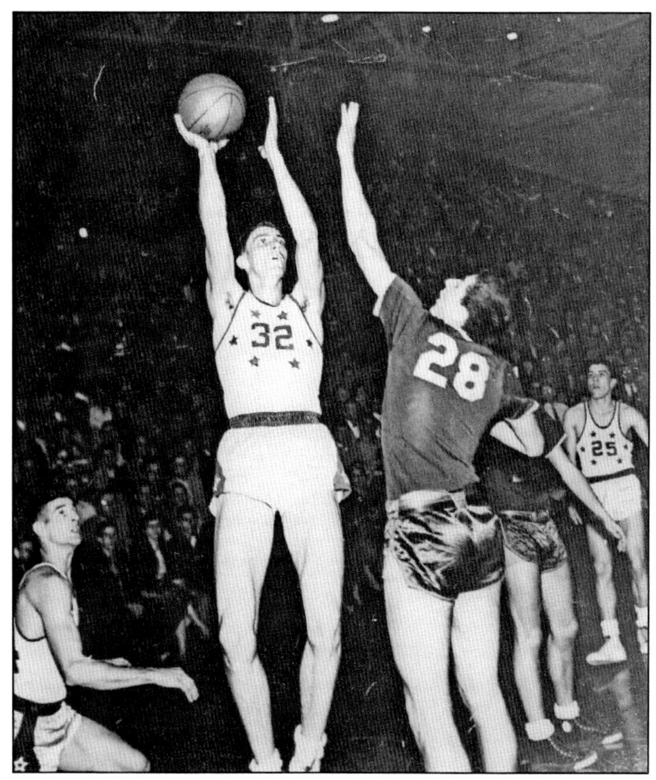

In Rio's 141-year history, no name has earned the institution the wide recognition accorded to Clarence "Bevo" Francis (1932–2015), whose two-year student career and basketball legacy seem forever embedded. As far away as Freetown, Sierra Leone, his name came up in a casual conversation coauthor Ivan Tribe had with a Sierra Leonian in 1979 when Rio Grande was mentioned.

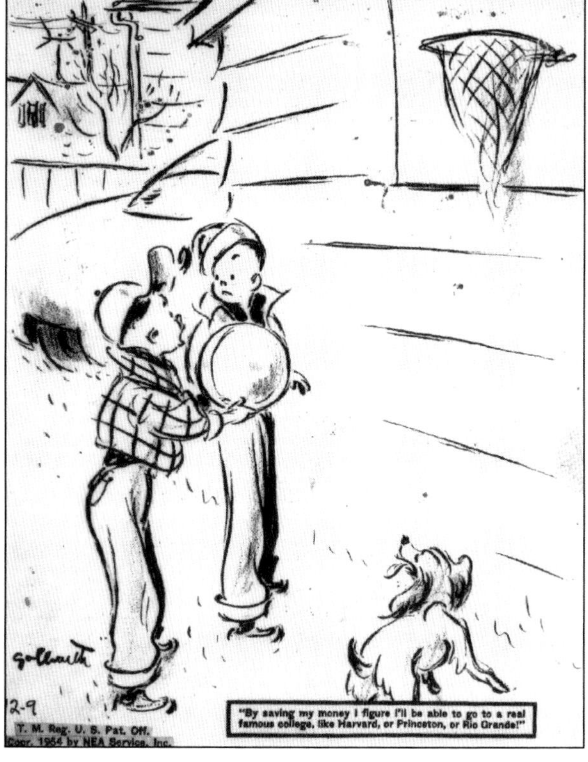

When Bevo Francis was the talk of the sports world, his name entered the national culture, as illustrated in this cartoon of two kids with a basketball. One says, "By saving my money and playing basketball, I figure I'll be able to go to a real famous college, like Harvard, or Princeton, or Rio Grande."

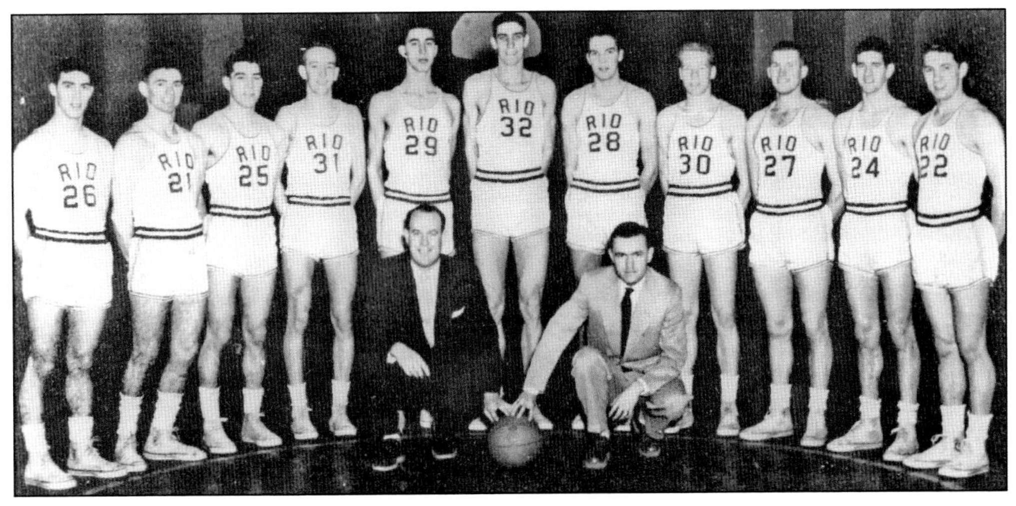

The 39-0 Redmen cage squad of 1952–1953 is sometimes considered the best small-college basketball team ever. Pictured from left to right are (kneeling) assistant coach Carroll Kent and coach Newt Oliver; (standing) John Viscoglosi, Jim McKenzie, Wayne Wiseman, Jack Gossett, Bill Frazier, Clarence "Bevo" Francis, Zeke Zempter, Dick Barr, Roy Moses, Bill Ripperger, and Bob Mundy.

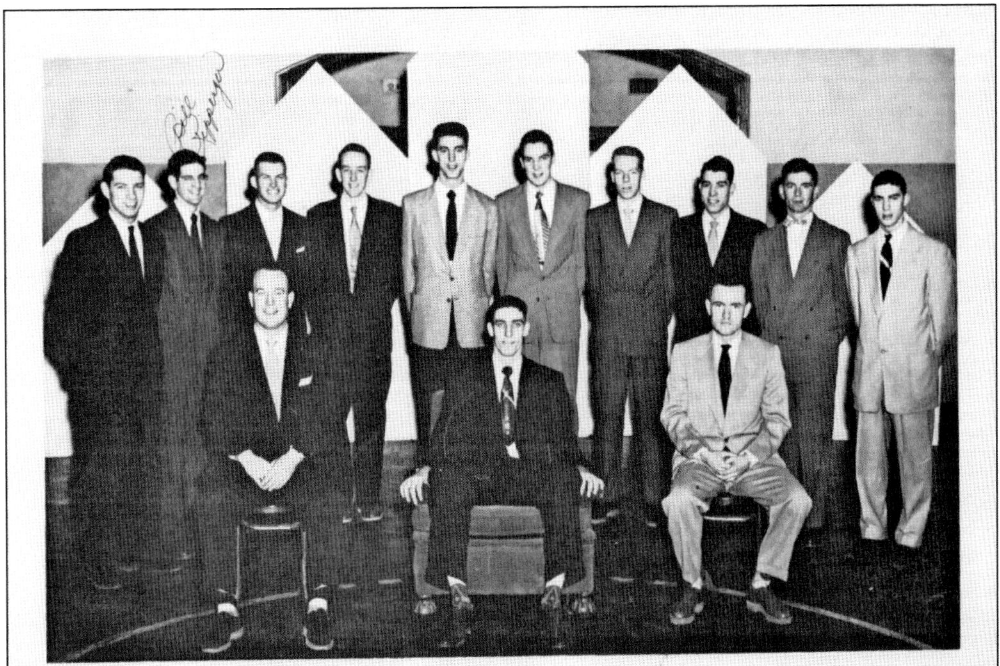

UNEQUALED---UNEXCELLED---UNDEFEATED

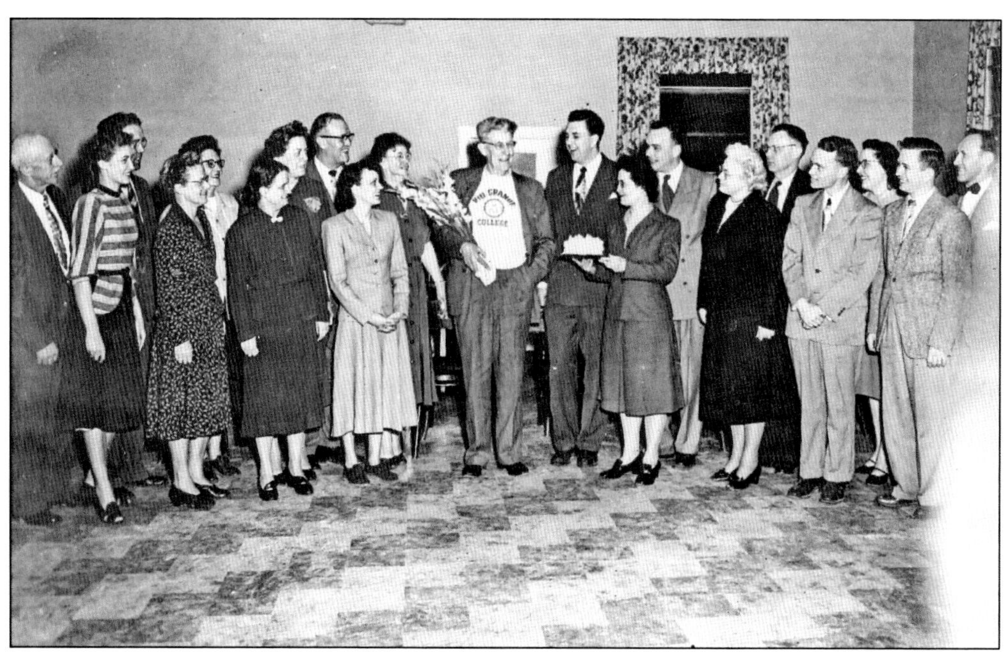

On his 75th birthday in 1952, the venerated William Lewis was treated by the faculty and students to cake and presented with a Rio Grande T-shirt, which he is wearing proudly, if not a bit underdressed from his usual, more formal appearance. Lewis was soon incapacitated and passed away in 1956, leaving his grieving widow, Mary, and a grieving college. The stage in Community Hall was completely covered with baskets of flowers from the Rio Grande College family.

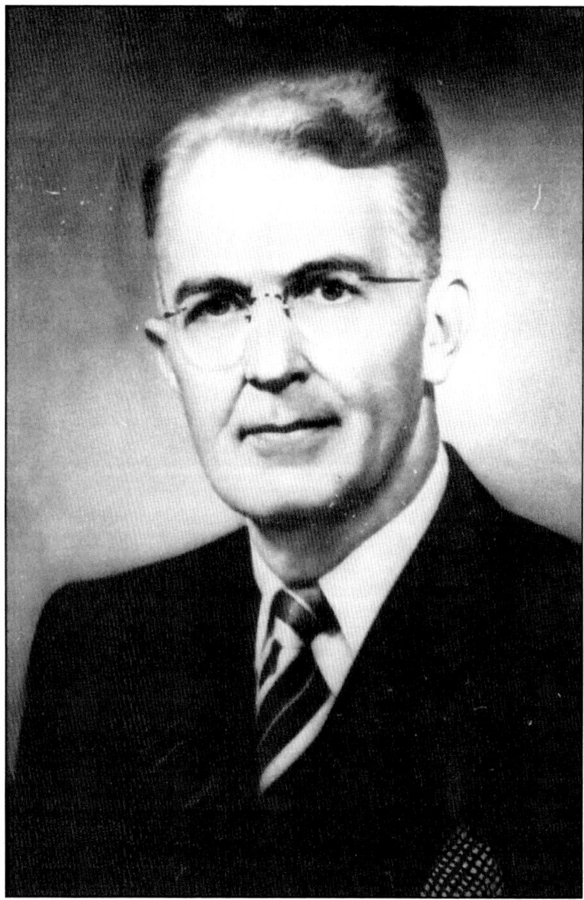

Guernsey County native Paul Revere Lyne (1896–1971) spent two six-year stints (1923–1929 and 1932–1938) as a coach and professor at Rio Grande College before becoming president in 1954, following the Bevo Francis era. In Lyne's eight years as leader, enrollment doubled but remained small by contemporary standards. Basketball remained respectable but not dominant. Lyne deserves much of the credit for this, as well as the measured growth.

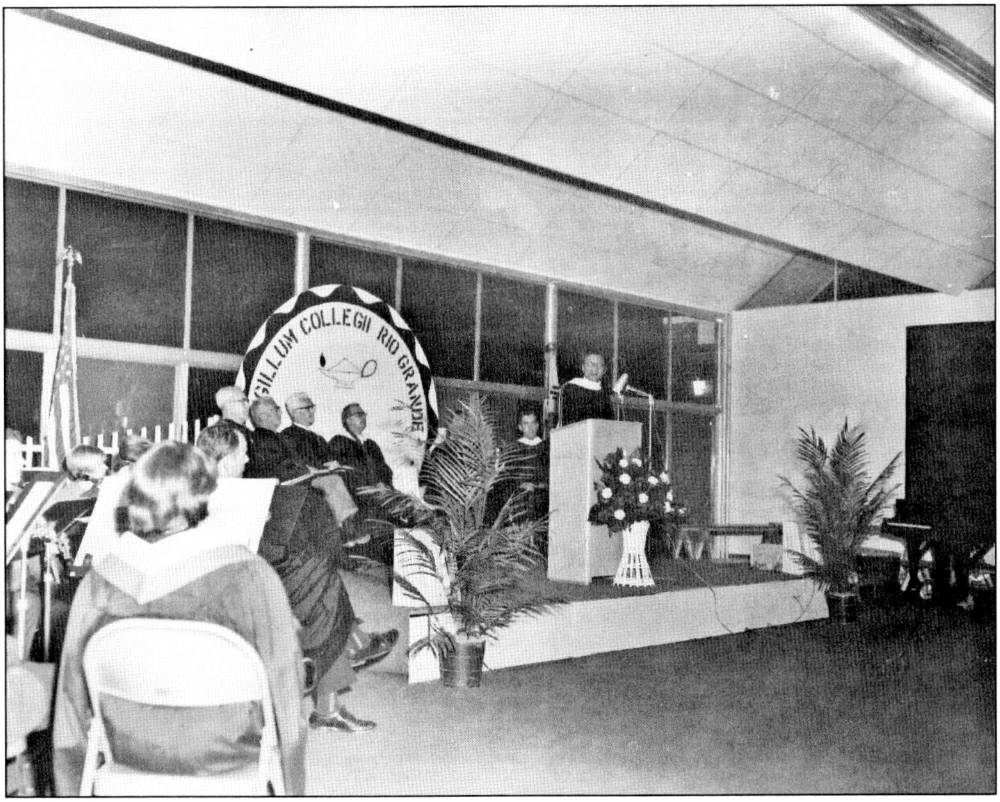

Tong Won Lee (class of 1951) later earned a doctorate from Oxford and held such South Korean government posts as special envoy and minister of foreign affairs. In November 1967, he returned to Rio Grande and received an honorary doctor of public letters; he remarked that "Rio Grande College has always remained very deep in my heart with lingering and beautiful memories."

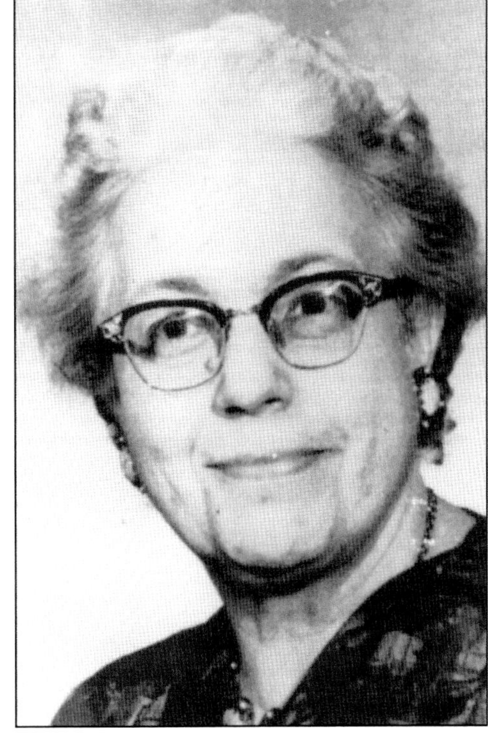

Clara Poston (1902–1990), a southern Ohio native, came to Rio Grande in 1948 and spent 23 years here. A stickler on quality grammar, she authored a popular workbook, *Laying a Foundation for Effective Speaking and Grammar*. She also played a key role helping President Christensen in his successful endeavor to secure North Central Association accreditation. Retiring in 1971, she eventually moved to Florida.

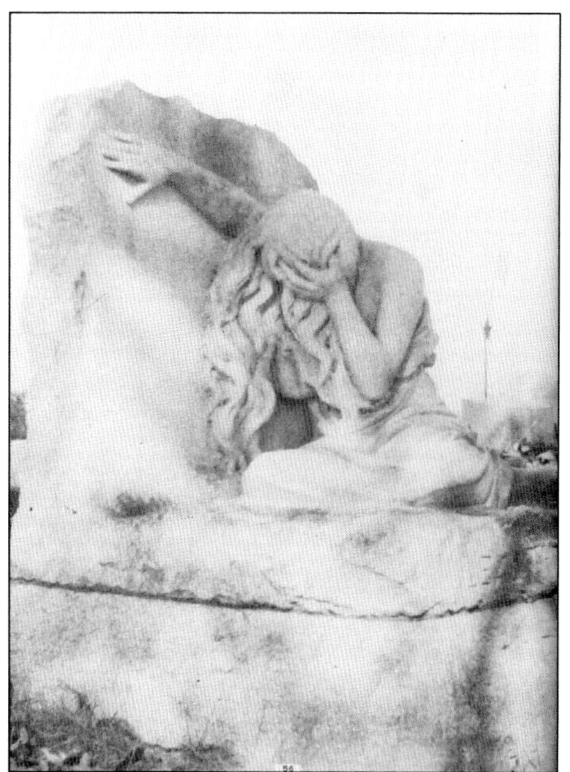

First mentioned in a 1930s *Grandion* as "a trip to the Virgin" and seen here from a full page of the 1950 *Grandion*, the gravestone of Clarissa Davis (1837–1910) in Calvary Cemetery has become the center of Rio Grande's greatest legend. Rio students have dubbed her "the Weeping Virgin." In actuality, Clarissa Davis was married and had four children. Whatever the reason, a trip to visit "the Weeping Virgin" is a ritual still followed by students and some faculty members.

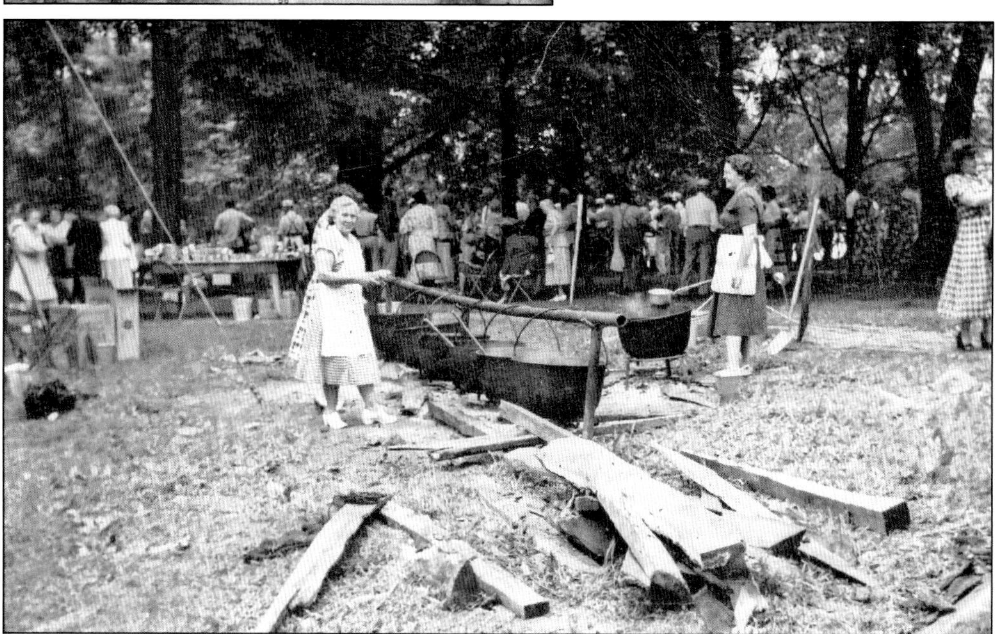

In the years after the Civil War, local communities held bean dinners, usually sponsored by the Grand Army of the Republic, as reunions or get-togethers for Union veterans and their friends. The Rio Grande one allegedly dates from 1872 and for decades took place on the Rio Grande College campus, as pictured in this 1955 scene. Currently, it is held in the Bob Evans Farm Shelter House.

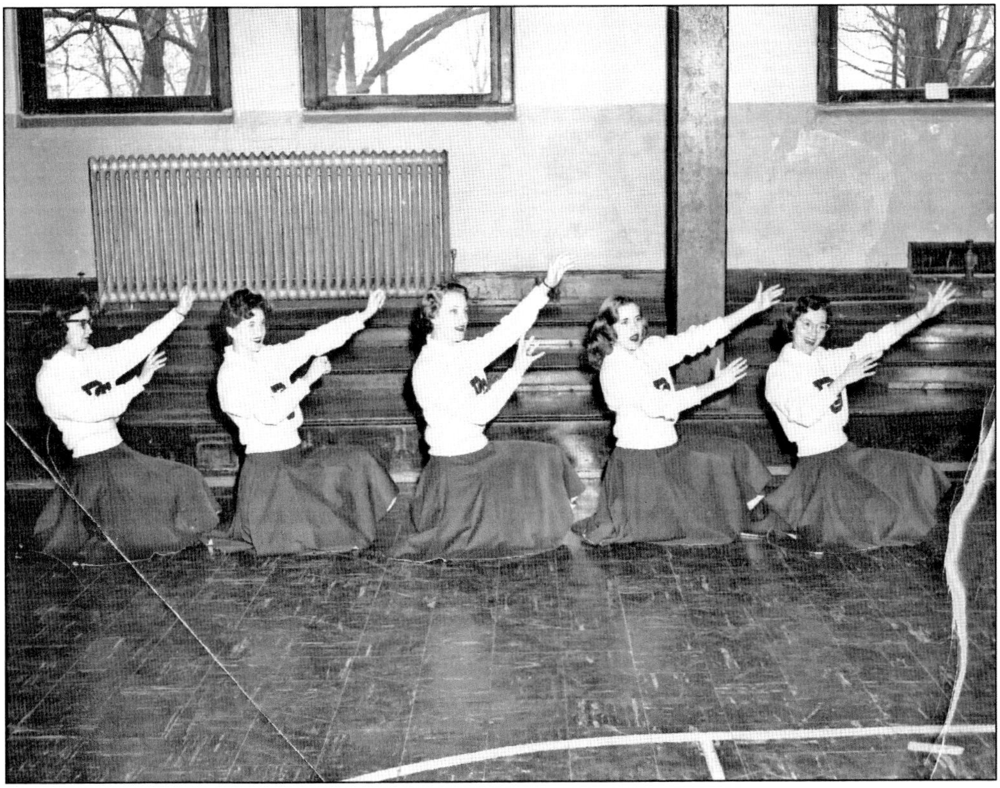

In the fall of 1956, the Rio Grande Redmen cheerleaders pose for this picture in Community Hall. From left to right are Joan Kelly (class of 1957), Erma Waller (class of 1957), Fern Oppy (class of 1957), Margaret Large, and Carol Goodrich. In the 2003 *Alumni Directory*, the first three are identified as retired teachers.

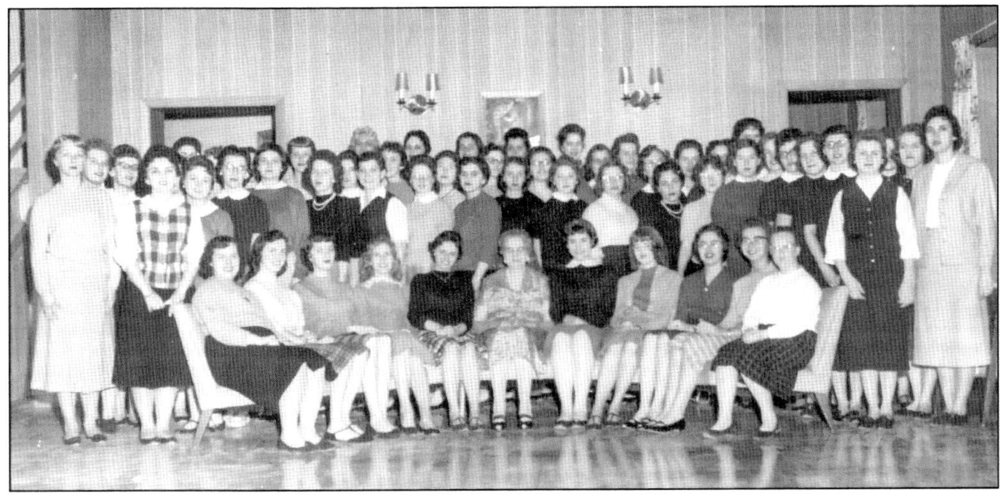

Davis Hall, named for the philanthropic Davis family of Oak Hill, became the first modern dormitory on the Rio campus. Built in 1957 on the corner that had been the site of Brockett Garden, it provided accommodations for over 100 female students. It led to the termination of Davis Cottage as housing for young ladies. In later years, more Davis money flowed into Rio Grande. Pictured here are the first residents of Davis Hall.

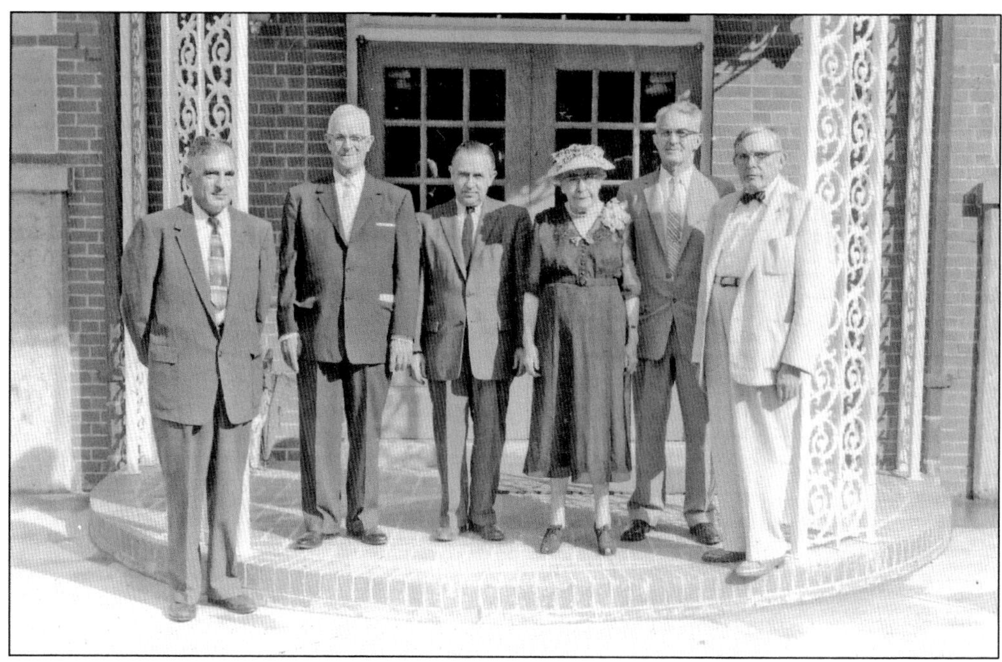

This group of trustees poses for a photograph at the May 1957 dedication of Davis Hall. From left to right are Francis W. Shane (?), Gallipolis; Frank C. Morrow, Wellston; Jack Stiffler Sr., Jackson; Margaret J Davis (principal donor), Oak Hill; Pres. Paul Lyne; and board chair J. Boyd Davis.

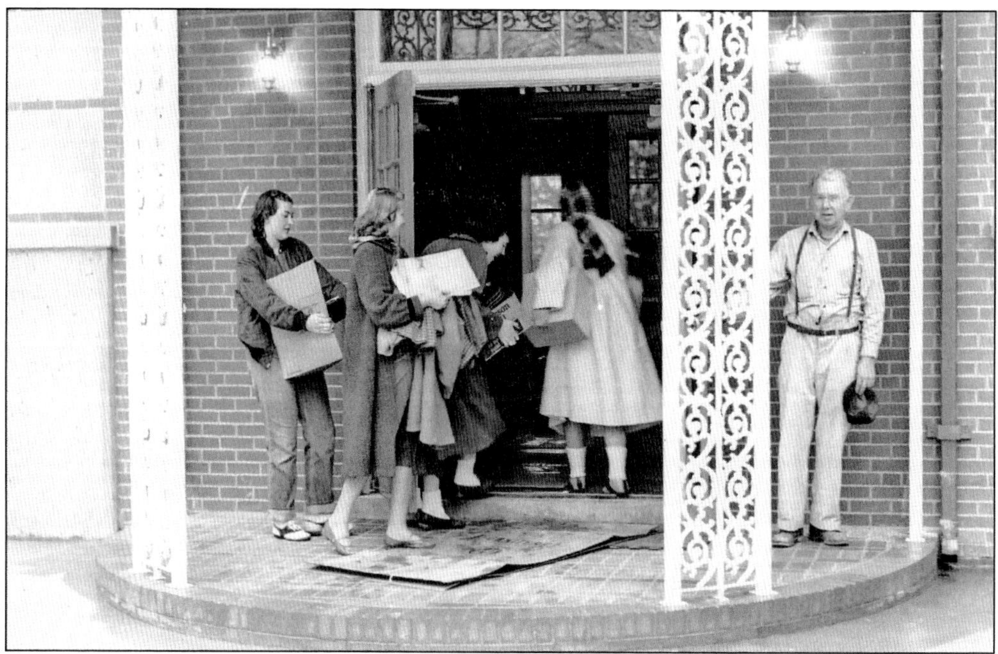

The opening of Davis Hall meant that female residents would now be housed on campus in a modern residence hall constructed to accommodate large numbers of students. Gone were the days of small groups of female students scattered about in small rooming houses. Here some of the first residents are seen on move-in day.

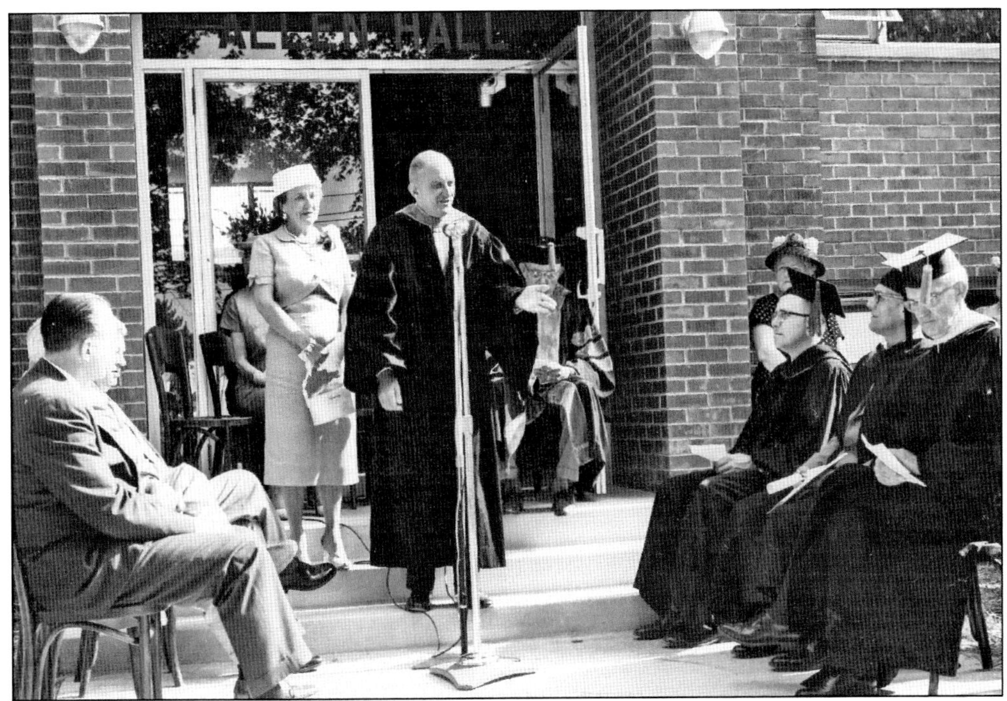

From his birth in the Boarding Hall, Don Allen (1904–1959) was closely associated with Rio Grande College. He was a 1921 alumnus and a major philanthropist, especially in his dozen years as a trustee from 1947. Allen was a major auto dealer, and his biggest achievements came with the funding of the building that bears his name and through providing athletic scholarships. He is pictured at the 1958 dedication of Allen Hall.

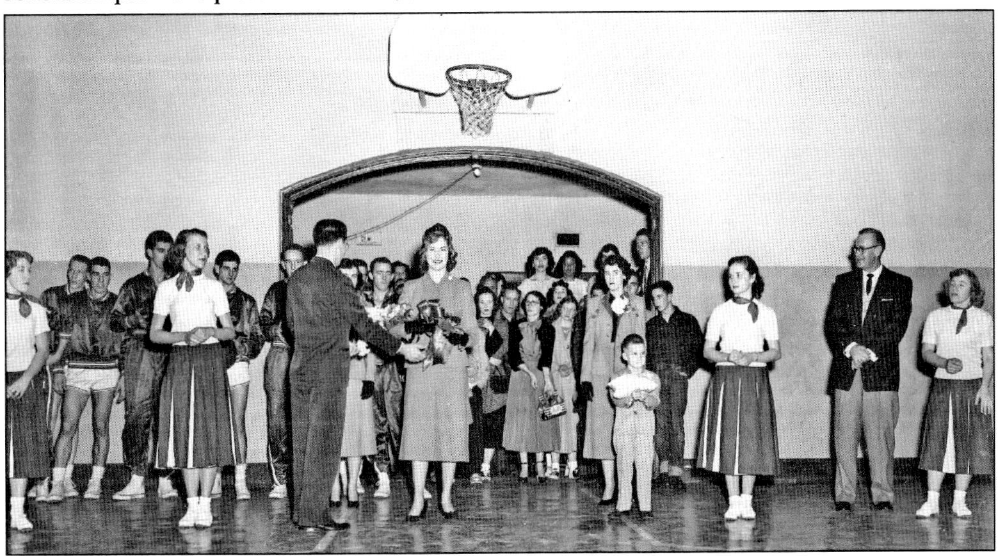

This picture of a 1950s-era homecoming in Community Hall illustrates some of the growing problems of that aging facility. It was cramped for basketball, lacking in adequate bathroom facilities, and run-down after years of minimal upkeep. Basketball games would soon be played entirely off campus—at Southwestern High School, Gallia Academy, and in Jackson. The basketball program was a band of vagabonds until the opening of Lyne Center in 1969.

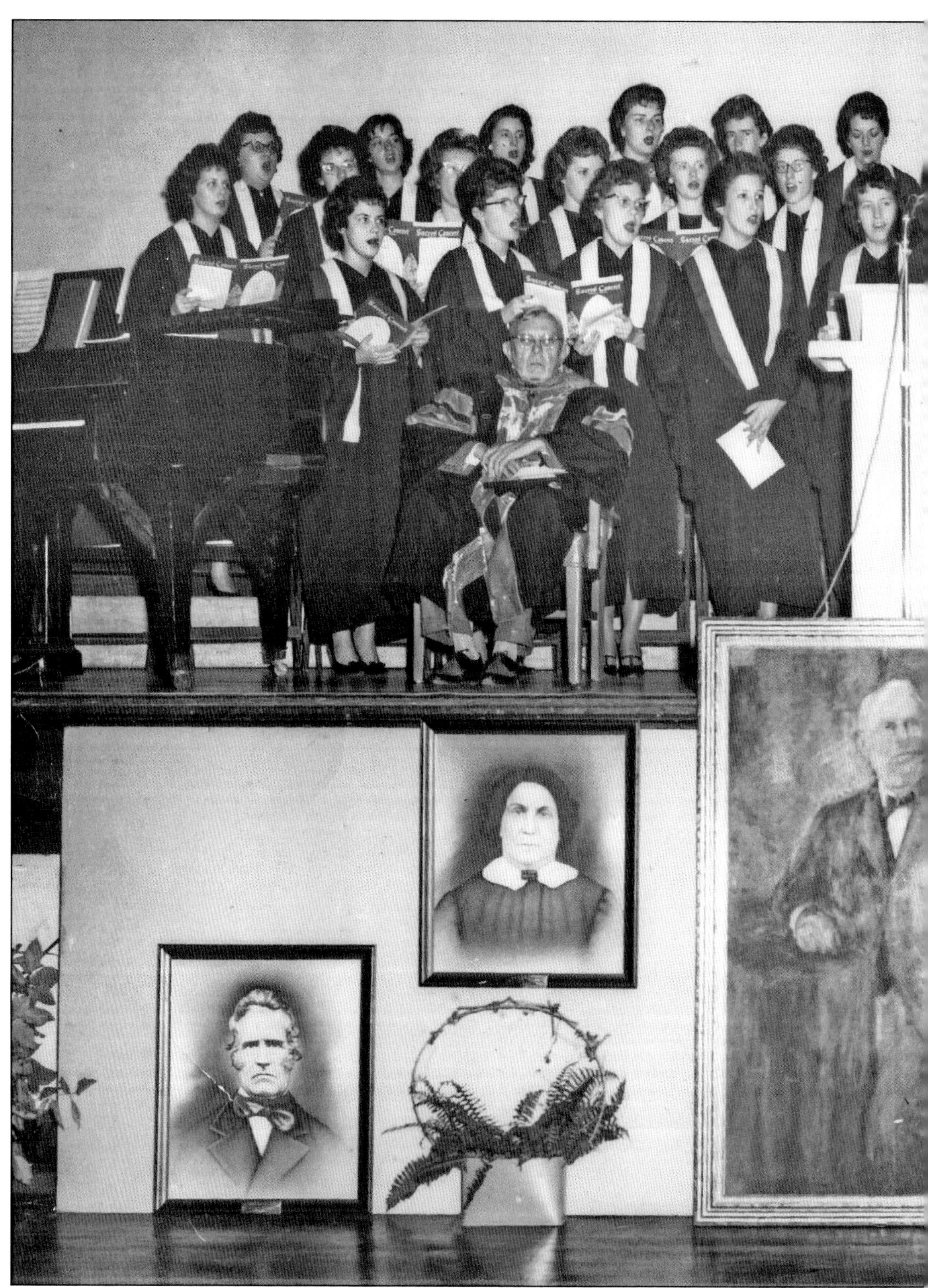

Founder's Day constituted a major activity on campus for many decades. This 1960 photograph shows the faculty and choir assembled on the Community Hall stage for the ceremony, with

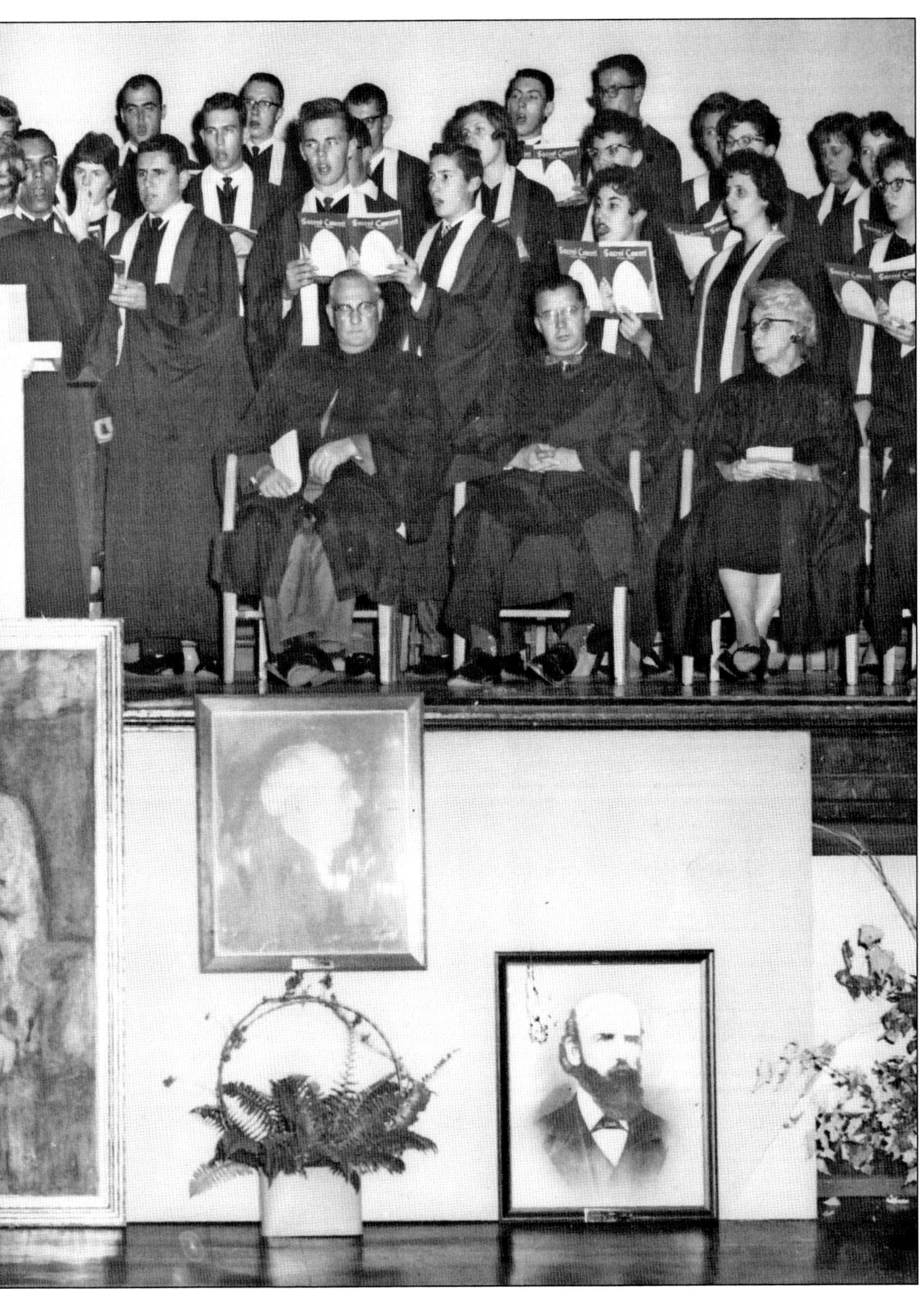

portraits of Nehemiah Atwood, Permelia Atwood, Ira Z. Haning, and two views of longtime president John Merrill Davis (1887–1911) in the front.

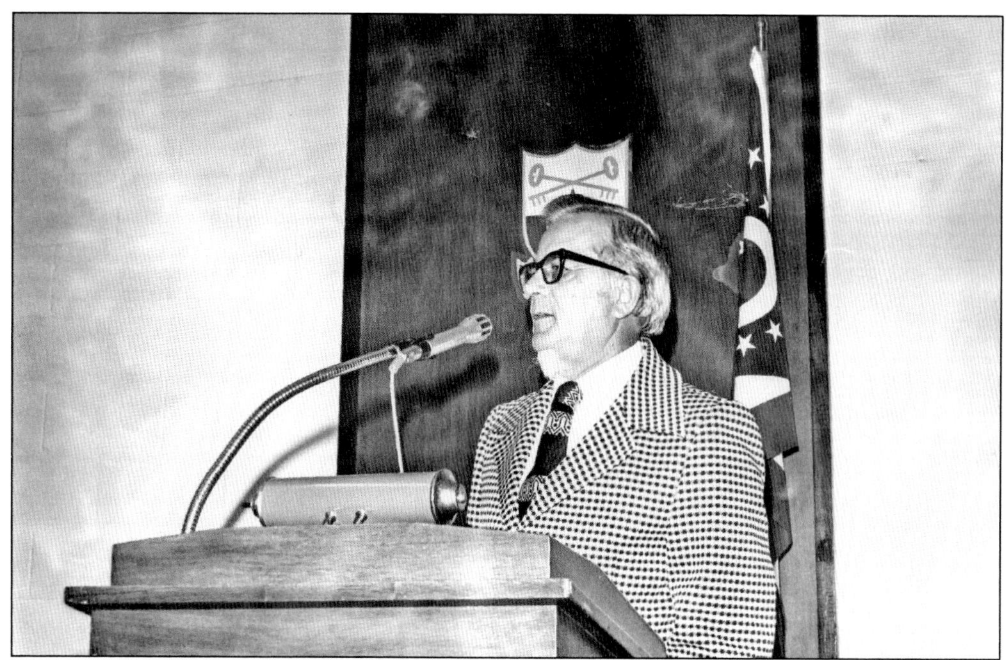

Alphus Christensen (1913–1992), who became president of Rio Grande on August 1, 1962, was the first executive to earn a doctorate. He was Minnesotan by birth and South Dakotan by residence, and his leadership brought may positive changes to Rio, including a new library, a dining hall, dorms, and, especially, accreditation and the community college by the time of his 1975 retirement.

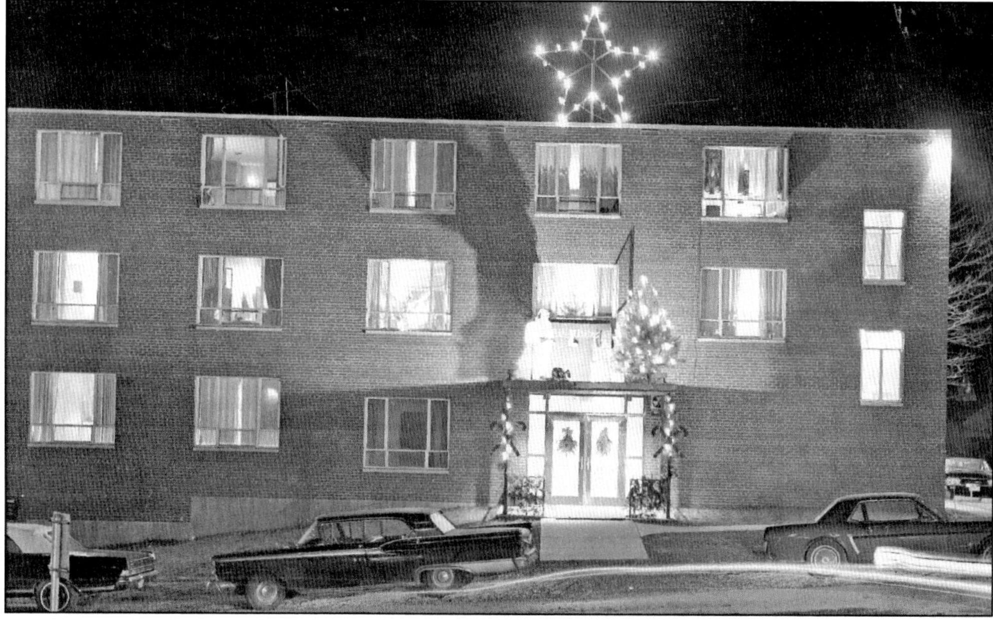

Moulton Hall was the first of three new dorms built in the 1960s. It bore the name of Albanus A. Moulton (1848–1888), who became one of the first professors and, in 1878, the second Rio Grande president. An able scholar of New England origin, Moulton suffered from consumption and eventually left Ohio in 1887 for Colorado, where he died the following year.

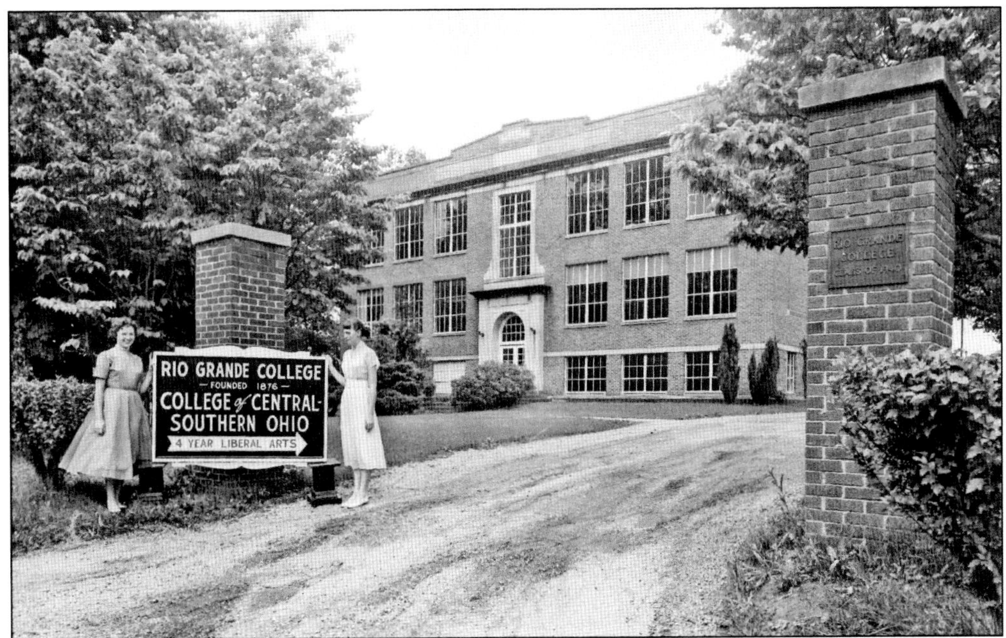

The Rio Grande community has sometimes been concerned that the name causes confusion with some undefined locale in Texas. Apparently, about 1960, someone thought to provide the school with a "sub-name," thus this sign identifying it as the "College of Central Southern Ohio." This name seems not to have caught either, and the more familiar sign, "Rio Grande College, 1876," was restored.

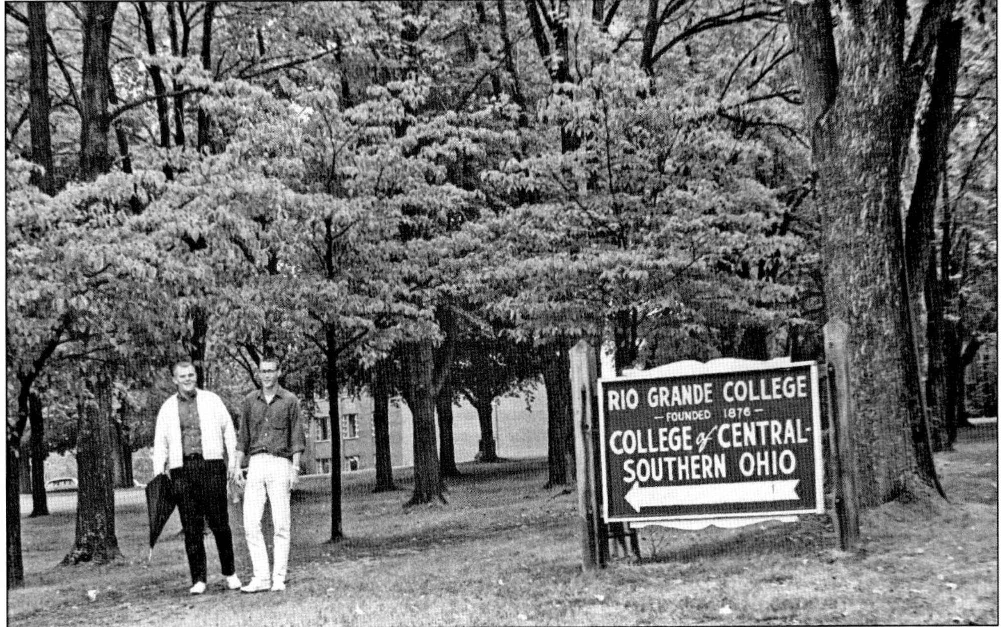

In addition to the one at the Atwood Drive entrance, another "College of Central Southern Ohio" sign stood at the corner of North and West College Avenues. With the new Allen Hall visible behind the trees, this photograph from 1963 shows students Jim Williams (left) and Walt Stiverson, both in the class of 1966. Both became Scioto County teachers.

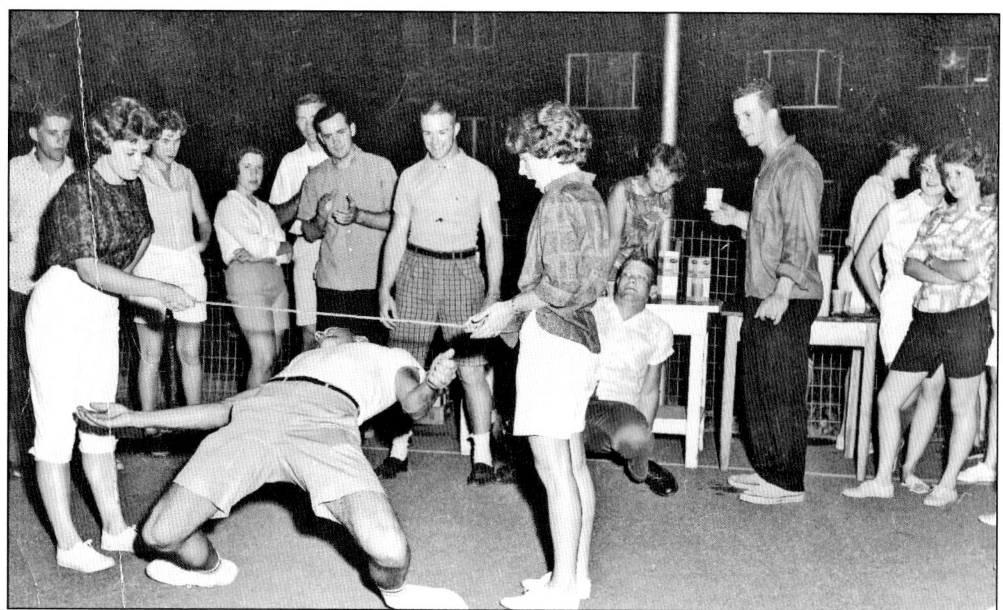

Dancing of any sort by Rio Grande students was not allowed until 1930. Since then, students have more than made up for that with May Day dances, homecoming dances, dance-a-thons for charity, and just about any other type of dance. Still, looking at this picture of 1962 students doing the limbo, one has to wonder just what the founders would have thought had they witnessed this.

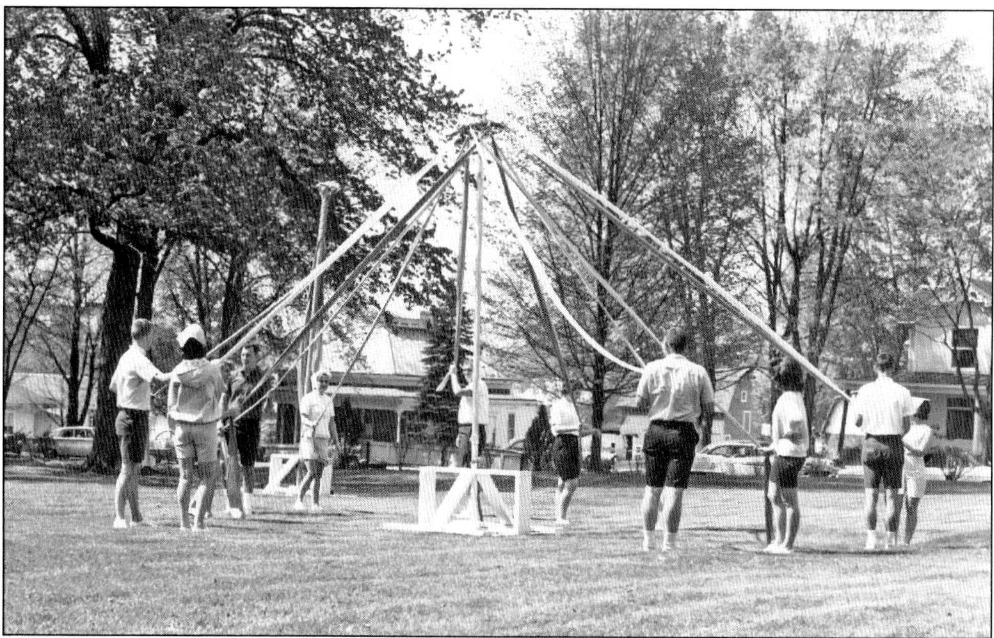

May Day weekend has always been a highlight of the spring at Rio Grande. Through 1963, a Maypole was actually set up on campus with a traditional dance. In the early 1960s, Prof. Zelma Northcutt was in charge, but it became more difficult to recruit participants. Other May Day traditions survived, but the Maypole as a tradition of ancient rites of spring did not. May Day is now celebrated with the Greek Games and a dance.

A widespread fad among collegians in the middle decades of the 20th century was trying to determine how many students could fit into a telephone booth. Rio Grande students were no exception. The 1962 photograph shows five inside and a sixth on top. Not only has this fad faded away, but telephone booths are now rare as well.

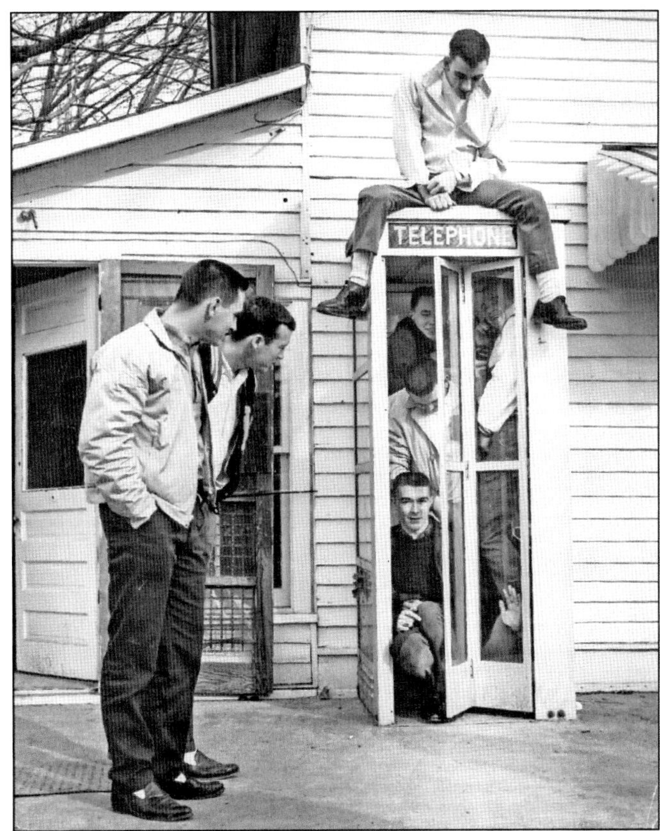

In a picture that may well be a visual description of the old saying "You and the horse you rode in on," a story by Lance Wilson in a 1966 edition of the *Signals* newspaper takes on the issue of students writing their names in a new sidewalk that had not yet dried. The horse was named Rocquinante, a takeoff of the famous steed ridden by Don Quixote.

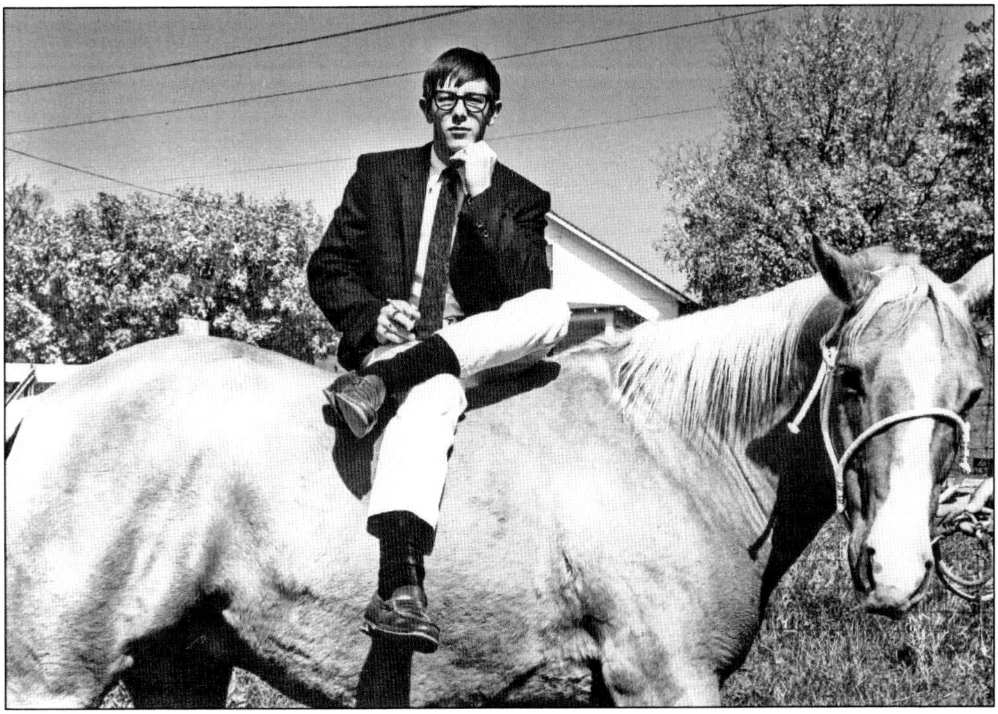

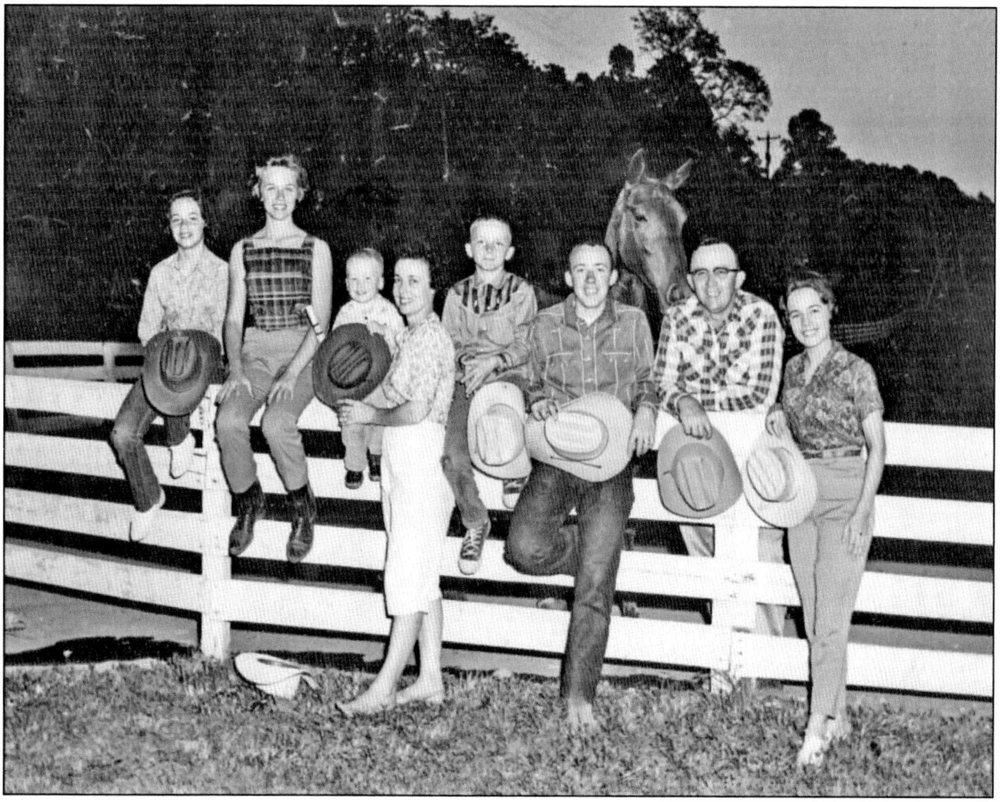

Bob Evans (1918–2007), a noted businessman, spent 11 years on the Rio Grande College Board of Trustees and an additional term on the Ohio Board of Regents, where his efforts founded the Ohio Appalachian Center for Higher Education. The entire Evans family is pictured here. From left to right are Debbie, Robin, Bobby, Jewel (Mrs. Bob Evans), Steve, Stanley, Bob, and Gwen.

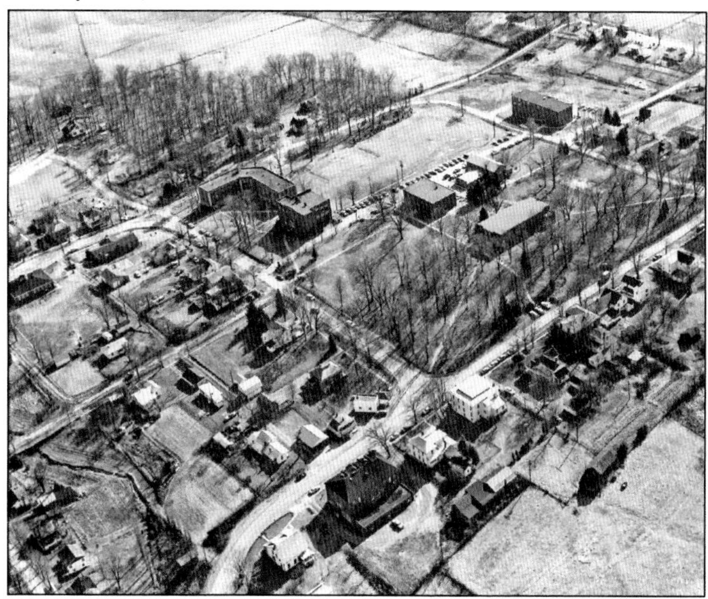

Many aerial photographs of the Rio Grande campus are obscured by heavy foliage. However, this one from about 1963 provides a clear view. Easily visible are Davis, Anniversary, Allen, and Moulton Halls. Also quite visible are Haning and Community Halls, Davis Cottage, Varney House, and the old student center. Davis Library, Florence Evans Hall (old Dining Hall), and additional dorms would soon be built.

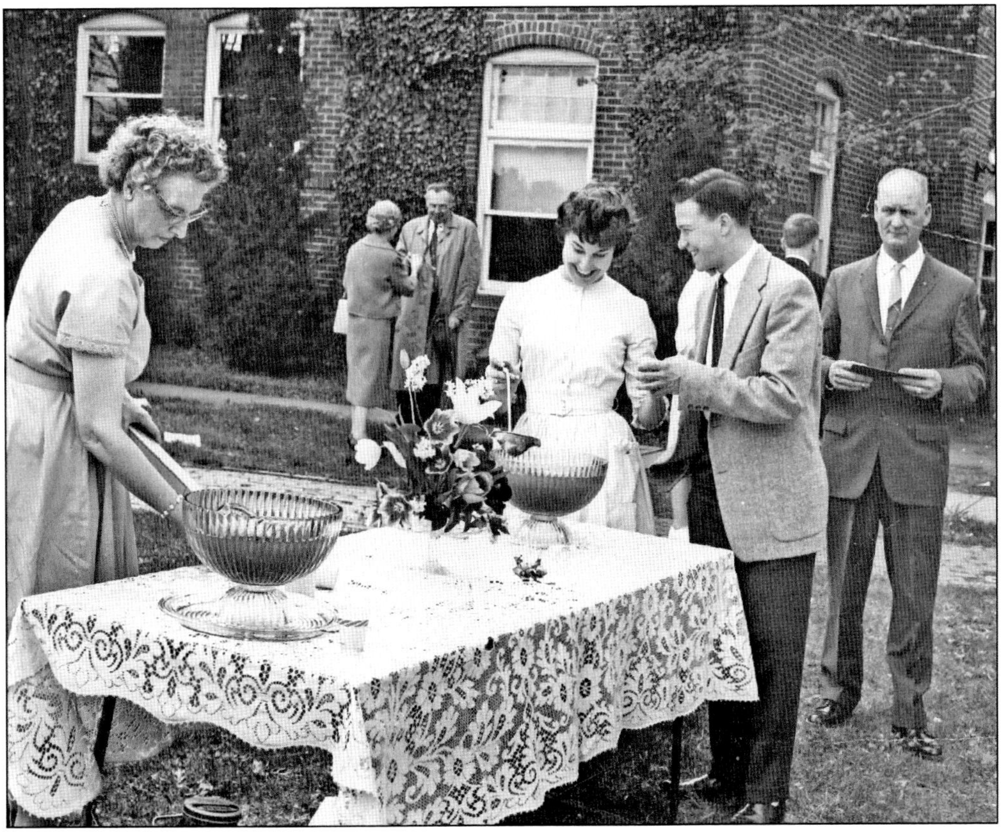

A long and continuing tradition at Rio has been serving punch and cookies to the audience at the conclusion of commencement exercises. This undated image illustrates the circumstance. Ivy-covered Community Hall is in the background.

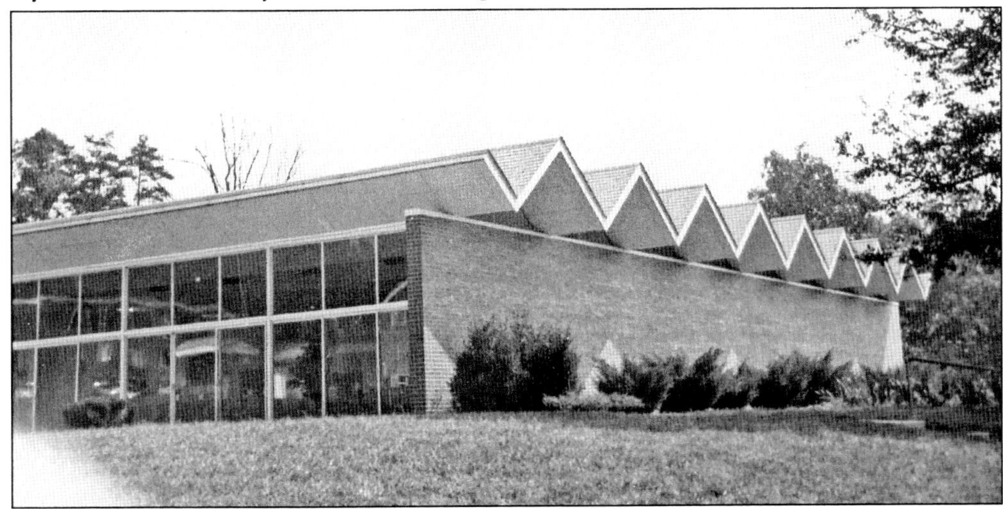

Completed in 1966 and known as the Dining Hall until 1983, this structure received its current name from a Jackson, Ohio, benefactor: Florence Evans. For some years, it served as home to the Emerson Evans School of Business. More recently, it houses a number of offices, including admissions and records, and is known as the "Reardon One Stop."

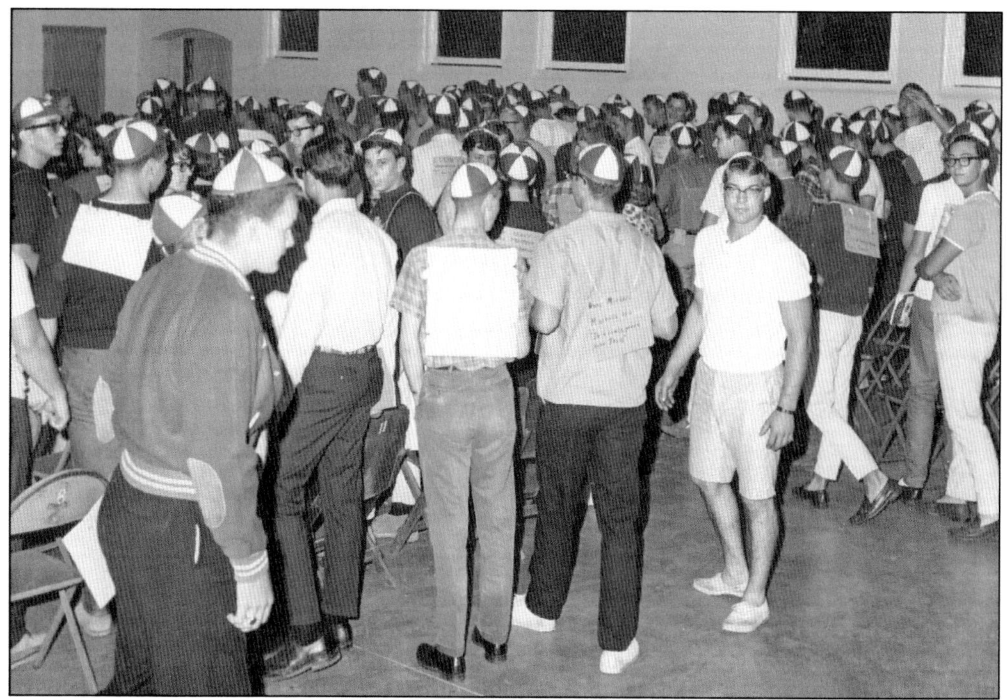

During Freshman Week from at least the 1930s up through the end of the 1960s, first-year students were subjected to a variety of mild hazing, including the wearing of beanie caps. This 1965 image shows a number of them in Community Hall. Afterward, this tradition mercifully died, as most commuters simply ignored such foolish activity.

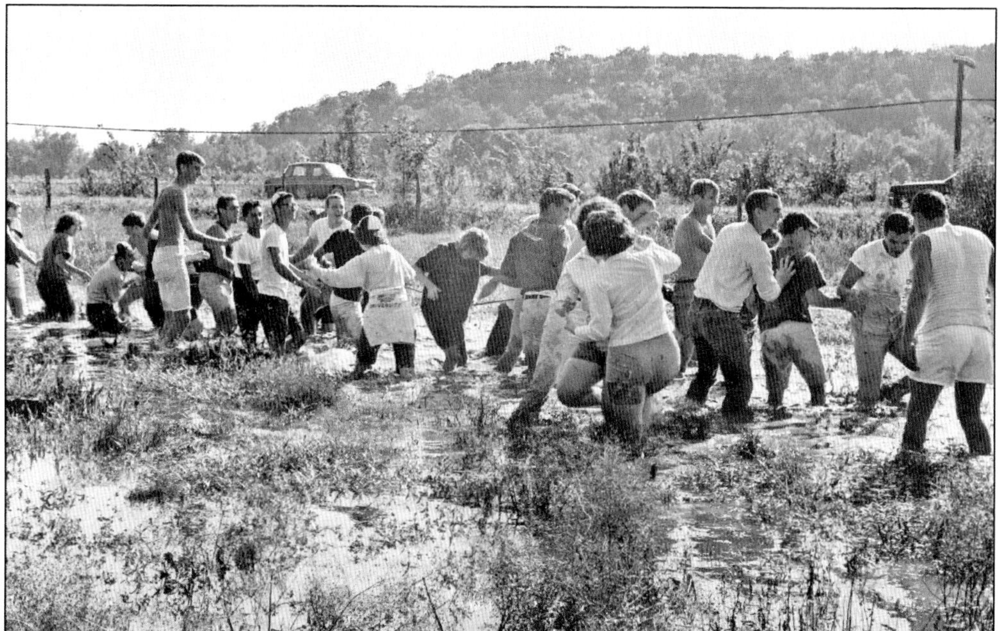

Another Freshman Week tradition that flourished for some years was the tug-of-war. The losers, and sometimes winners as well, got dragged through the mud. Although dirtier than beanie wearing, this event—as pictured in 1965—also passed into history.

Rio Grande's new Jeanette Albeiz Davis Library opened in the fall of 1965, providing the college with a building used almost exclusively for library purposes. It received its name from the wife of longtime trustee Sam Davis (1957–1975). After more than half a century, it continues to occupy a prominent spot on the URG campus. The location had previously been part of the college football field.

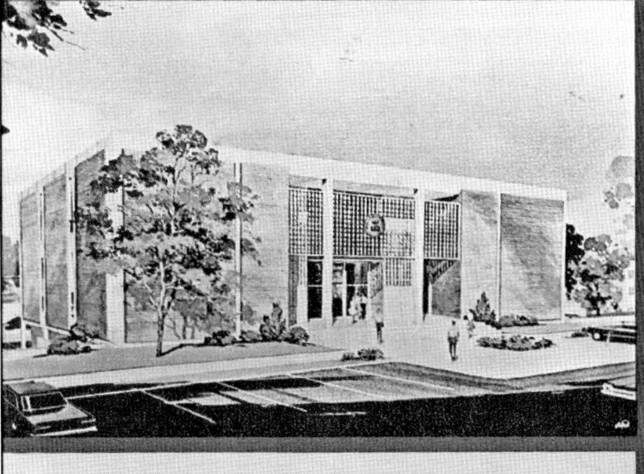

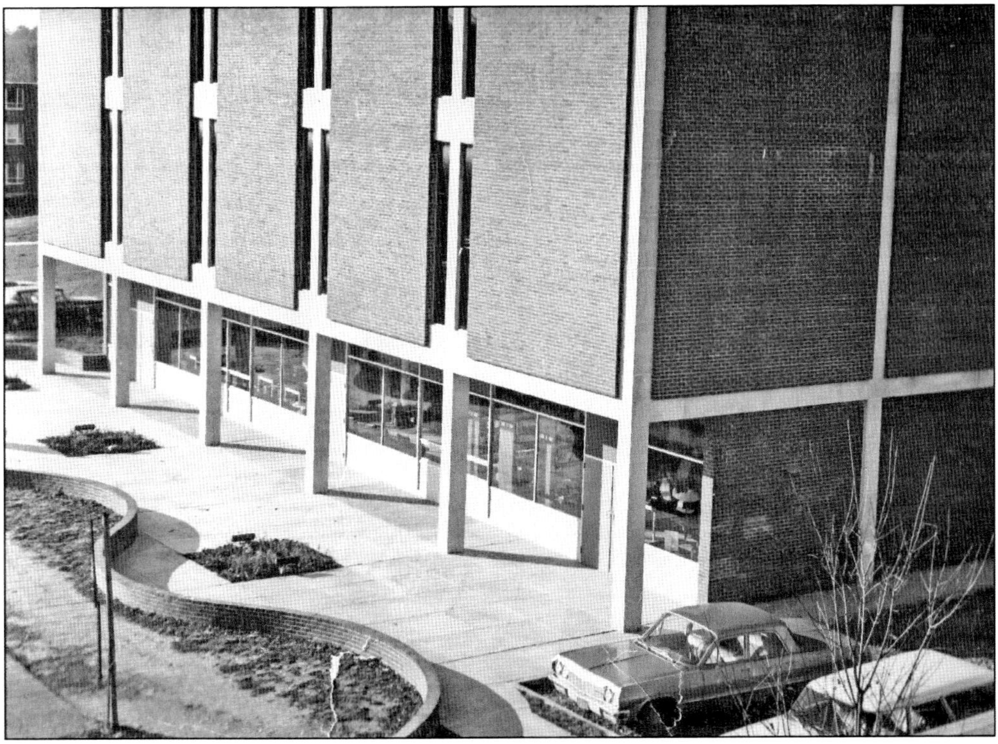

Photographers from outside Rio Grande College who take pictures for recruiting brochures and catalogs often view beautiful campus scenes that elude those who are at Rio on a daily basis. Such is this image of the rear of Davis Library, a half century old in 2016, that those entering from the front hardly notice. This angle is commonly observed only through the windows of a portion of Davis Hall.

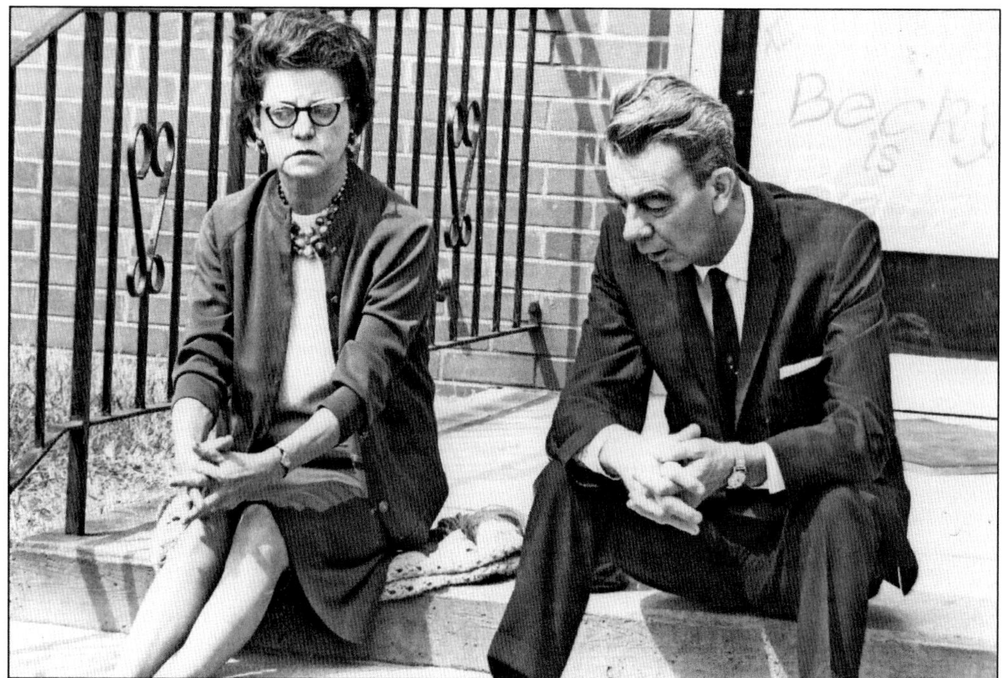

John J, Graham (1914–1988) and his beloved wife, Pauli (1913–1973), came to Rio Grande in 1966. John was an old friend of President Christensen from their days as college debate coaches. John and Pauli were brought in to teach communication and help with the move for accreditation. Legends with their students, many of whom speak of them with an almost godlike love, these two unique and dynamic individuals left a mark on all Rio Grande students since. From 1974 until the 2016–2017 academic year, former students have taught speech at Rio Grande.

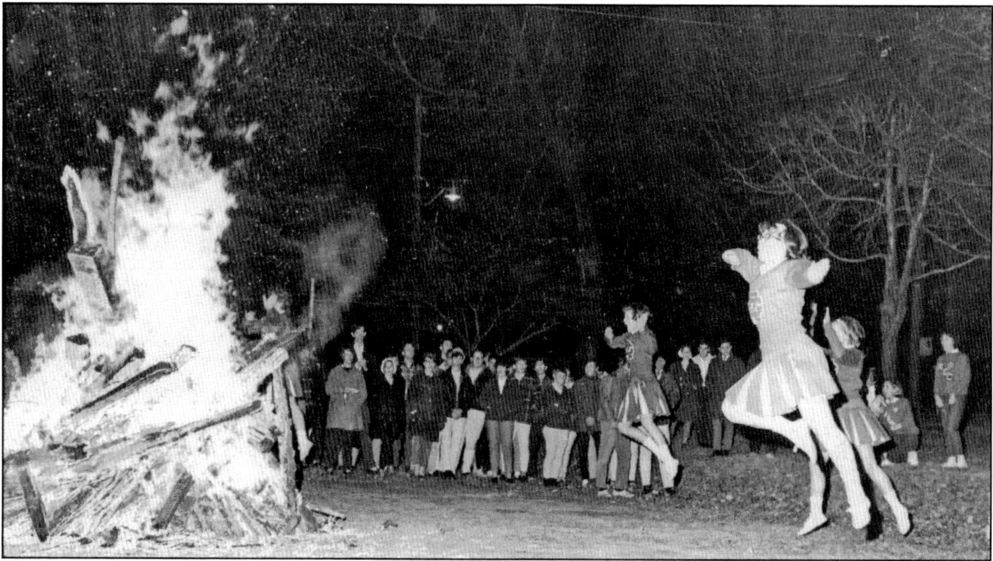

Bonfires were common on campus in the 1960s as a venue for pep rallies. In this picture, cheerleaders seem to be taking flight into the bonfire itself. It is hard to determine if the rallies ever helped with victory, but the students always attended and had a good time.

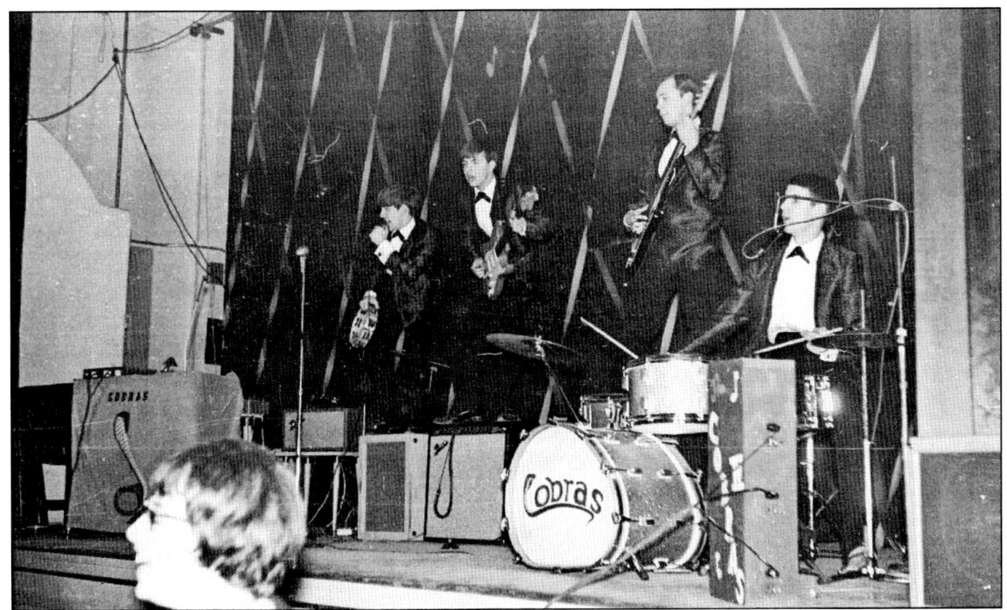

A band made up of Rio students in the late 1960s, the Cobras often played dances at Rio Grande and other venues in southeastern Ohio. Shown here in performance in Community Hall are Stephen Miller on bass, David Miller on lead, Dave Littler on drums, and vocalist Rex Prater. As of the fall of 2016, a variation of the group has continued to rock on. (Courtesy of alumnus Erik Miller, son of Stephen.)

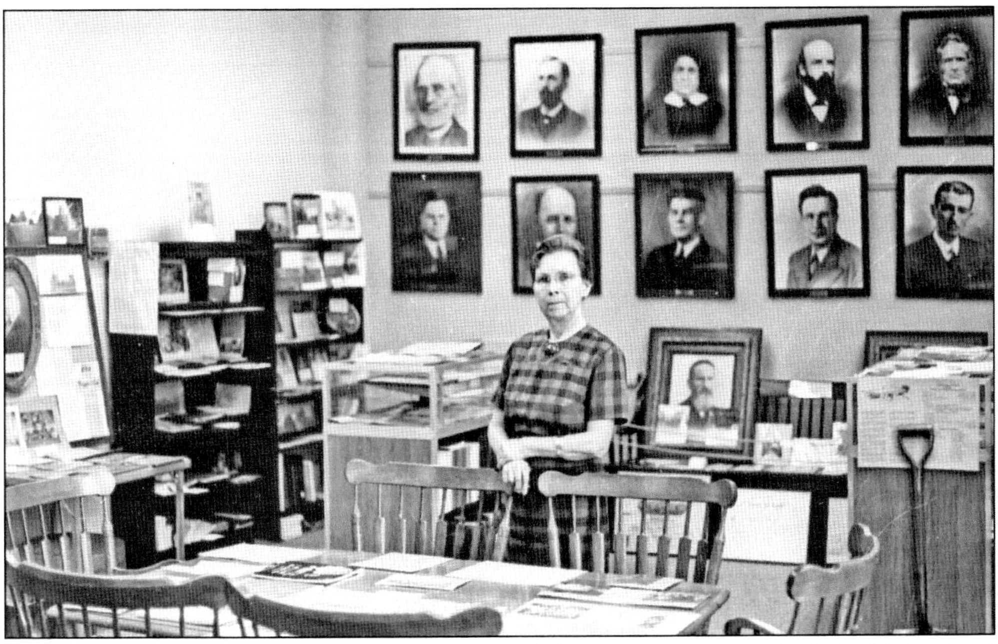

Mary Lintner came to Rio Grande in 1922 to teach home economics at both the high school and the college as part of the Smith-Hughes Act. In 1923, she married Dean William A. Lewis, but she continued teaching until 1929. Following her husband's death, she held a part-time position as curator of the library's Heritage Room until overtaken by age and her own death in 1978.

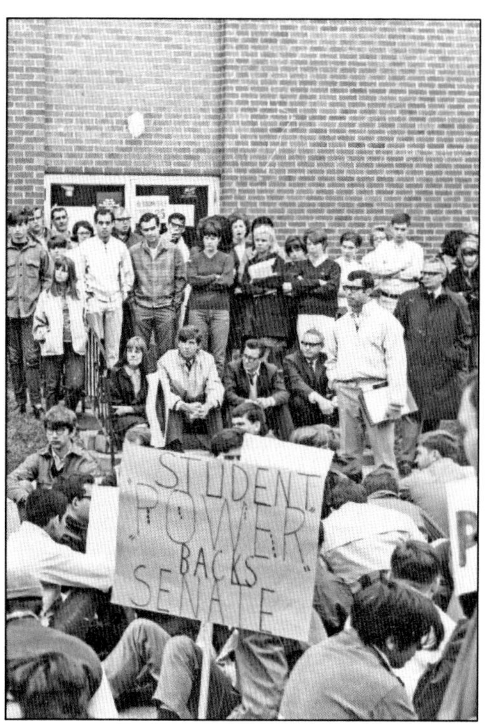

The social change and turmoil of the 1960s had a profound effect on Rio Grande. The call for more social freedom and a resistance to authority came to a head in 1969. On March 18, 1969, one student was arrested and 40 were suspended for participating in a protest on the library steps.

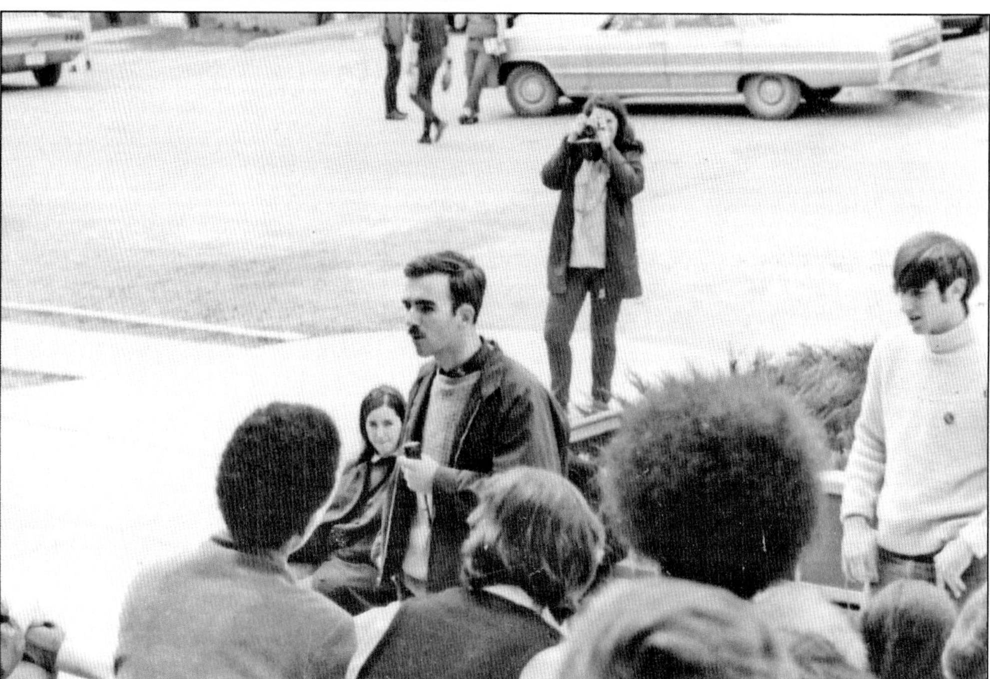

Mike Graham (class of 1970) was the son of John Graham and the student body president. Pictured here with the microphone speaking to students, he walked the tightrope of being the son of a very active faculty member and also a person of deep convictions for student rights. The storm of 1969 was weathered with little damage, and Mike would become a lawyer deeply involved in the fight for social justice.

Five

FROM ACCREDITATION TO UNIVERSITY 1969–1989

With North Central Association accreditation achieved and an enrollment that swelled to 850 in 1969–1970, the Rio Grande community had some reason for optimism. However, such hopes were short-lived, as a new crisis soon appeared. The termination of conscription, coupled with the all-volunteer military, caused widespread enrollment decline in all colleges; the decline tended to be more acute in smaller schools such as Rio, where the numbers dropped to 750 in 1971–1972.

Conditions demanded new innovations to stem the reversing tide. A short-term solution created a new scholarship program. Creation of a four-county community college district promised more long-range stability: students in the district would pay a lower tuition rate, funded by a district one-mill tax levy. The initial $1,000 scholarship plan brought in 155 new students, and the May 1974 passage of the Gallia-Jackson-Meigs-Vinton levy produced positive results. Student numbers slowly and steadily increased again. Alphus Christensen, having achieved the major goals of accreditation and the community college, retired after the May 1975 graduation exercises.

Short-term presidencies of Paul Hines and Thomas Quick had little impact but also did little damage. Paul Hayes—in two stints (1977–1983 and 1986–1991)—chose to build on the Christensen legacy. He successfully achieved more cooperation between the separate boards of trustees and initiated new technical programs, some of which endured, while those that failed to attract students were terminated. Absorbing the Holzer School of Nursing into Rio Grande College ranked as his best move to most, with expanding the Emerson Evans School of Business and strengthening existing programs not far behind. A three-year interregnum of the unpopular Clodus Smith left no long-term negativity. The public funding placed new emphasis on FTE (full-time equivalent) numbers.

By the 1980s, the vast majority of students were commuters. However, sports teams—for both males and females—continued to do well, and campus organizations flourished. In August 1989, with an FTE number of 1,738 and a head count of 2,012, Rio Grande College, following similar action in like-sized schools, became the University of Rio Grande.

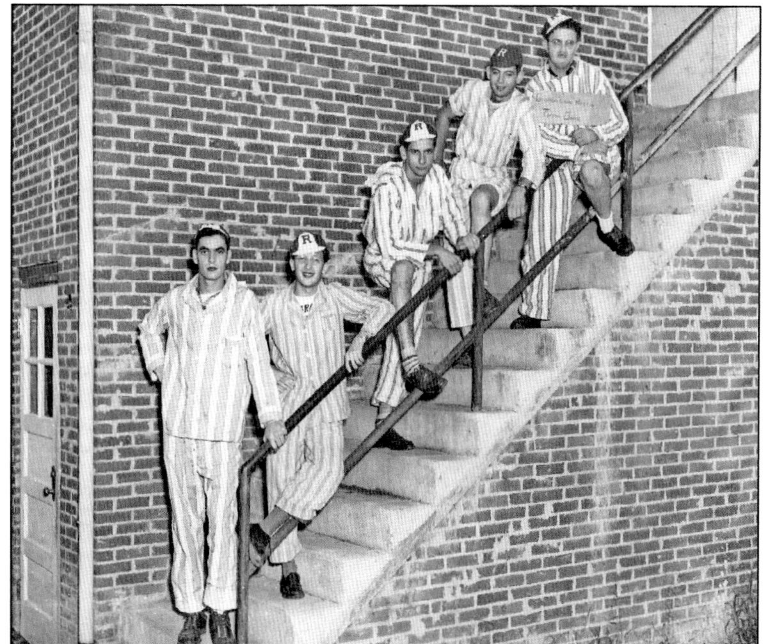

This pajama-clad quintet pictured on the steps of the old Student Center in the late 1960s undoubtedly shows participants in the waning years of Freshman Week. Except for the person shown at the top of the stairs, who carries a sign identifying himself as Charles Martin, the others have not been identified.

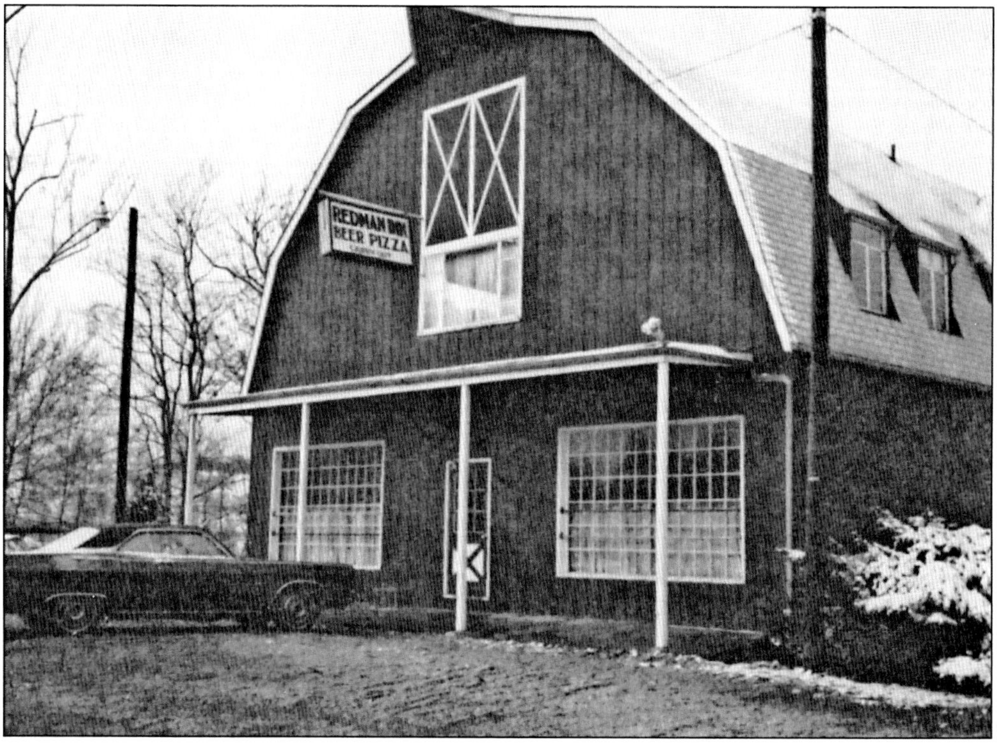

Most of the original founders of Rio Grande College were equally active in the temperance movement, and Raccoon Township had a long dry tradition. However, by the later 1960s, student attitudes had changed. Springfield Township was wet, and the Redman Inn became a favored student watering hole until well into the 1980s. The structure was later turned into apartments.

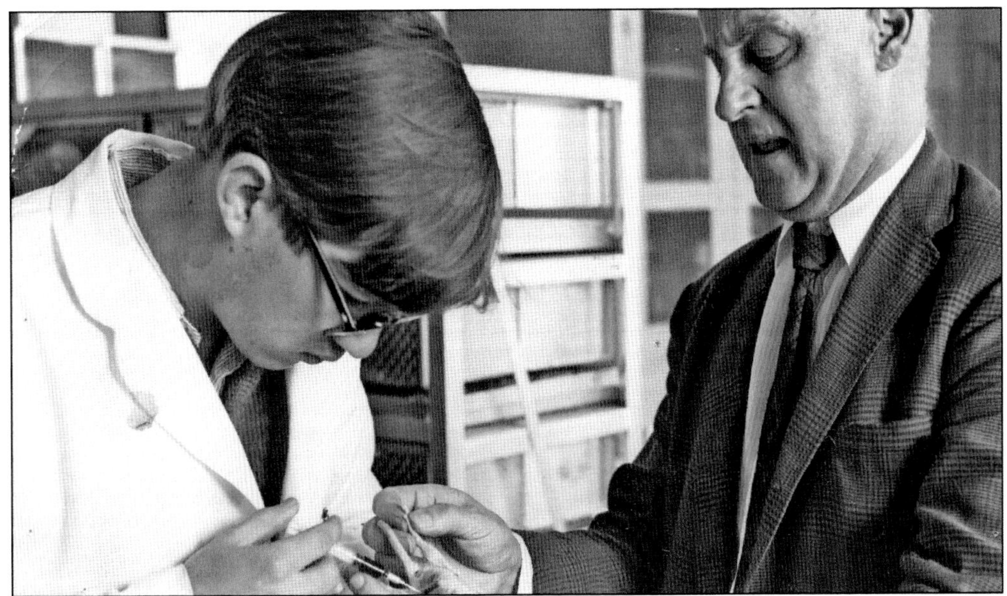

Biology professor Lloyd Carr (1917–1976) may well have been the best-educated Rio Grande faculty member. He studied at the Sorbonne and held a doctorate from the University of Paris. A Renaissance man, Carr was also a Virginia folksong collector. He joined the science staff in 1963 and dropped dead near the library on October 4, 1976. Carr is pictured here with an unidentified student injecting a lab rat.

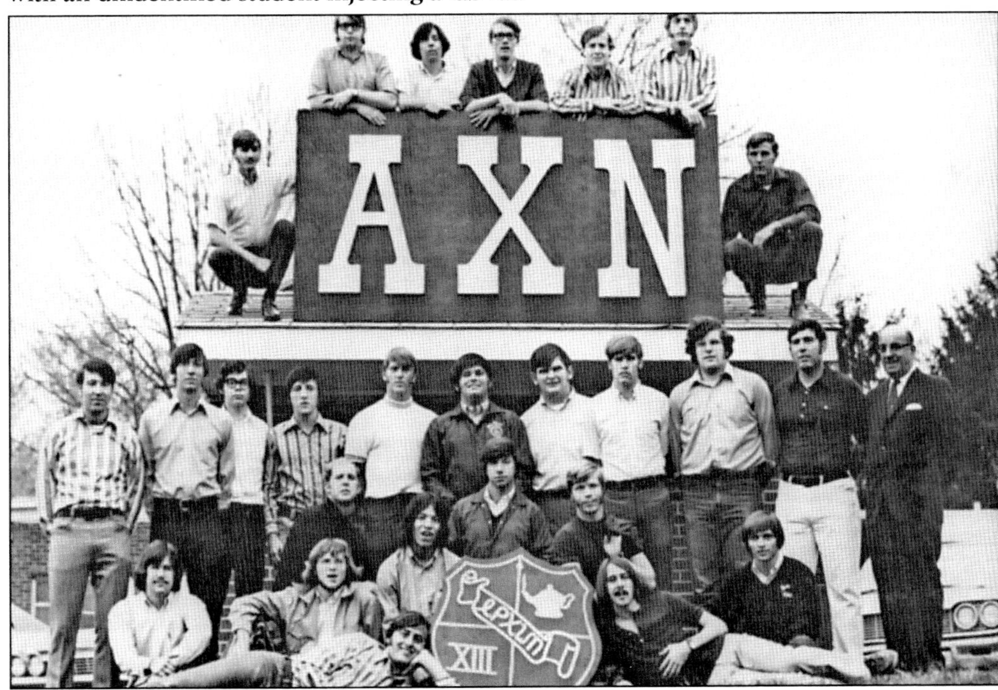

The Fraternal Order of Archon, or Alpha Chi Nu (AXN), is the oldest of current campus fraternities, founded during the 1958–1959 school year. It engaged in a wide variety of service and social activities, including sponsoring queen candidates for homecoming and May Day. Dean Brown was a longtime advisor. This and subsequent Greek photographs date from 1971.

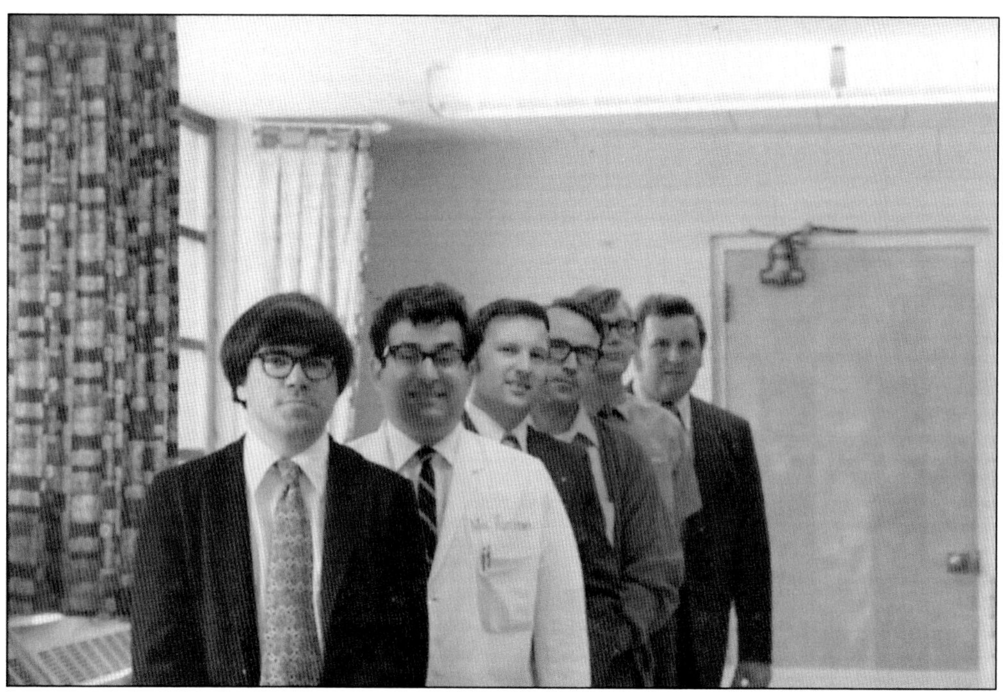

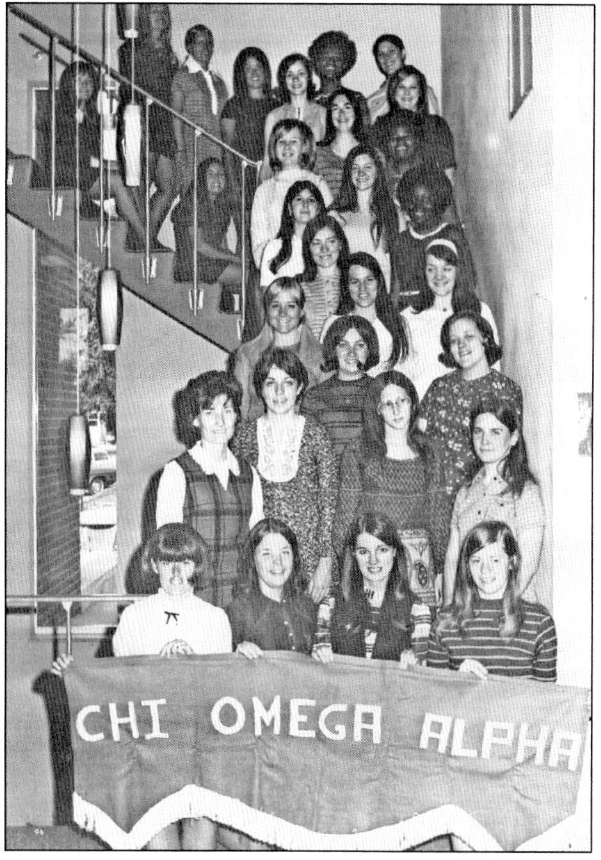

In 1971, the math and science faculty poses for a group photograph. From left to right are T. Michael Rhodes, Ronald Tucceri, Charles Withee, Benjamin Forshey, Russell Eubanks, and H. Paul Lloyd, who eventually moved to the Education Department. All except Eubanks devoted most of their professional careers to "Old Rio." Tucceri taught chemistry; the others, mathematics.

The oldest current campus sorority—Chi Omega Alpha, or Athena—dates from March 10, 1959. It later changed its name to Phi Sigma Sigma and remains thus known in 2016. In addition to its normal service and social activities, it participates in the Adopt-a-Highway Program.

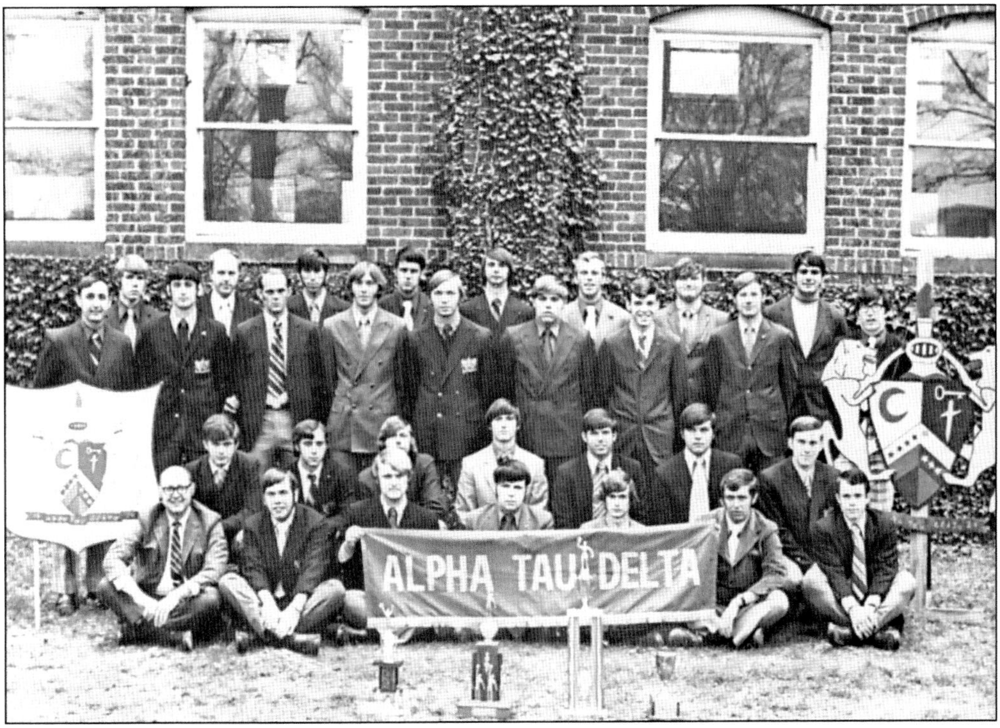

Alpha Sigma Phi fraternity dates from April 22, 1972, under that name, but it had earlier been known as Alpha Tau Delta (as pictured). Charter members include two who went on to have longtime Rio Grande connections: track coach Bob Willey (class of 1973) and trustee Jack Finch (class of 1974). Jack Payton (class of 1975) served as Gallipolis City Schools superintendent.

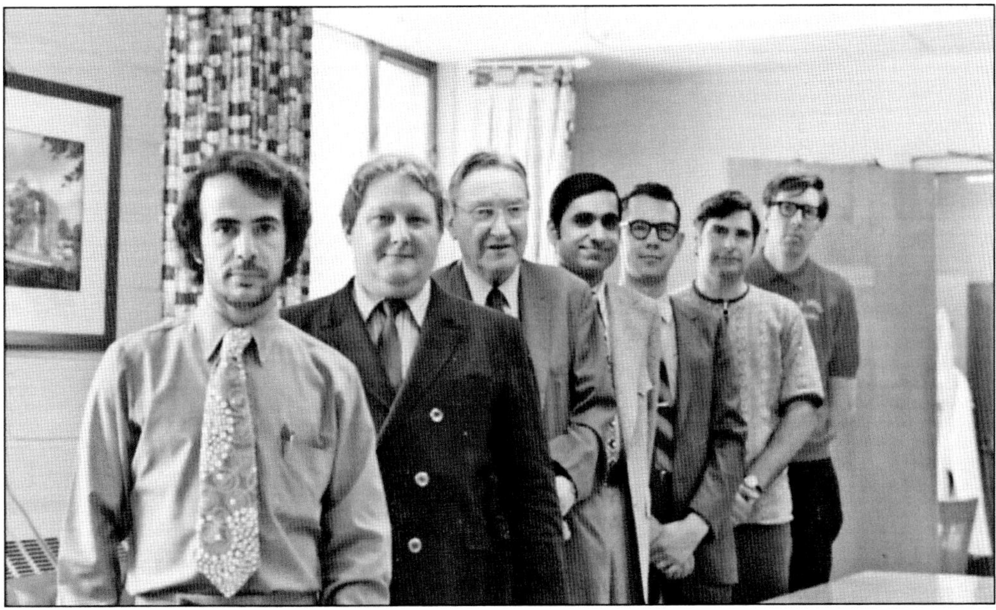

The social science faculty in 1971 consists of, from left to Paul Angelides (political science), Sam Smith (history and political science), J. Sherman Porter (political science), Kris Kool (economics), James Clark (business), Frederick Snuffer (sociology), and Robert Leith (history).

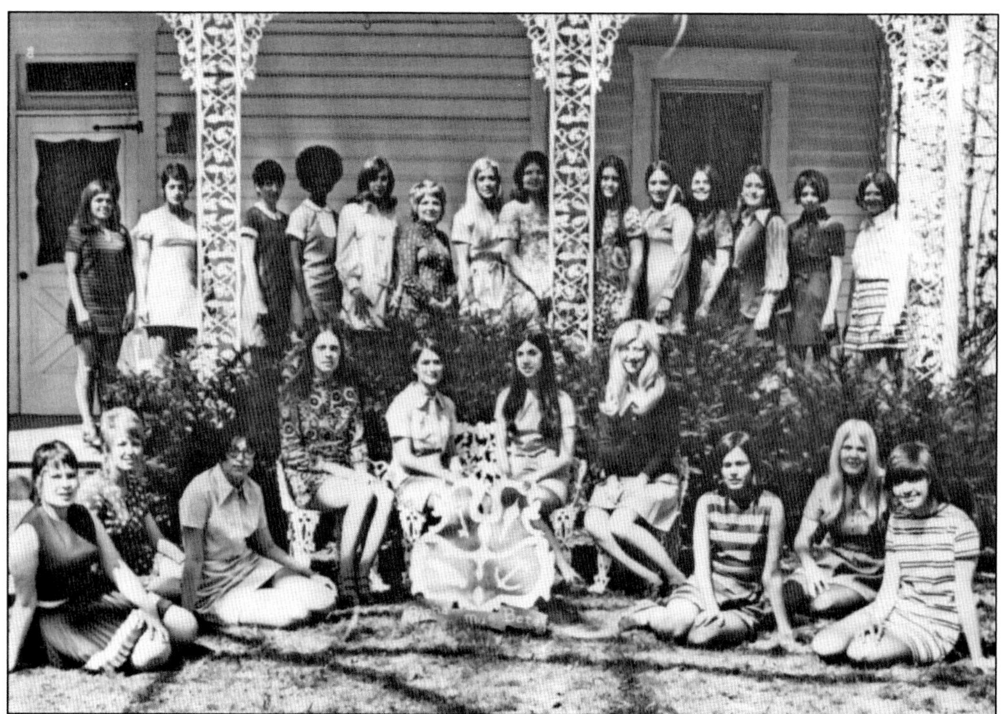

Alpha Mu Beta sorority dates from 1965 and remains active after more than 50 years. It is self-described as a "sisterhood of friendship and cooperative learning." Along with members of Chi Omega Alpha and Zeta Theta Chi, several Alpha Mu Beta sisters have been homecoming and May Day queens.

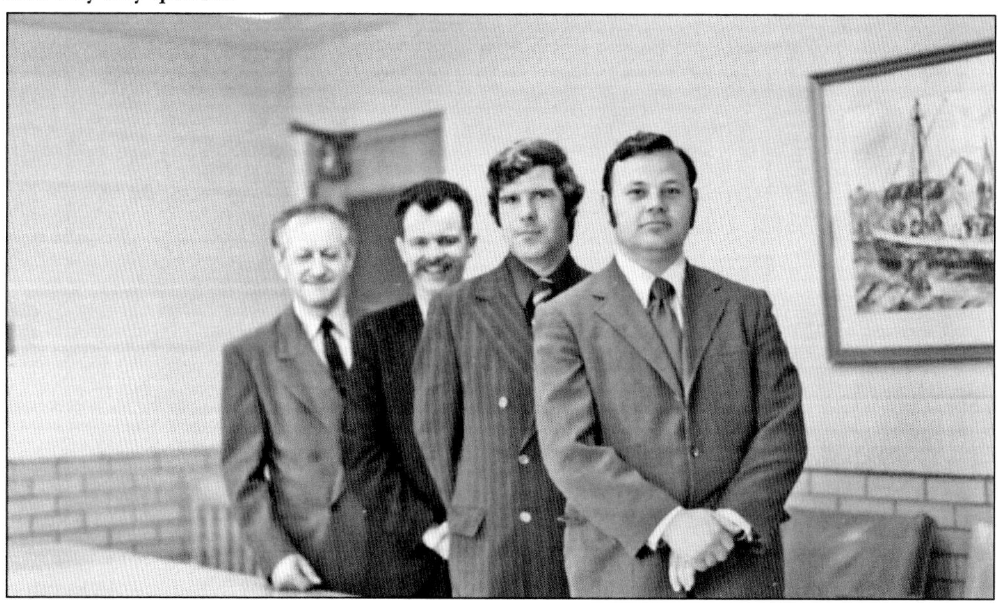

Four members of the wide-ranging humanities staff are, from left to right, Jan Simko (literature), T. Vail Palmer (philosophy and religion), Jack Hart (literature), and Lewis Rutherford (communications). The approximate date is 1971. As of January 2017, Hart is still a very active professor of English.

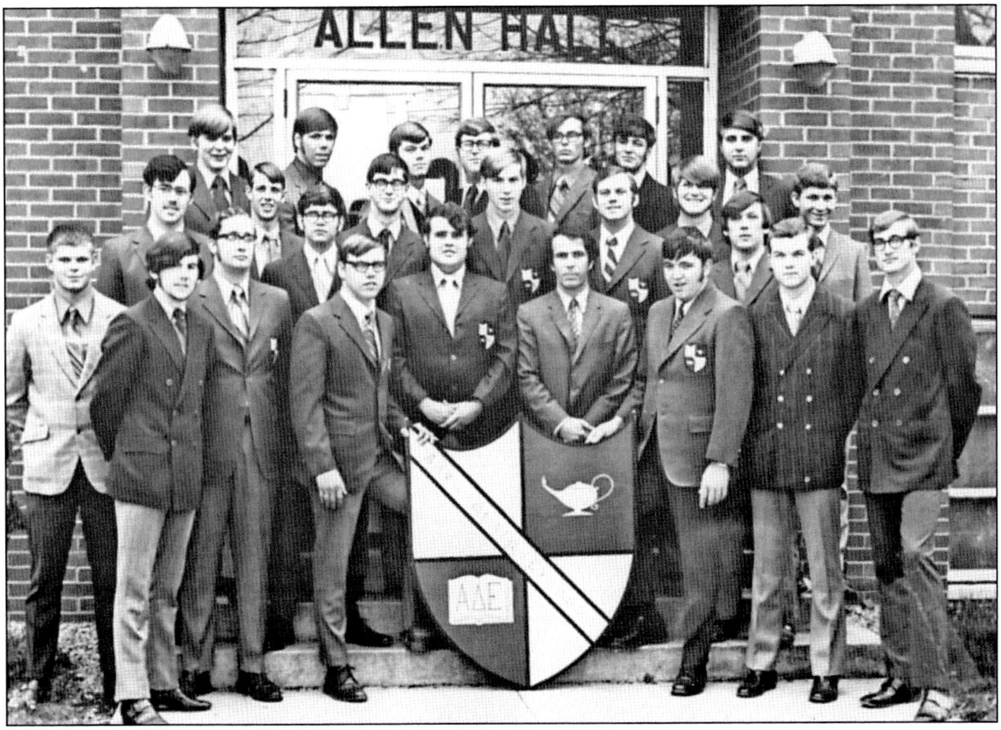

Alpha Delta Epsilon fraternity was founded in the fall of 1968 to "promote scholarship and a close brotherhood." In 1985, the group changed its name to Tau Kappa Epsilon when it took a national affiliation. Members include William Hull (class of 1991), who attained a scholarly reputation writing three chapters in a biographical study of vice presidents before he was claimed by cancer.

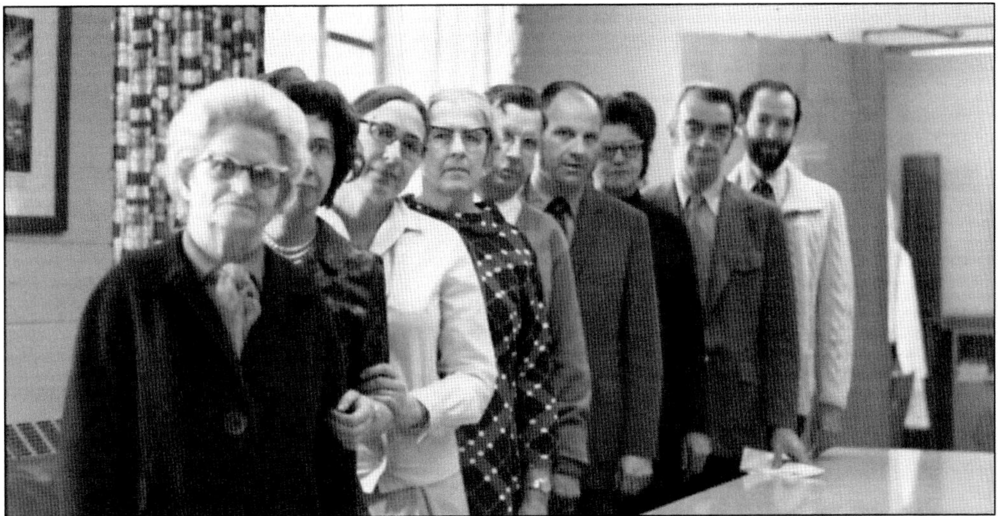

This faculty group shot from the early 1970s covers instructors in a wide variety of subjects. From left to right are Zelma Northcutt (music and history), Marjorie Harrison (English), Shirley Mason (art), Ruth Thomas (English), Luther Tracy (English), Merlyn Ross (music), Pauline D. Graham (English and communications), John J. Graham (communications), and John Bernard (communications).

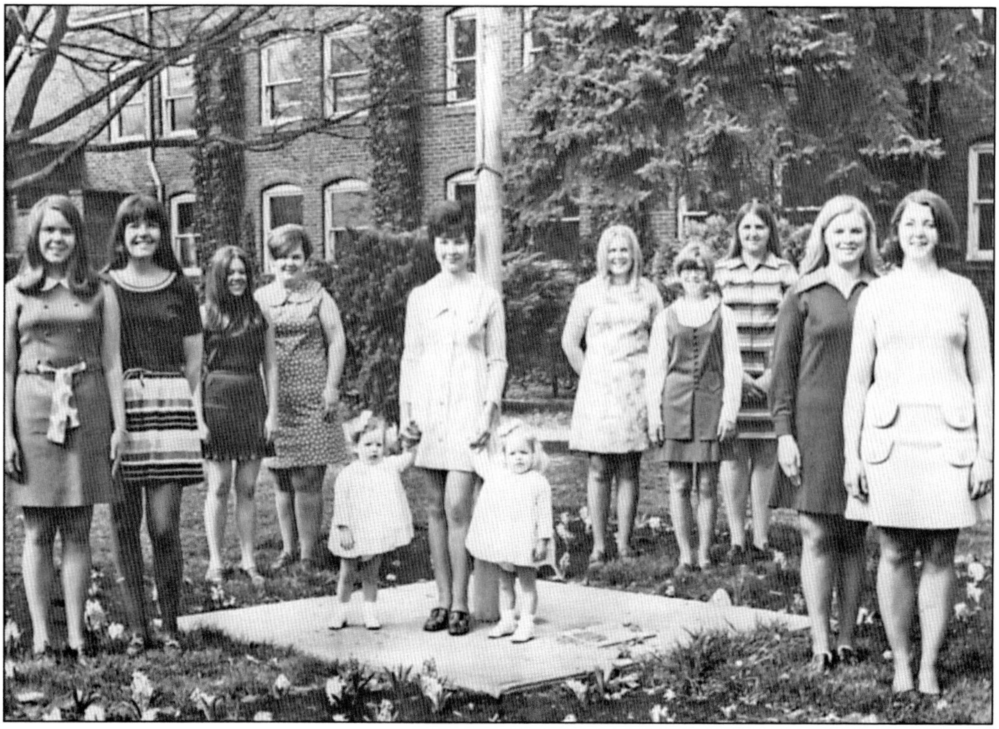

Founded in 1959 as Zeta Chi, this sorority later became familiarly known as Zeta Theta Chi. In 1986, it went national as Alpha Sigma Tau. For several years, it and Athena ranked as the two leading female Greek groups. Later, in the mid-1990s, Alpha Sigma Tau disbanded and then rejuvenated under the old Zeta Theta Chi name.

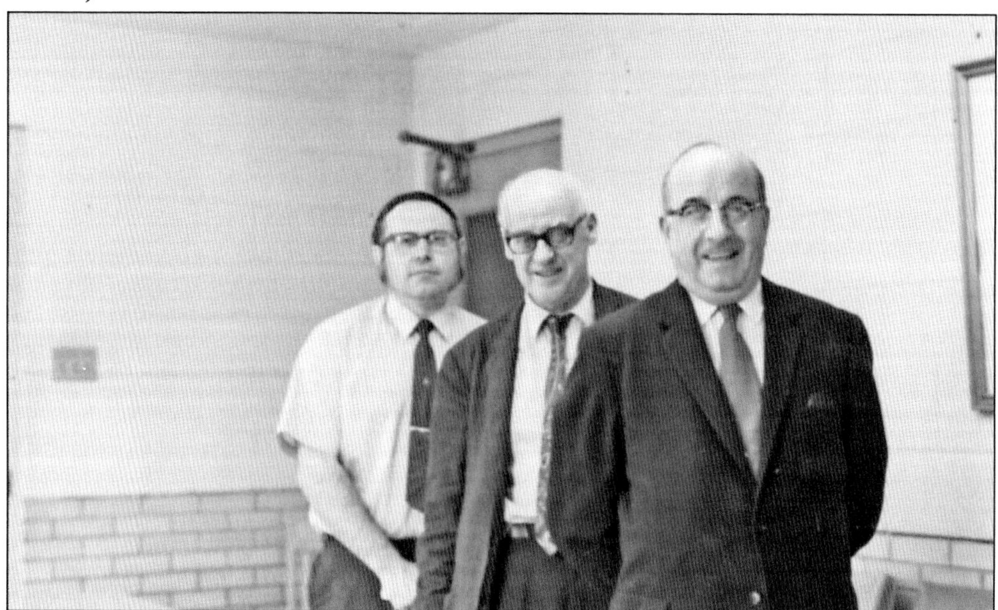

Three professors of the 1972 science faculty pictured here are, from left to right, George Ossman (physics), Lloyd Carr (biology), and Arthur Espensceid (department chair and chemistry). For some reason, Ron Tucceri (chemistry) is in the photograph with the mathematics instructors.

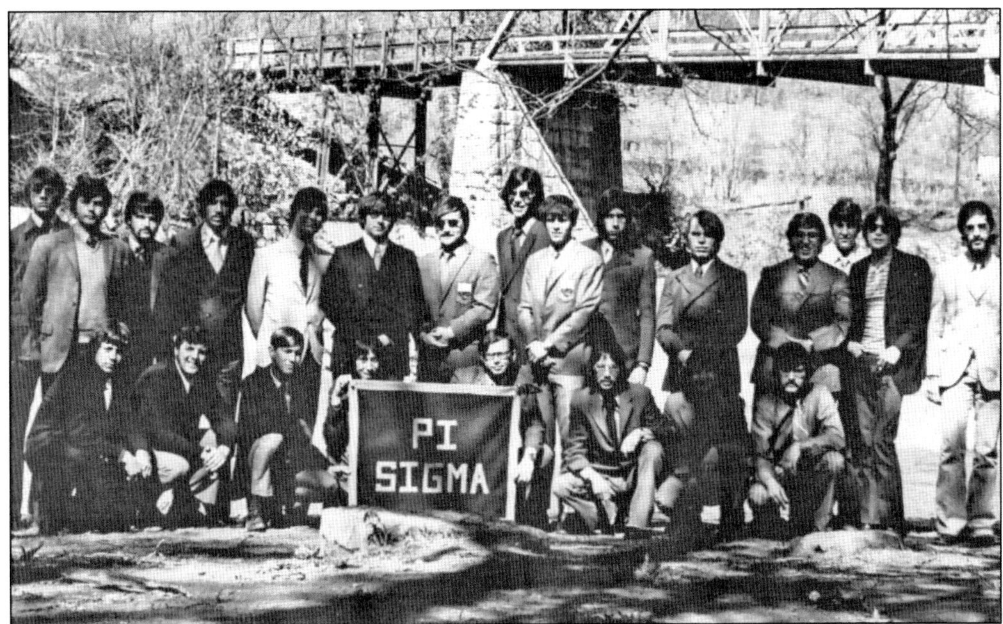

Pi Sigma (later Sigma Pi) fraternity dated from 1963 and focused on "brotherhood, truth, knowledge and secrecy." It was apparently the first campus group to confer honorary membership on Bevo Francis. According to one story, the entire group went streaking by the Dining Hall windows during 1974, when that phenomenon was a national fad.

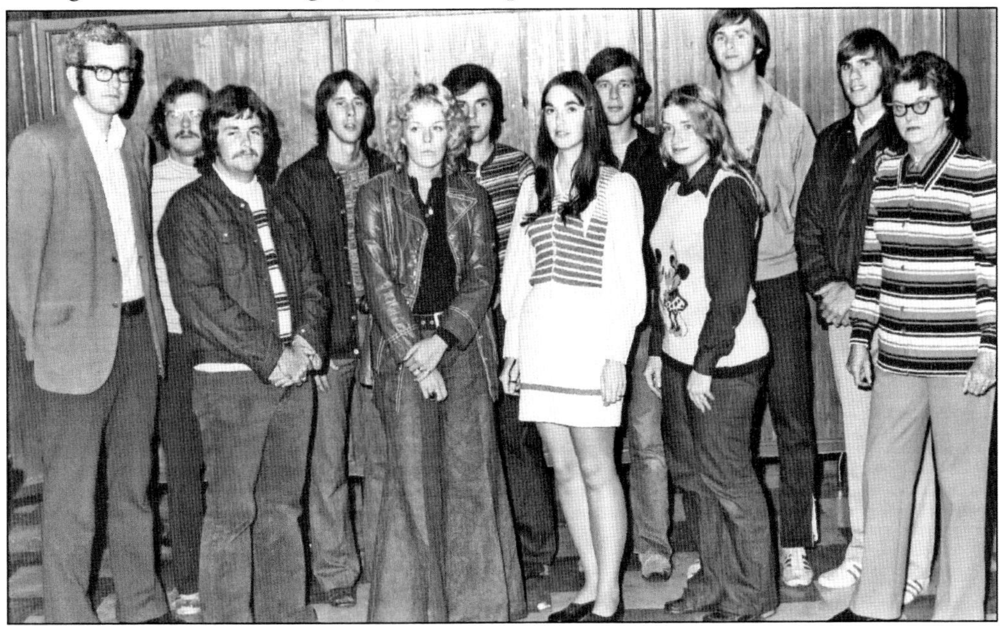

In this picture of the 1972–1973 student senate, Clyde Evans (far left) is one of the advisors, along with Pauli Graham. Evans (born 1938) grew up in Rio Grande but went to Union College to play basketball and earn higher degrees. He returned to Rio in 1966 as director of admissions, eventually rising to vice president and provost. His principal achievement came in the form of four successful terms in the Ohio General Assembly, after which he joined the URG Board of Trustees.

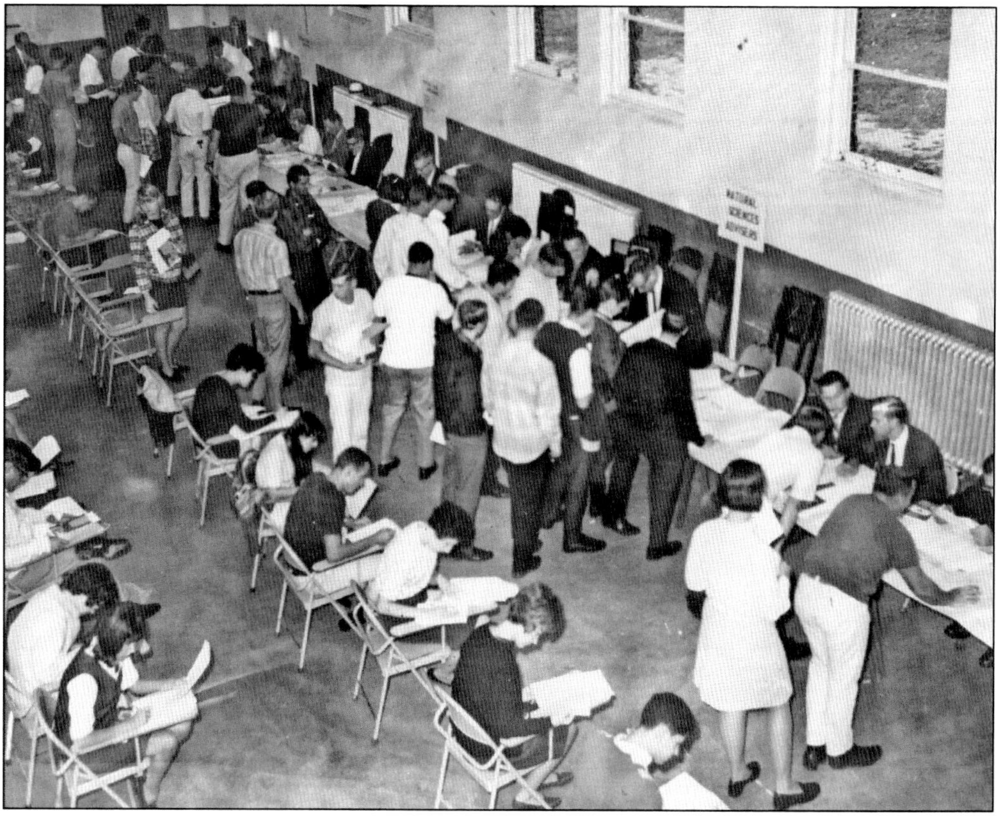

First-day registration at Community Hall in the 1970s could sometimes have challenging and confusing moments for new students. For others, it might be a smooth process. One person called it the freshman's first introduction in getting "the Rio Runaround." After the demise of Community Hall, the process relocated to Davis Career Center.

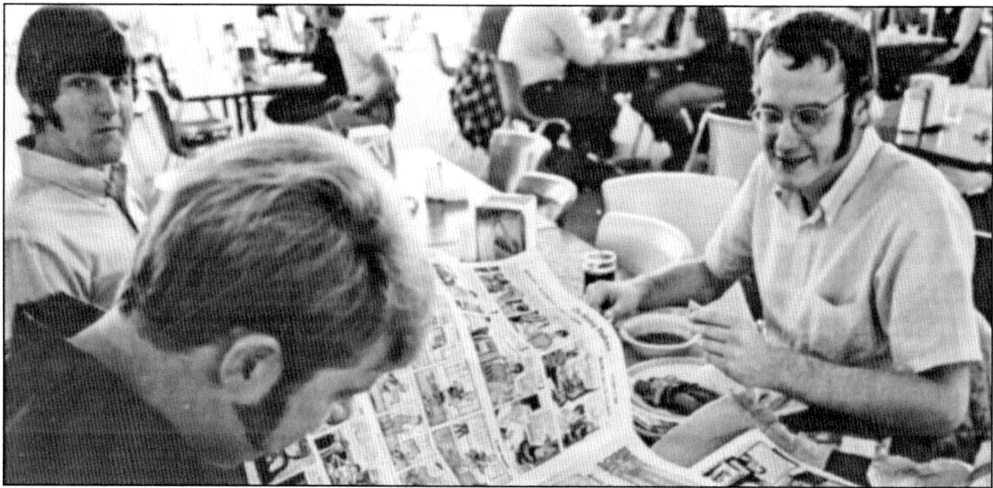

In this picture of a leisurely Sunday lunch about 1972, Ray Matura (with sideburns) and two other students are discussing the great ideas of the day. Ray was then an instructor and resident director of Boyd Hall. Being a Sunday, breakfast was not served and lunch invariably was fried chicken (one piece per person) with mashed potatoes and gravy.

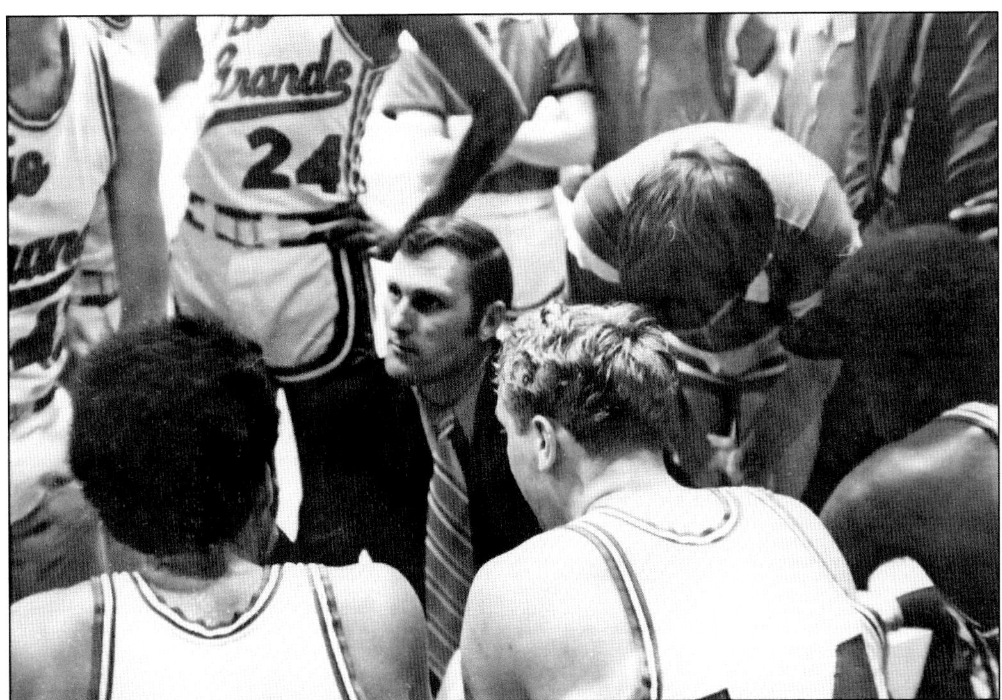

Art Lanham came to Rio in 1960 to take over the athletic department and coach basketball. A Navy veteran and a graduate of Union College, "the daddy" guided the basketball program into its best era since the Bevo years and into the new Lyne Center. He coached the Redmen from 1960 until 1980. The program was handed over to John Lawhorn and then Earl Thomas, who guided the Redmen into the Final Four of the NAIA for the first time. Art's son Jeff is now the athletic director, and Art's granddaughter Maddie played for the Redstorm softball team.

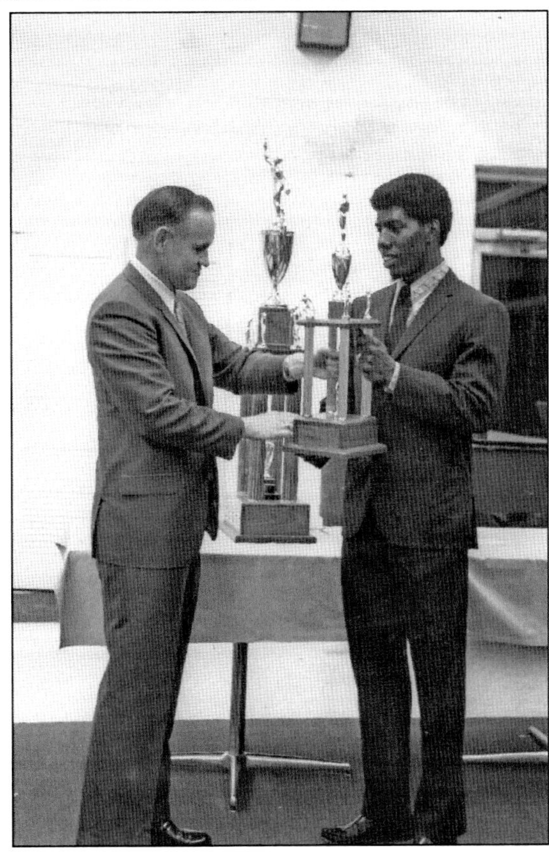

Bob Lawson (class of 1970), seen here receiving a trophy from the legendary Newt Oliver, is one of Rio's most gifted and talented students of all time. A member of the URG Athletic Hall of Fame, Bob was a brilliant student, a gifted singer, a versatile actor, and a great all-around guy. After receiving his doctorate, he has worked at Marshall University and Shawnee State, been a motivational speaker and author, and continued to teach.

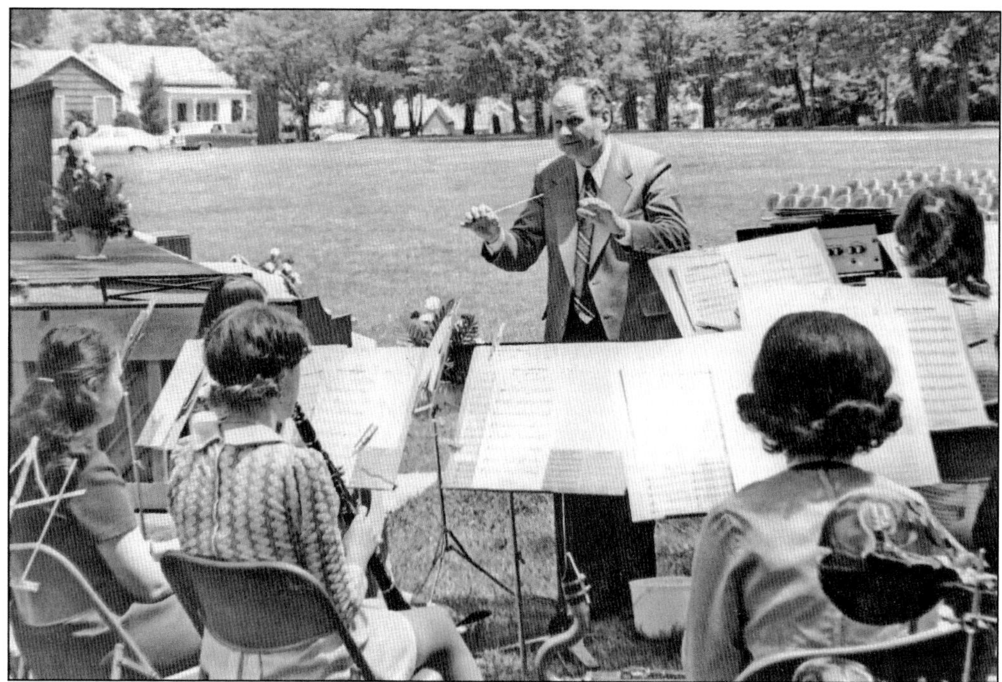

Darwin native Merlyn Ross (1932–1986) spent 20 years (1966–1986) on the Rio Grande music faculty, during which time he made the Grande Chorale vocal group a real showpiece. He was also the music director at Grace Methodist Church in Gallipolis. Ross became the first winner of the Edwin A. Jones Award in 1985, and the atrium in the Fine Arts Center bears his name. Sadly, Ross died the following year. To his former students and Grande Chorale artists, Merlyn bequeathed a deep love and passion for music and the arts.

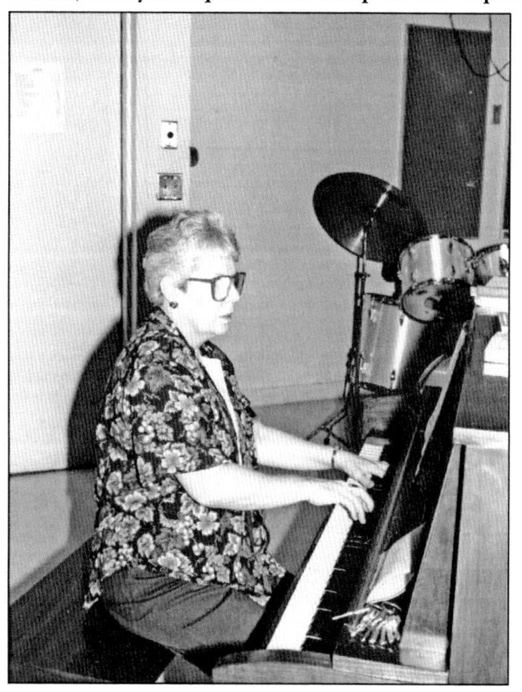

Edie Smith was born in Seneca Falls, New York, in 1931. She attended Oberlin College and graduated from Ohio University. On June 18, 1954, she married Merlyn Ross, and they literally spent a lifetime making beautiful music together. Wherever one saw Merlyn, one could be assured that his favorite piano player would never be far from his side or the keyboard. Edie taught piano at Rio Grande, played piano for musicals directed by Ed Roark (class of 1967), created RSR Enterprises with Roark and Patsy Schuldt (class of 1968), and began playing the piano and organ at Grace Methodist Church in 1956, a role she still fills in 2017.

Ed Roark (1943–2003, right) is seen here receiving a scholarship during his student years at Rio Grande from Herman Koby. Ed directed theater with a passion and flair seldom seen outside of Broadway. A gifted actor, singer, and dancer in his own right, Ed was able to draw every ounce of talent out of an actor. His favorite saying was "There are no small parts, only small actors." Among the shows he directed were *The Trojan Women*, *Anastasia*, *Fiddler on the Roof*, *Man of La Mancha*, and a Neil Simon festival—three major shows in production at the same time. Simply put, he was brilliant, and his untimely passing is still felt by many.

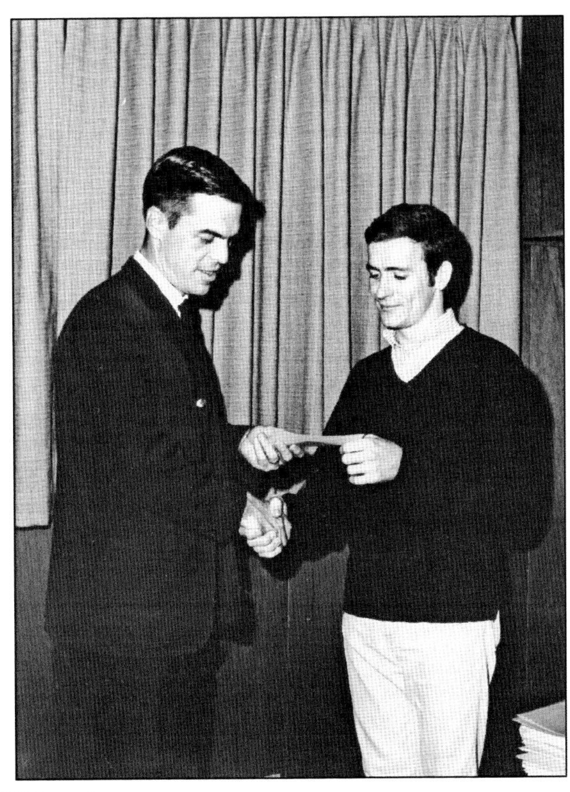

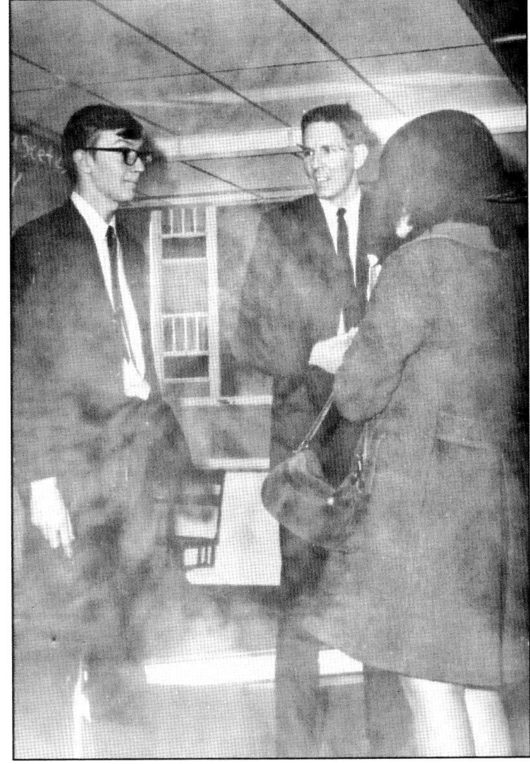

Bernie Murphy (class of 1968, left) spent many years at Rio Grande holding a number of mid-level administrative posts ranging from admissions counselor to director of continuing education before moving on to greener pastures in the late 1980s. To the right are history professor C. Robert Leith (class of 1965) and Leith's wife, Diane (class of 1970).

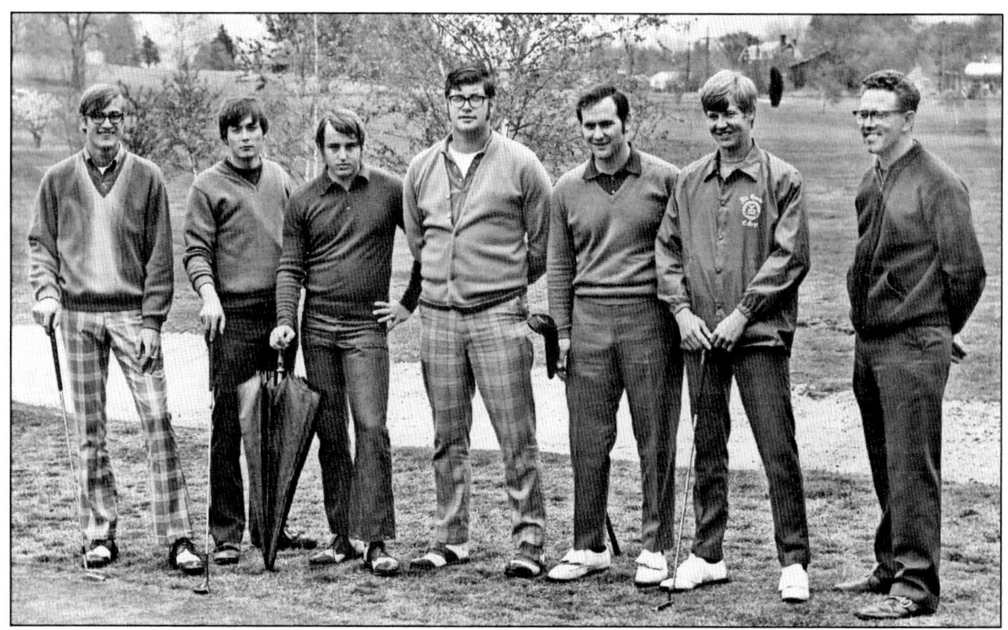

Off and on over the decades, Rio Grande has fielded an intercollegiate golf team. The 1971 squad, from left to right, Gene Grabiec, Chuck Kramer, Dave White, George Pope, Al Mascioli,and Joe Gullion, is shown with coach John W. Shupert (also a member of the mathematics faculty).

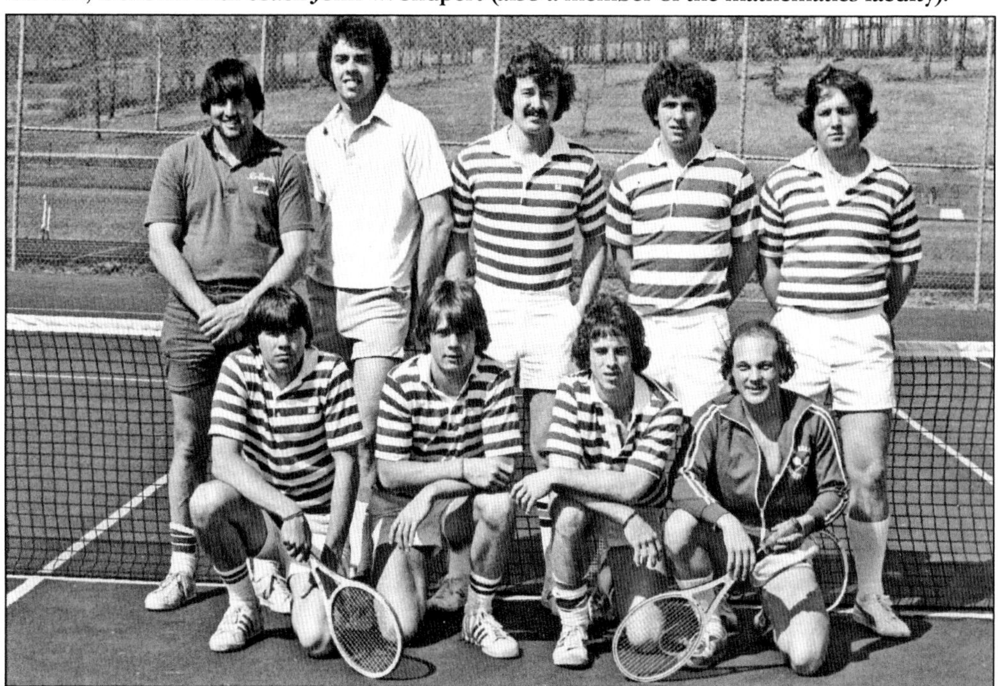

The 1978 men's tennis team photograph includes, from left to right, (first row) Dan Purcell, Phil Alban, Roger Butner, and Ed Boone; (second row) coach Tom Meadows, Gil Price (best known for basketball prowess), Dave McDowell, Mark Swain, and Scott Epling. The team had an 11-3 record on the season but dropped to fourth place in the Mid-Ohio Conference Tournament.

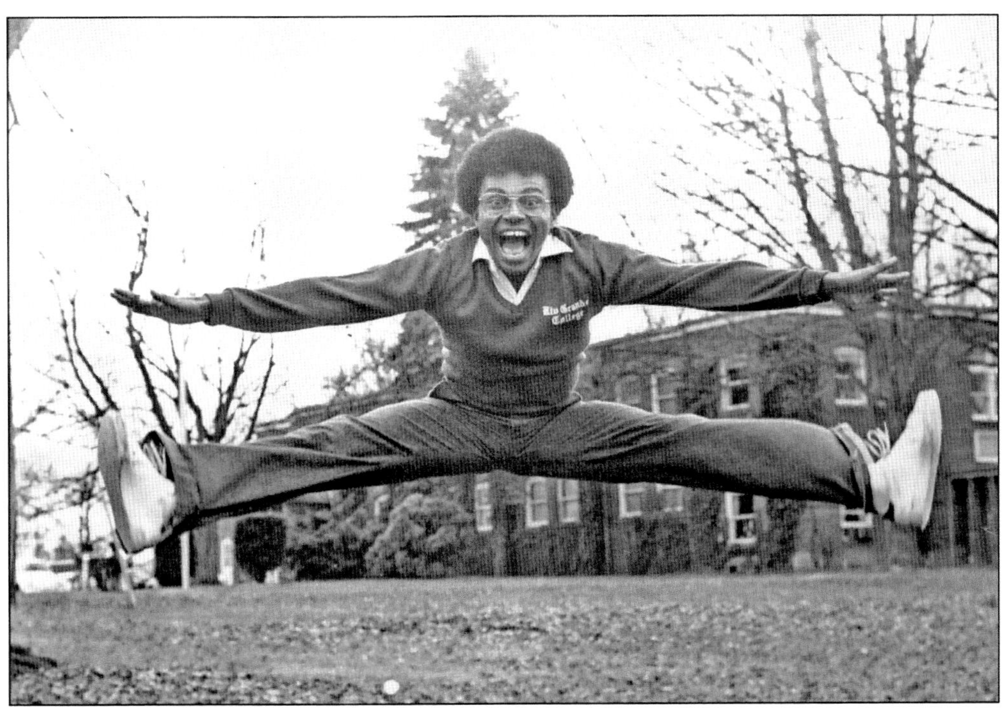

One of the best and most enthusiastic Rio Grande cheerleaders was James "Buzzy" Barksdale, shown here in the midst of a jump doing a split. After graduation, Buzzy taught in the Columbus public schools and proved to be an accomplished musician as well. Sadly, he passed away all too soon in 1985.

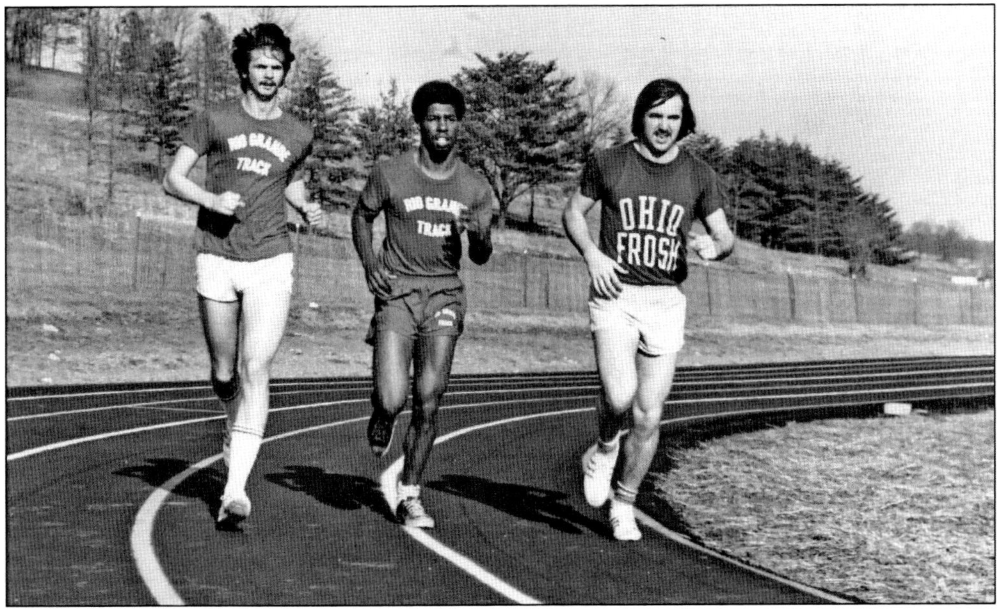

Robert Willey (class of 1973, left) and Robert Lawson (class of 1970, center) are both members of the Rio Grande Athletic Hall of Fame. They are seen here running side by side. From 1976 to 1980 and again since 1980, Willey has been a member of the physical education faculty and coached both track and cross-country. He is also an Alpha Sigma Phi brother.

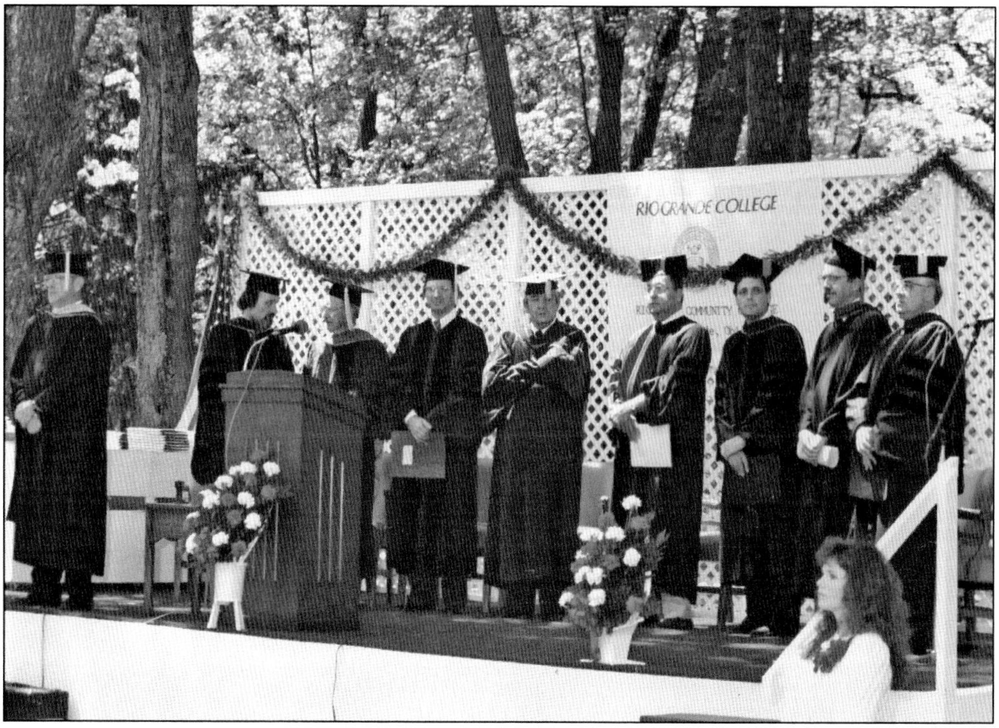

Paul C. Hayes (1922–2014) served as Rio's president from 1976 until 1983 and again from 1986 until 1991. Although sometimes more arbitrary than many faculty would have liked, he proved to be an effective executive, with both substantial enrollment growth and an impressive building program accomplished during his years. He retired to Wilmington, Ohio. Hayes (center, arms crossed) is seen here during the presentation of an honorary doctorate to Ron Glover, a Rio alum who went on to be the president of American Express.

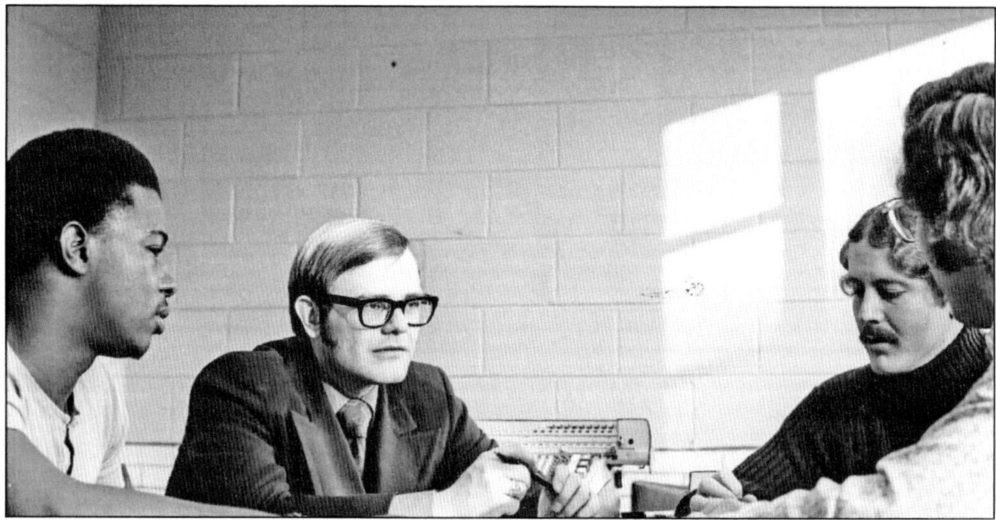

Dean S. Brown (1940–2005, class of 1965) joined the Rio Grande staff in 1966 as an admissions counselor, rising to director of admissions, dean of students, and vice president for enrollment management and institutional advancement. Closely associated with the Fraternal Order of Archon, he perished in an auto accident while still on the job.

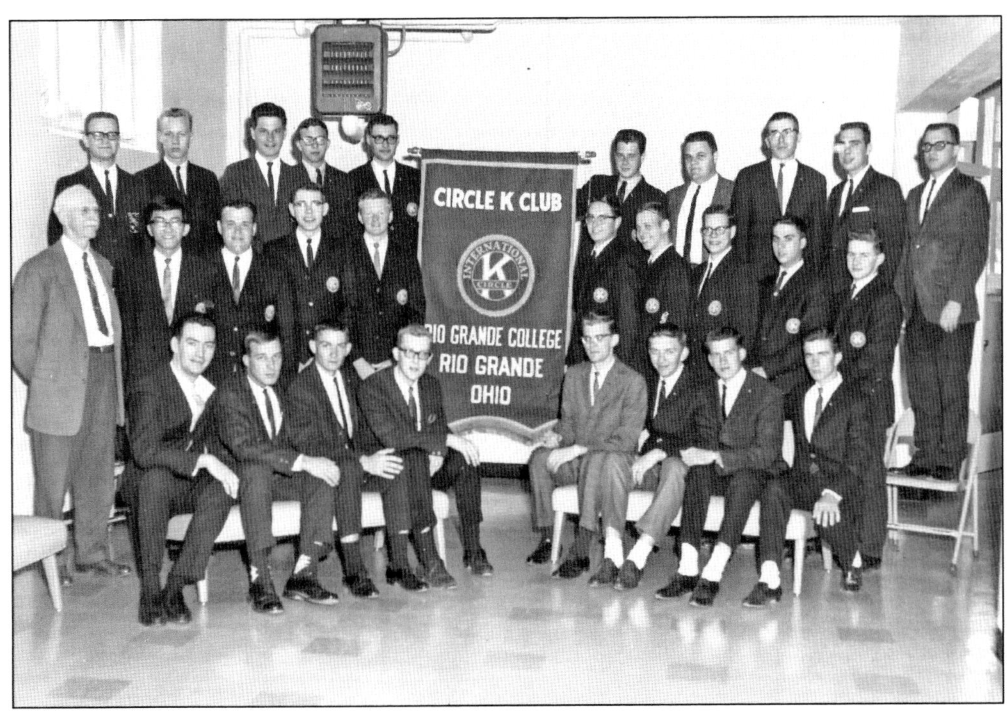

Circle K was a male service club affiliated with the Kiwanis organization. It flourished on the Rio Grande campus for several years in the 1960s and 1970s. The chapter was especially active during the time when elderly economics professor Fred Bouic (standing at far left) served as the club advisor. Bouic, an inveterate joiner during his long life, was also an active Odd Fellow, Mason, and Shriner.

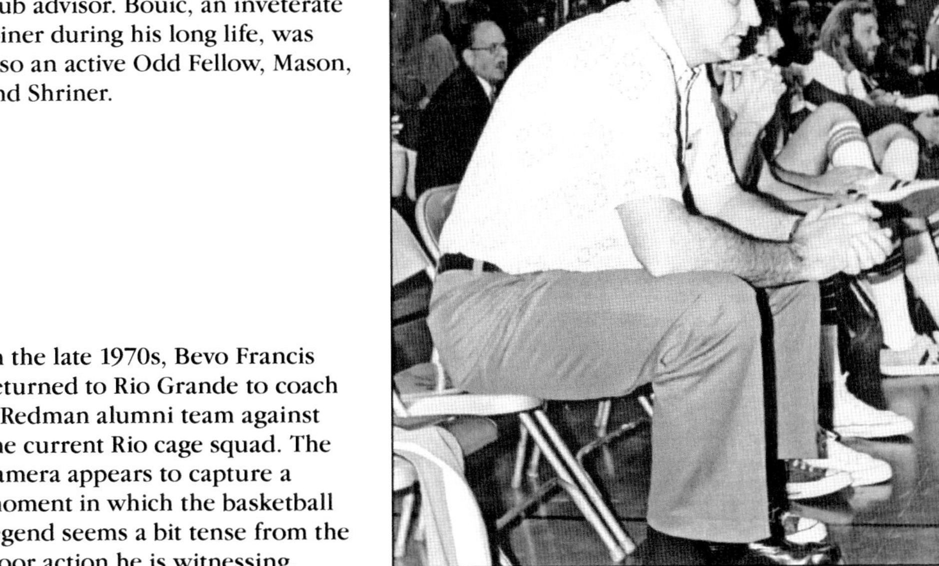

In the late 1970s, Bevo Francis returned to Rio Grande to coach a Redman alumni team against the current Rio cage squad. The camera appears to capture a moment in which the basketball legend seems a bit tense from the floor action he is witnessing.

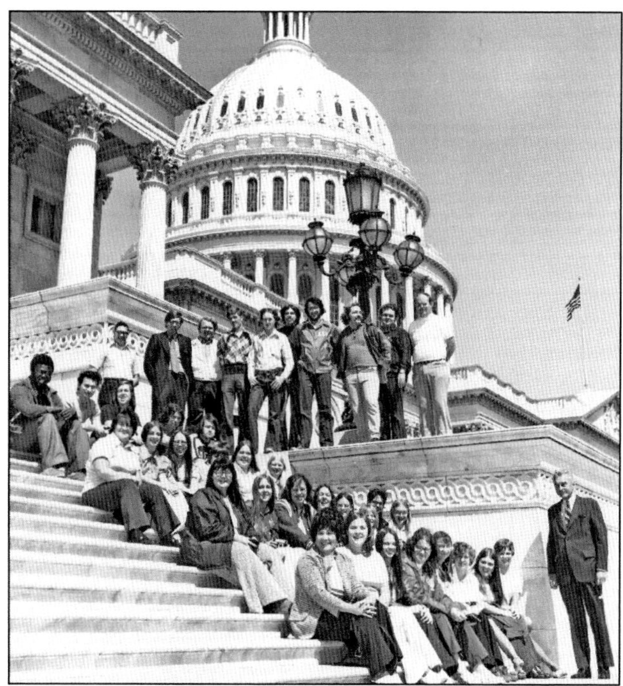

Student trips to Washington, DC, invariably include a trip to the Capitol and a photo op with their congressman. This 1972 photograph shows a group of history students on the steps. Standing second from left in the top row is Prof. C. Robert Leith. Congressman Clarence Miller is standing at lower right.

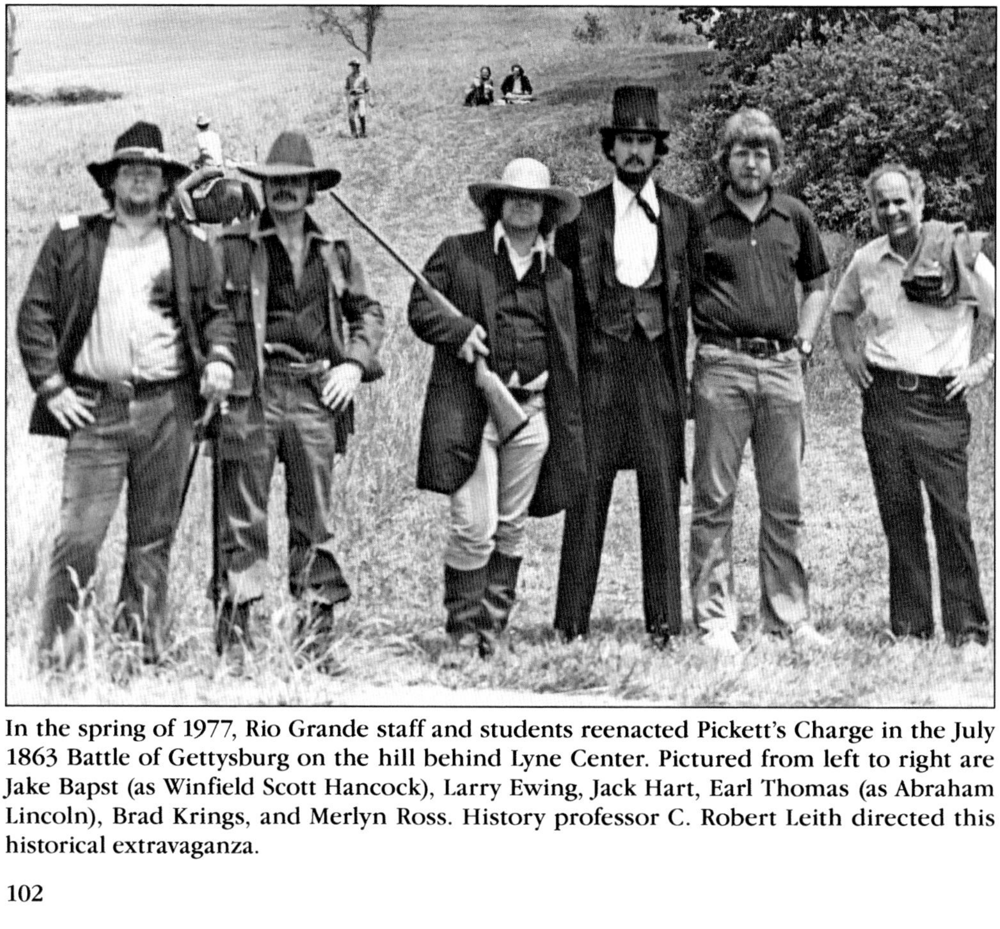

In the spring of 1977, Rio Grande staff and students reenacted Pickett's Charge in the July 1863 Battle of Gettysburg on the hill behind Lyne Center. Pictured from left to right are Jake Bapst (as Winfield Scott Hancock), Larry Ewing, Jack Hart, Earl Thomas (as Abraham Lincoln), Brad Krings, and Merlyn Ross. History professor C. Robert Leith directed this historical extravaganza.

Henry "Skipper" Johnson (class of 1978) of Gallipolis played both basketball and baseball during his Rio Grande years. He is pictured here in uniform as a pitcher for the Redmen nine. Skip was always kidded for his close resemblance to a Philadelphia Phillies pitcher of the time, Charles Hudson. Skip has stayed active in sports, especially volleyball.

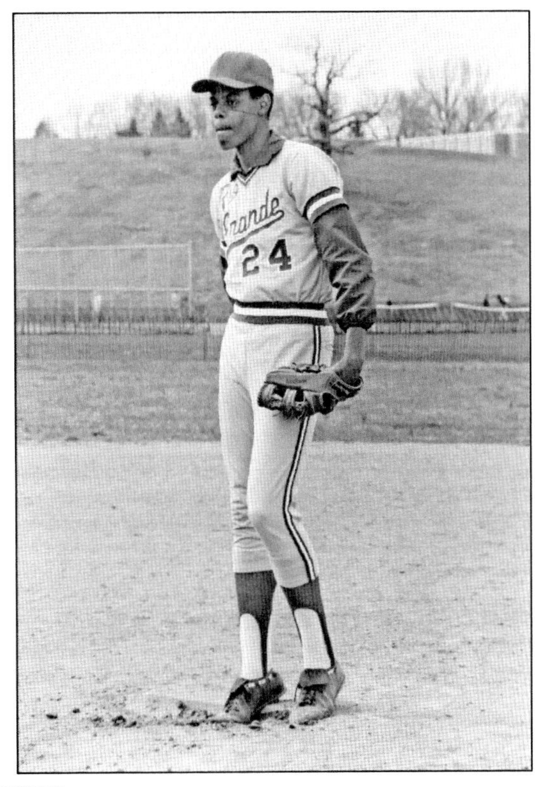

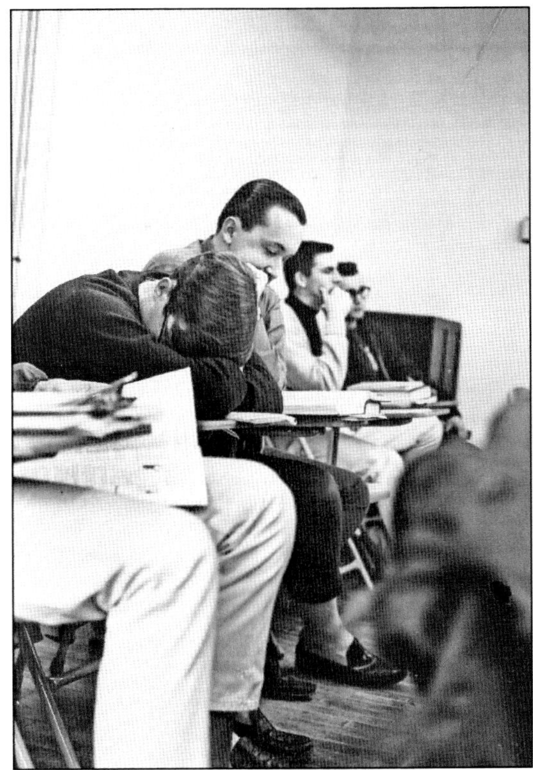

Were it not for the desks, these unidentified students could be from any time from 1876 until tomorrow. Sometimes late nights, ill health, or even a less-than-thrilling lecture could cause this. However, as a student by the name of "Bat" Topping writes in the 1916 *Grandion*: "Fierce lessons, Late hours, Unexpected company, Not prepared, Kicked out!"

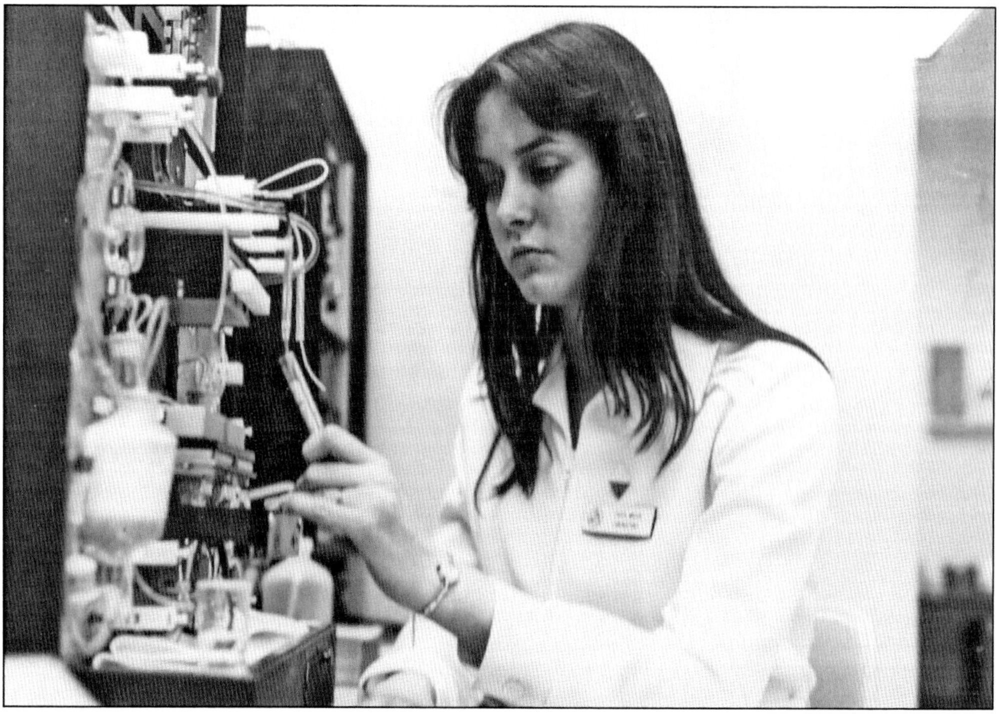

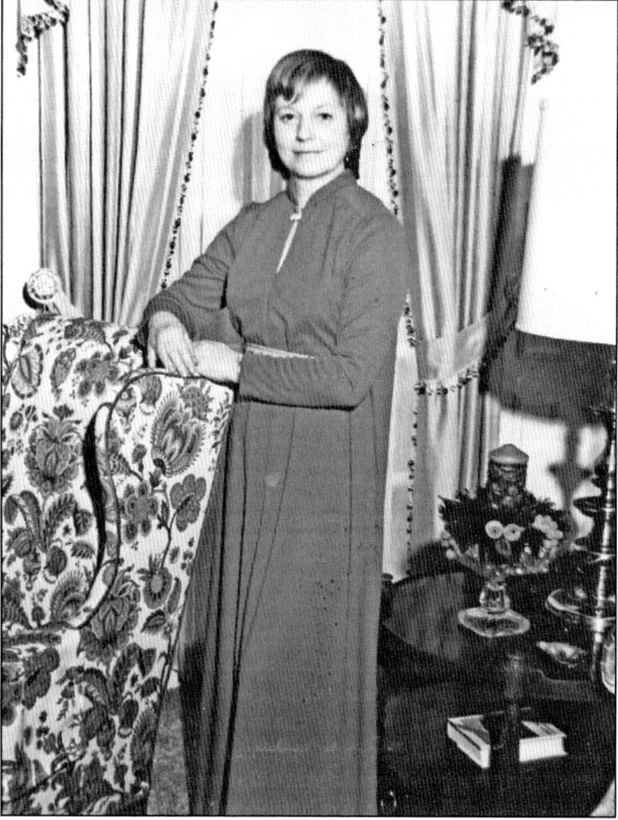

Faith White McKinniss (class of 1981) is pictured here as a microbiology student. For many years, she has been employed at the Holzer Medical Center and has been quite active in Cub Scouts, being among other achievements a holder of the Silver Beaver Award. Her husband, Terry McKinniss, is the middle of three brothers to earn degrees from Rio.

Phyllis Williamson came to Rio Grande College in 1946 as a first-year student and remained for two years. After marriage to Warren Sheets, she transferred to Ohio Northern, where her husband graduated from law school, and they later returned to Gallia County, where he became a noted attorney. Phyllis spent eight years on the private college board (1979–1987) and also served on the community college board.

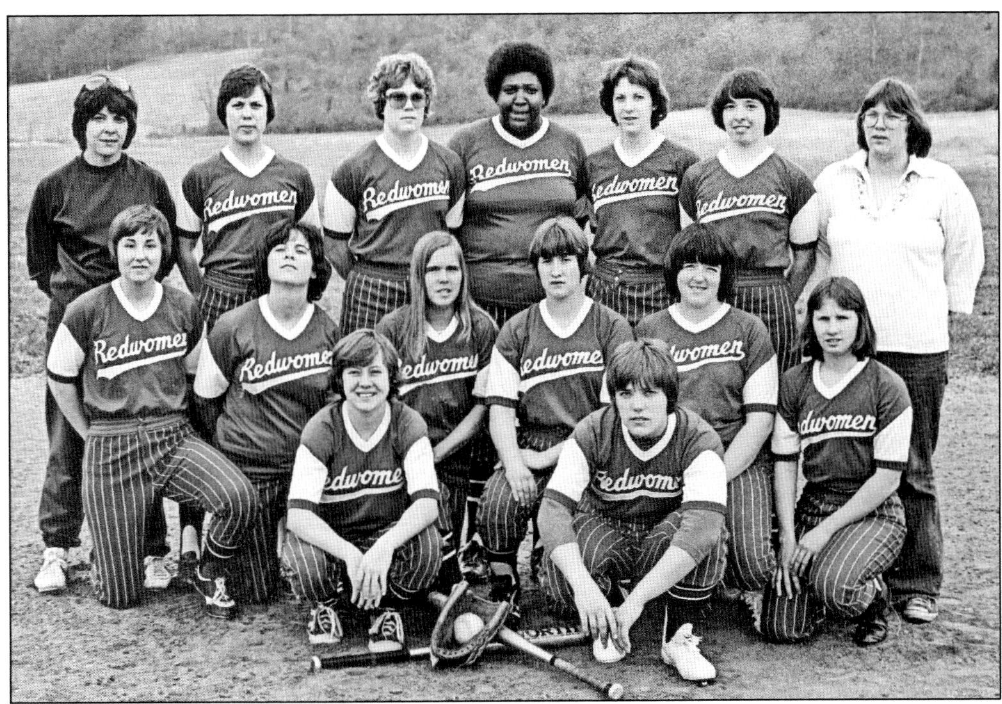

The Rio Grande girls' softball team had a successful 11-3 record in 1978. The team photograph includes, from left to right, (first row) Jackie Moore and Pam Mercer; (second row) Kim Baker, Diane Carsey, Terri Koster, Kaye Woodard, Kim Grueser, and Karen Boggs; (third row) coach Diane Lewis, Margaret Hackett, Denise Radcliffe, Deb Seay, Kim Ramsey, Pam Eshenaur, and Cheryl Smith.

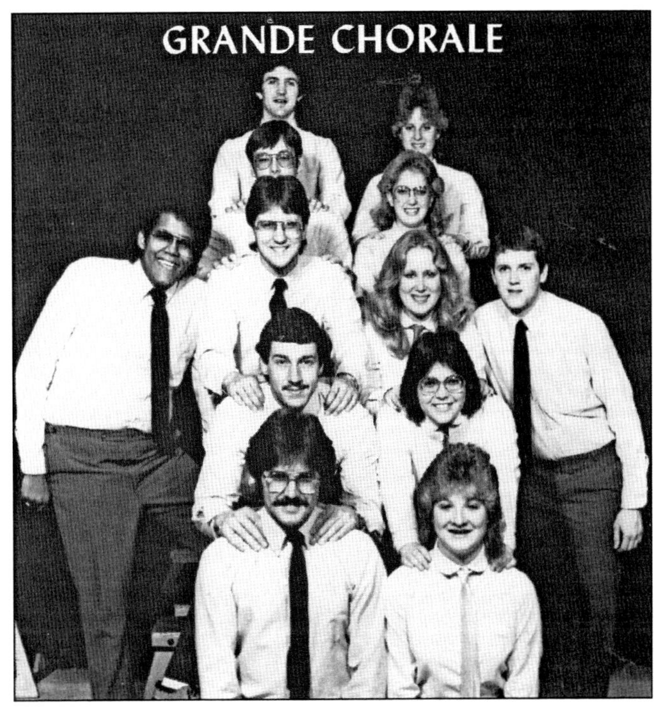

The 1984–1985 Grande Chorale consists of, from left to right, (first row) Marty Glassburn and Rhonda Leach; (second row) Kent Walker and Jean Ann Vance; (third row) Rober Gordon, Richie Steele, Kelli Kemper, and Matt Woodyard; (fourth row) Devana Savage and Patty Lehmann; (fifth row) Larry Payne and Pam Beegle. Gordon later became city manager of Gallipolis and a research associate at Ohio University's Voinovich Center.

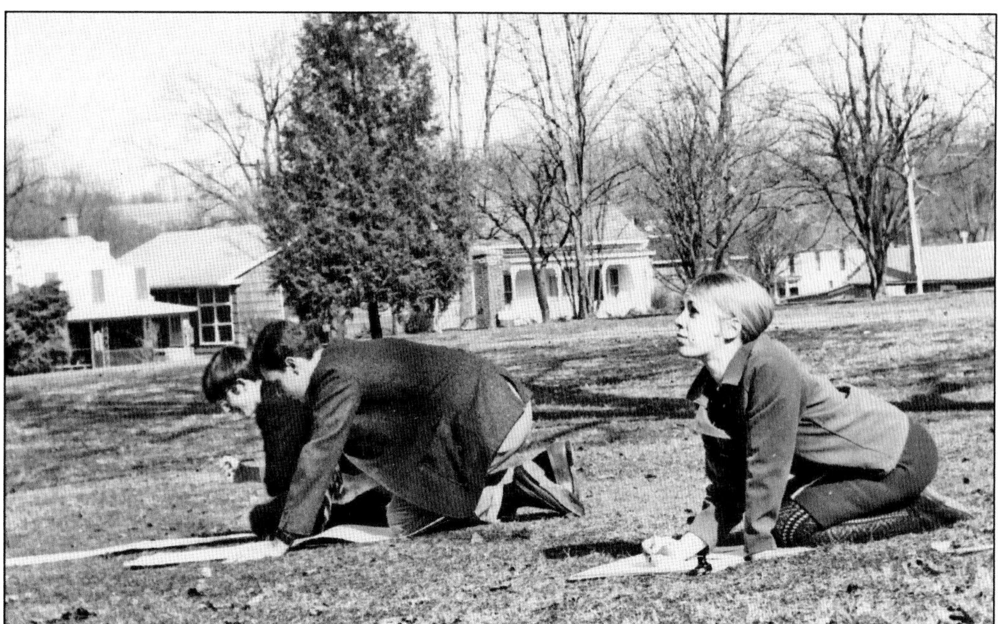

Here is another picture that is timeless. An art class sketching on the campus green would have been as familiar a sight in 1920, 1940, 1960, or 1980 as it is today. The original 10 acres given by Permelia Atwood have witnessed many such sights, as well as graduations, May Day celebrations, outdoor classes, or young lovers looking for a secluded spot under the trees.

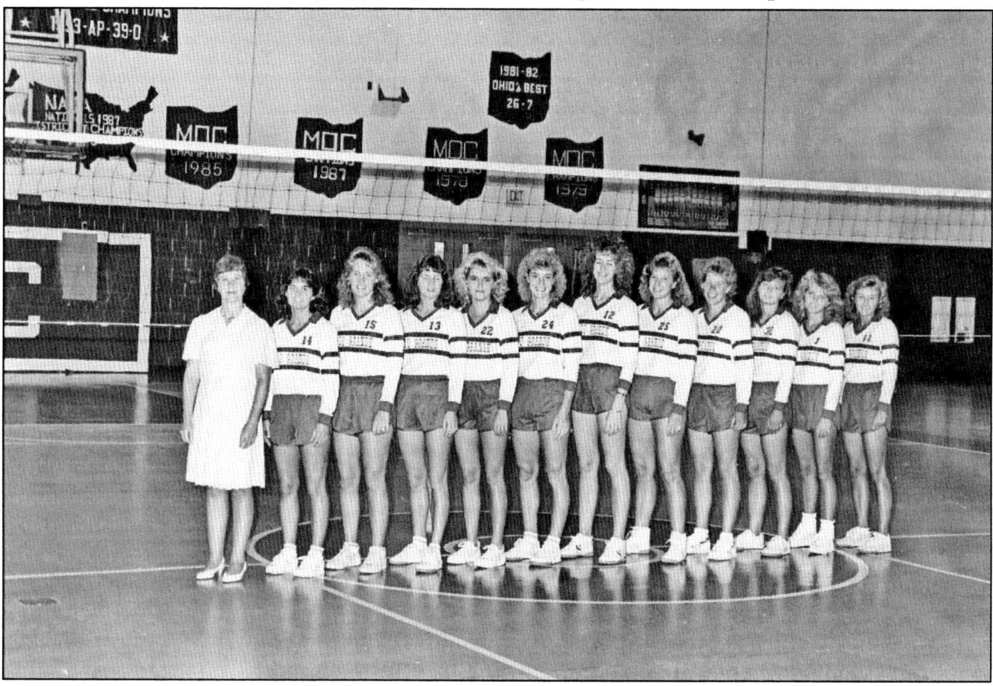

Other than basketball, intercollegiate volleyball is the leading women's sport. The 1988–1989 team had a quite successful 32-10 season. From left to right are coach Patsy Fields, Lori Storer, Kris Cochran, Sharon Headings, Robin Sharp, Sheila Brammer, Teresa Zempter, Shelley Hoop, Kris Williams, Shannon Huston, Lori Gampp, and Lisa Schmeltzer.

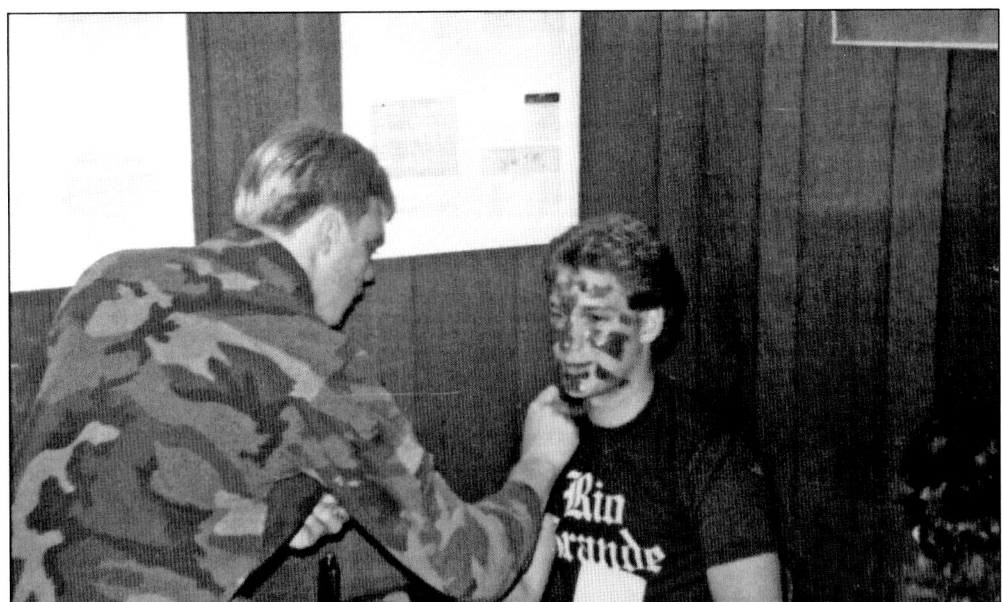

The ROTC program at Rio Grande started in the fall of 1984 and flourished until the late 1990s, when cuts in the defense budget caused its demise. In this image, Cadet John Harris is seen receiving a face camouflage treatment. Many students in the program have had notable Army careers, including Garry Thompson, Sandra Pummell, Nathan Swindler, Bradd Schultz, and Rae Ellen Keene-Schultz.

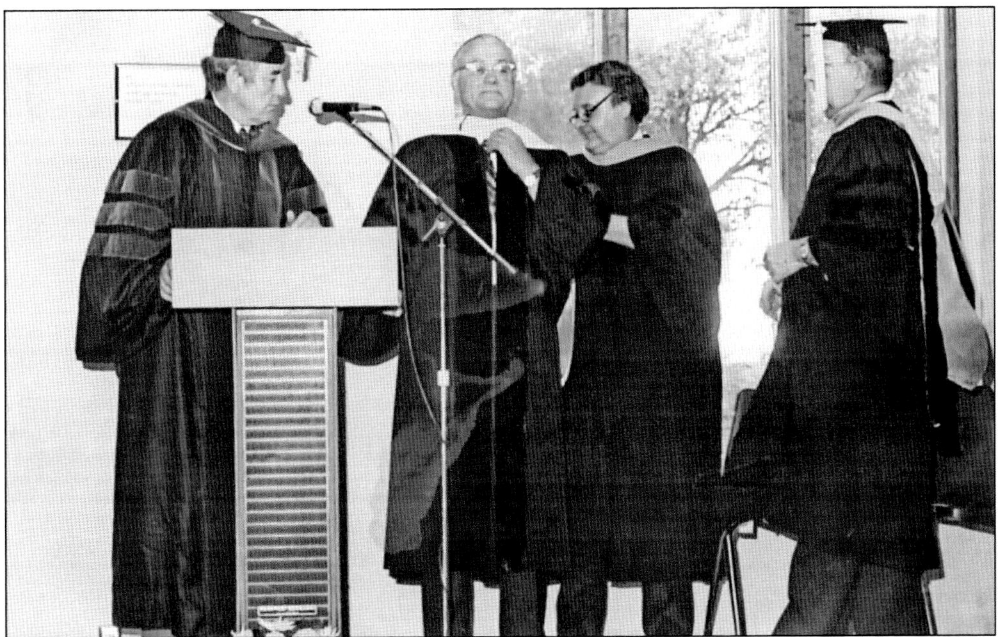

On September 24, 1983, Ohio State's legendary ex–football coach Woody Hayes visited the Rio Grande campus to inaugurate the Language Arts 101 speaker series in the new Berry Fine Arts Center. While there, he also received an honorary doctorate, the awarding of which is pictured here. From left to right are Rio president Paul Hayes, Dr. Wayne Woodrow "Woody" Hayes, and two unidentified trustees.

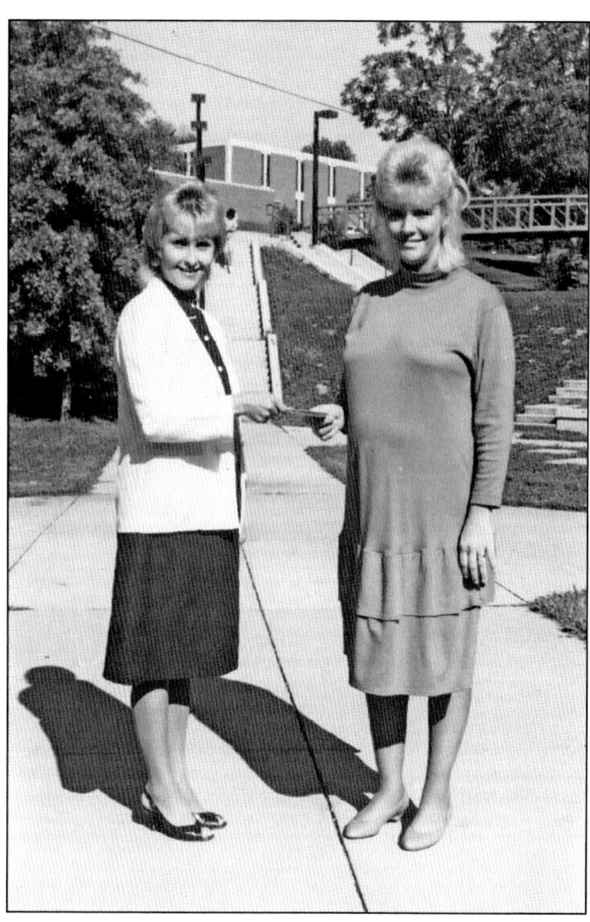

In 1981, Rio Grande College fully absorbed the Holzer School of Nursing, appointing Janet Byers as dean. By 1988, the program had been in full swing for several years. In this 1989 photograph, Dr. Byers presents an award to soon-to-graduate Meigs County student Brenda Russell.

In addition to commencement exercises, the Holzer School of Nursing has pinning and capping ceremonies each spring to honor successful students. The 1989 capping ceremony on the stage of the Berry Center's Alphus Christensen Theater is pictured here.

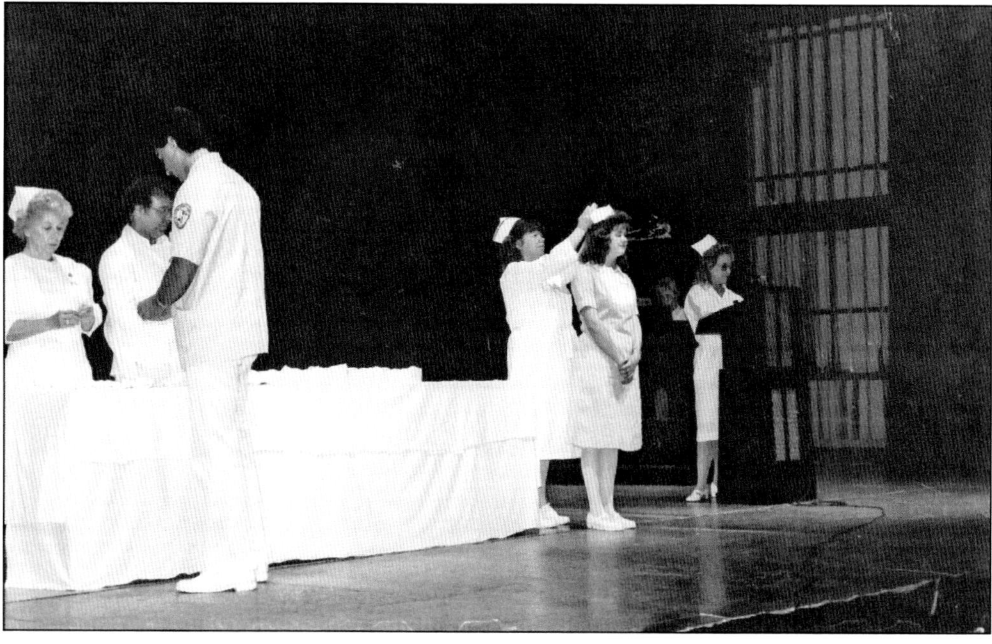

Six

From a New Name to a New Century 1989–2016

When Rio Grande College became the University of Rio Grande, the change could best be described as cosmetic. The majority of students—in the community college—still came from the four counties and the state of Ohio. Over the years, foreign students from such locales as Nigeria and Japan came and largely went. More recent ones hailed from lands with a strong soccer tradition, but the largest numbers arrived from Gallia, Jackson, Meigs, and Vinton or adjacent counties. More parking spaces for commuters became a necessity. New classroom buildings, such as Robert Wood Hall, McKenzie Hall, and Bob Evans Farms Hall provided the campus with a more modern appearance.

In 1991, Paul Hayes retired for the second time, succeeded by a southerner, Barry Dorsey. For better or worse, the new executive preferred to lead by what he termed "consensus." Critics might label this "indecisiveness." Full-time equivalent numbers peaked at 1,939 in 1992–1993, but head count was slightly higher the following year at 2,173 and was 2,313 in 2000–2001. By the beginning of the 21st century, 41 of 80 teaching faculty had doctorates. Toward the end of the Dorsey years, dissension between the private board and community college trustees created a matter for concern, but it managed to be resolved during the brief interim presidency of Don Wood, a private college trustee who was sandwiched between two other brief presidencies. Having gone to a quarter system in 1974, the school reverted to semesters in 2001. Potential enrollment declines were partly offset by the opening of a Meigs Center near Pomeroy, a McArthur Center in the former Vinton County High School, and in 2015 a center in Jackson.

Dr. Michelle Johnston, another southerner, took the presidency in October 2014. Her approach helped instill a more positive outlook for most. Still, the old problems of enrollment and money loomed ever-present, a tradition that has remained unchanged for 140 years.

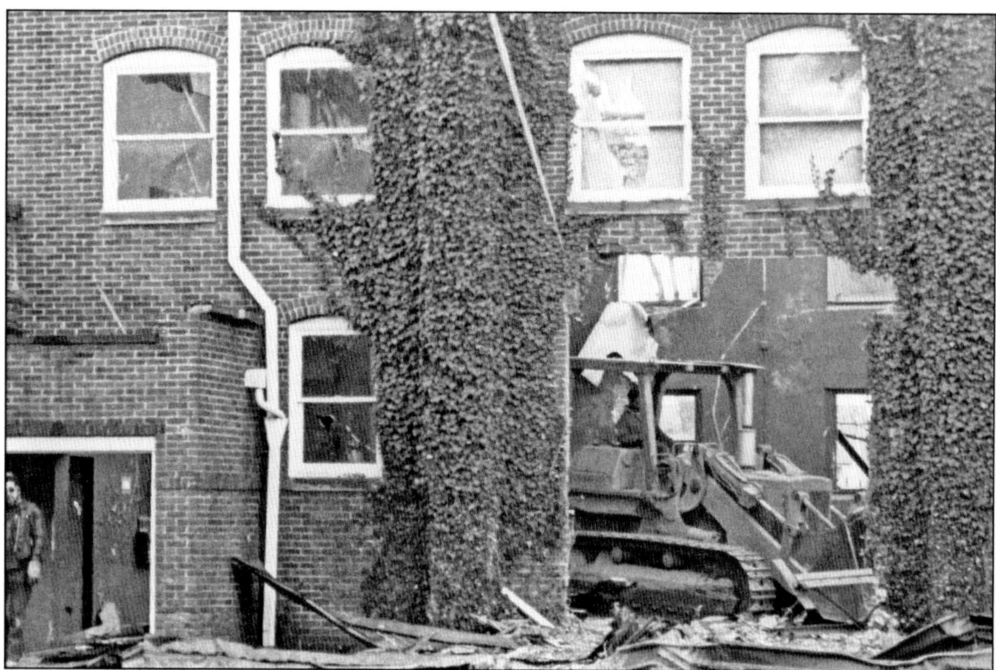

Although Community Hall had become woefully inadequate by the mid-1970s as a theater building, it nonetheless had become near and dear to many students, especially to those who participated in theater productions. A few students—some of whom feared Rio Grande might be turning into a tech school—even protested its 1978 demise, but when the new Berry Fine Arts Center replaced it, Community Hall was mourned no longer.

The second new building in the first Paul Hayes era, the Berry Fine and Performing Arts Center, dedicated in February 1981, contained a new theater (subsequently named for Alphus Christensen), a glass-enclosed atrium (named for music professor Merlyn Ross), and classrooms designed for photography, fine arts, and music classes. Namesake John Berry was a former trustee and philanthropist. In this picture, the cast of *Fiddler on the Roof* takes a curtain call.

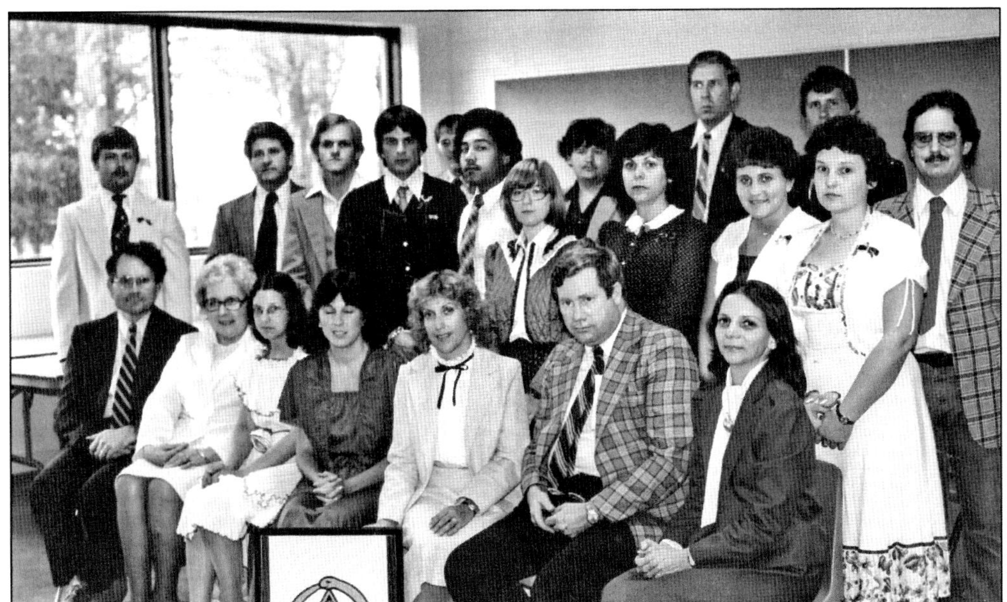

The Rio Grande history honorary society, Phi Alpha Theta, dates from 1982. Pictured are, from left to right, (first row) Barry Thompson, Jean Cooper, Pearl Cantrell, Cindy Preston, Brittina Green, Ivan Tribe, and Marcella Barton; (second row) Jeff Young, Robert Pfeifer, James Oliphant, David Burgess, Randy Ferguson (partly obscured), Mike Gore, Dianna Sturgill, John Barcus, Dorothy Costilow, Beverly Mahle, Carmen Manuel, and Gene Welch; (third row) Robert Leith and Kevin Lloyd.

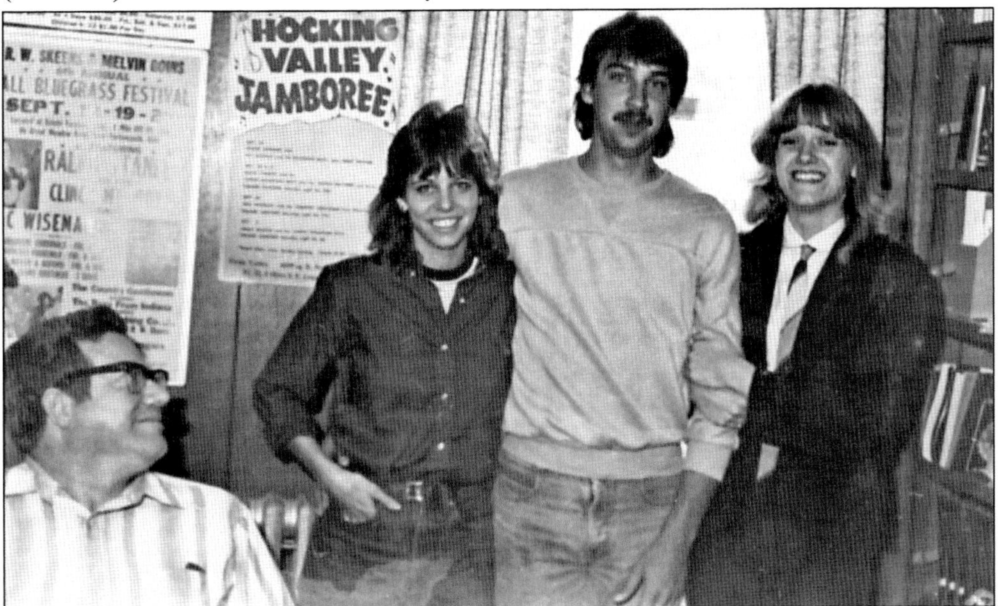

Dr. Ivan Tribe began his annual spring open house in 1982 to celebrate the cleaning of his office. This 1983 photograph shows Tribe seated at left, with his first student hostesses, Donna Pasquale (class of 1984) and Lori Meadows (class of 1984), on each side of the next host, Rick Stalder (class of 1985). Pasquale and Meadows became teachers at Washington Elementary in Gallipolis. Stalder taught physical education in Cincinnati.

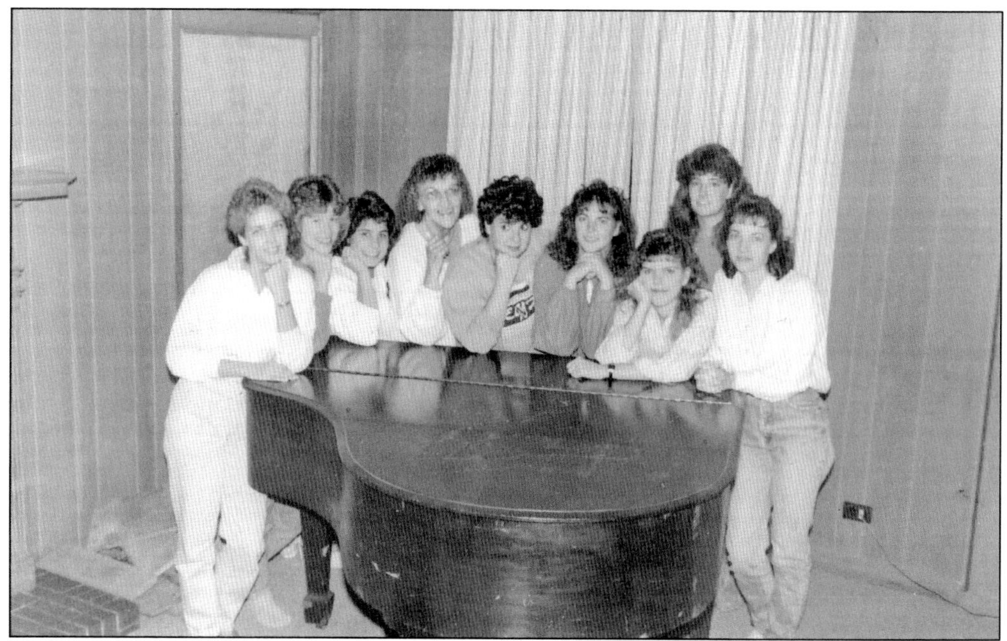

Resident assistants play key roles in dormitory life, helping the head resident and younger students. This 1988–1989 image shows, from left to right, Brenda Long, Sue Ann Hardy, Mimi Rentz, Doris Ross (longtime head resident), Laura Haverkos, Bev Huber, Sherri Cooke, Leah Myers, and Kristi Smith.

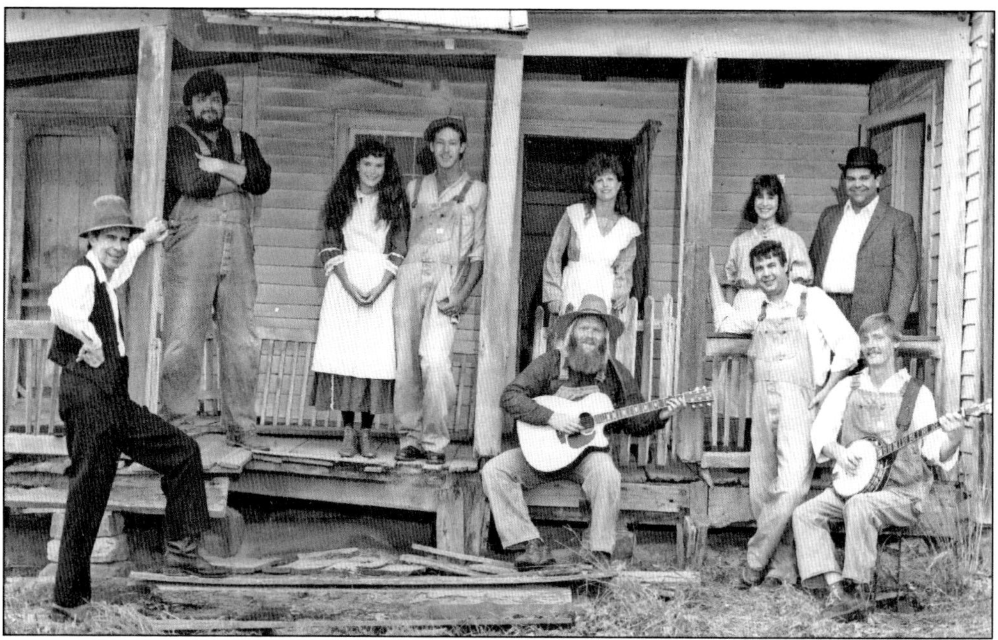

Greg Miller, who took over the fine arts program in 1985, adapted the Kermit Daugherty novel *Out of the Red Brush* (1954), about southwest Jackson County, for a stage production. When the novel first appeared, it was considered "off-color" but by the 1980s was much less so. Presented numerous times in the Christensen Theater, it also enjoyed a run as an off-Broadway production.

In 21 years on the Rio Grande faculty, Dr. Marcella Barton, a University of Chicago PhD, was both a quality and popular professor. During her Rio years, she served a term as president of the Ohio Academy of History, directed the Madog Welsh Studies Center, and produced a quality scholarly study of St. Teresa of Avila. Upon retirement, Barton moved to Florida.

The corps of officers for Phi Alpha Theta in 1988 consists, of from left to right, Anne Keating of Wellston, Marsha Shook of Coalton (who subsequently obtained a doctorate from Ohio University and is a key figure at its Voinovich Center), Marilyn Maynard of Jackson, and Billy Joe Adkins of Oak Hill.

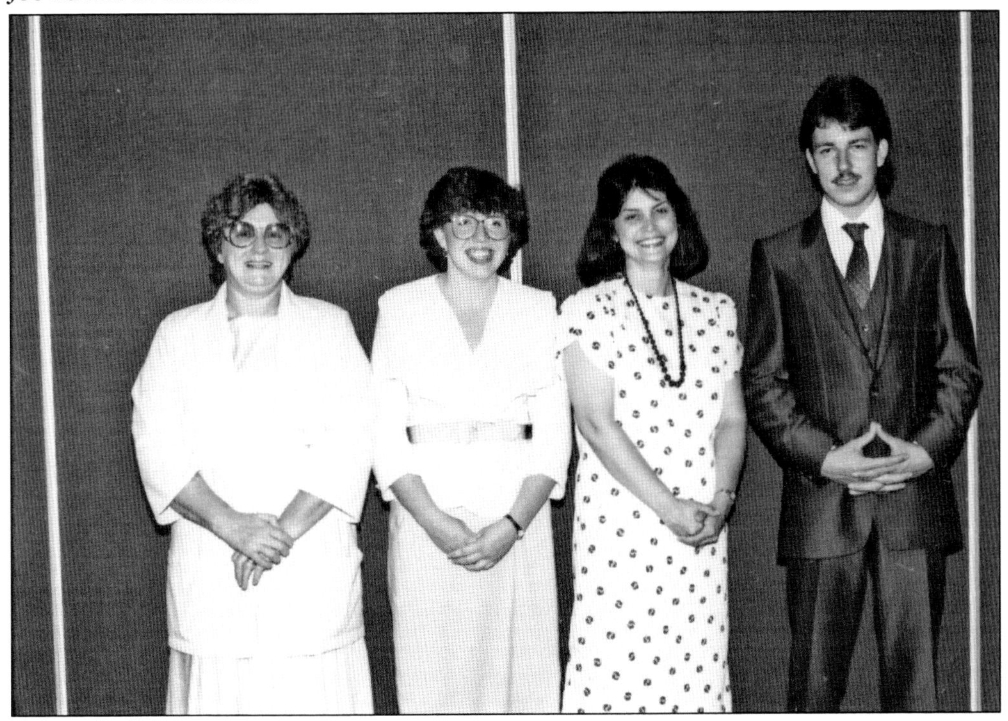

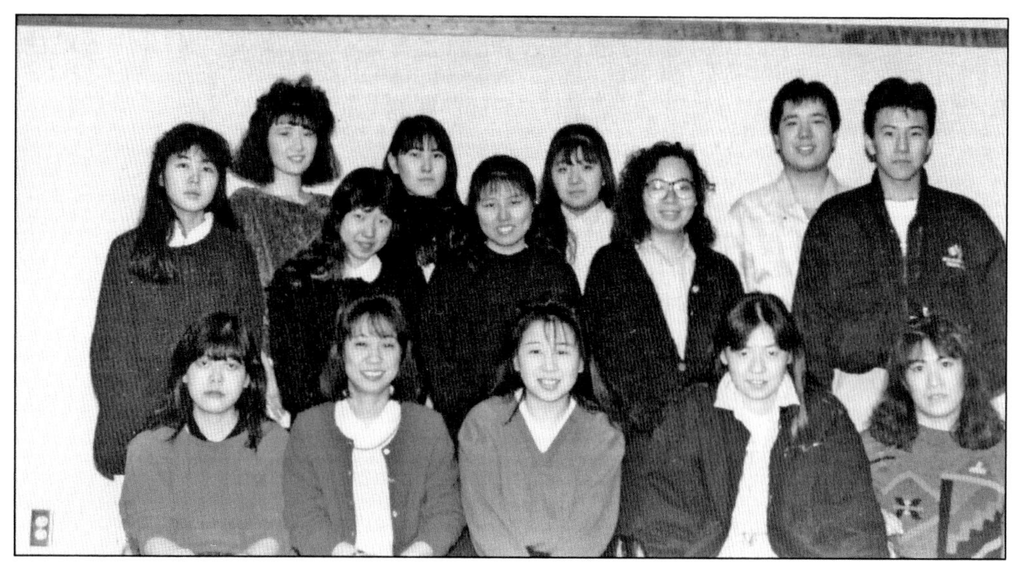

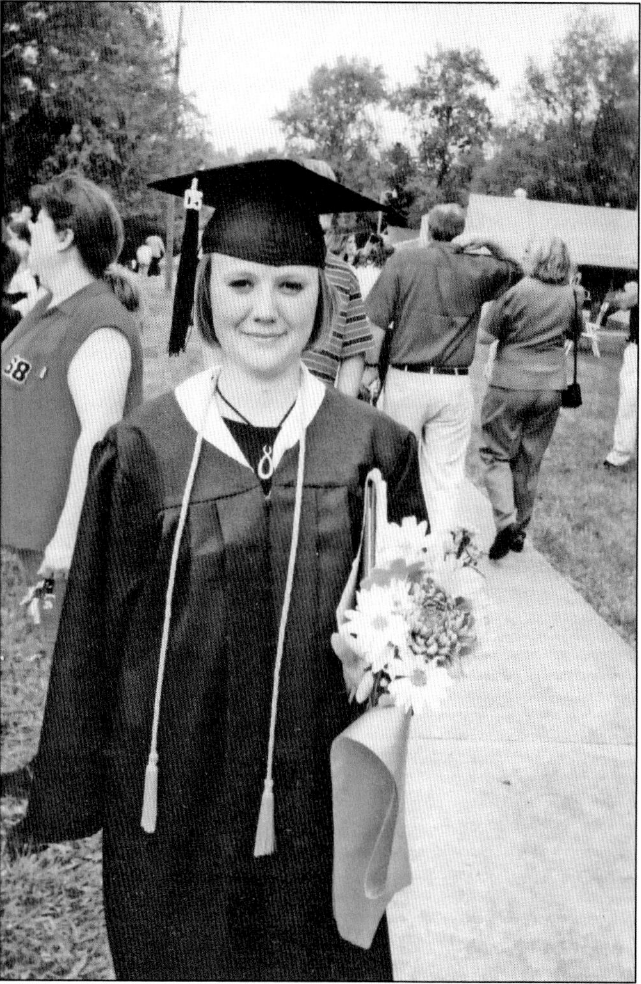

In the late 1980s, Rio Grande had a large Japanese student contingent. This 1988–1989 group shot shows, from left to right, (first row) Yoshika Ninomiya, Kayo Takamayu, Natsuko Kabutomori, Yuko Ishii, and Atsuko Yamazaki; (second row) Yoshiko Yashida, Yuko Hinzwi, Junko Hoizumi, Kazumi Iwasee, and Shinishi Kouteka; (third row) Myamke Yoshida, Junko Hirota, Kyuko Kawakami, and Akiyo Nakajima.

The 21st century brought a new coterie of international students to the URG campus, including some from former Iron Curtain countries. One of the more memorable was Lilya Dvornichenko, to whom someone gave the sobriquet "Ukrainian Sweetheart." She is pictured here at her graduation. Not pictured is her close friend Diana Ter-Ghazarian, who hailed from Armenia.

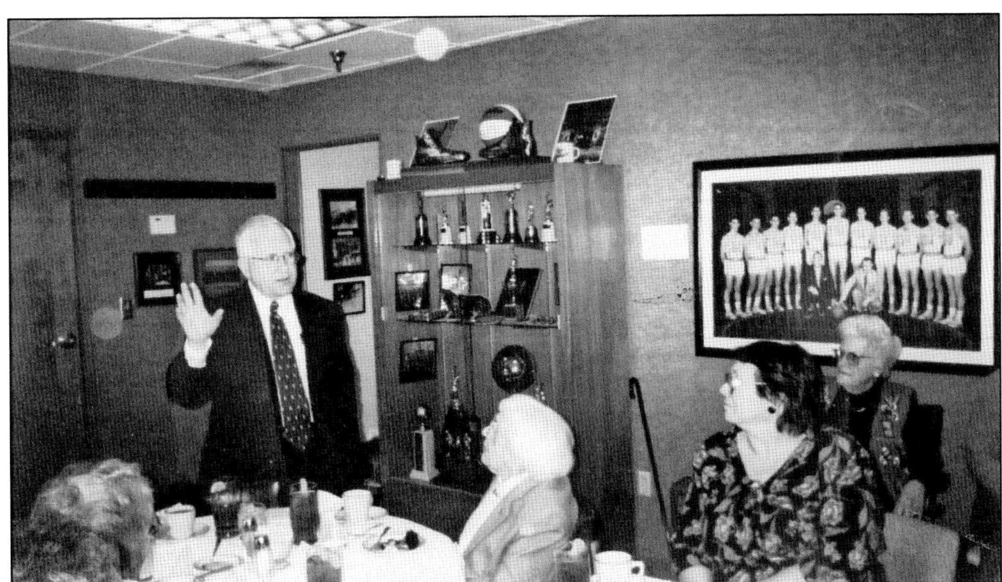

Barry Dorsey (born 1942) became Rio Grande's longest-serving president since John Merrill Davis, occupying the office from 1991 until 2006. A native of North Carolina, he once served on the staff of Sen. Sam Ervin. Dorsey once taught at Radford University but had mostly been on the staff of the Virginia Council of Higher Education. After retirement, he returned to Virginia.

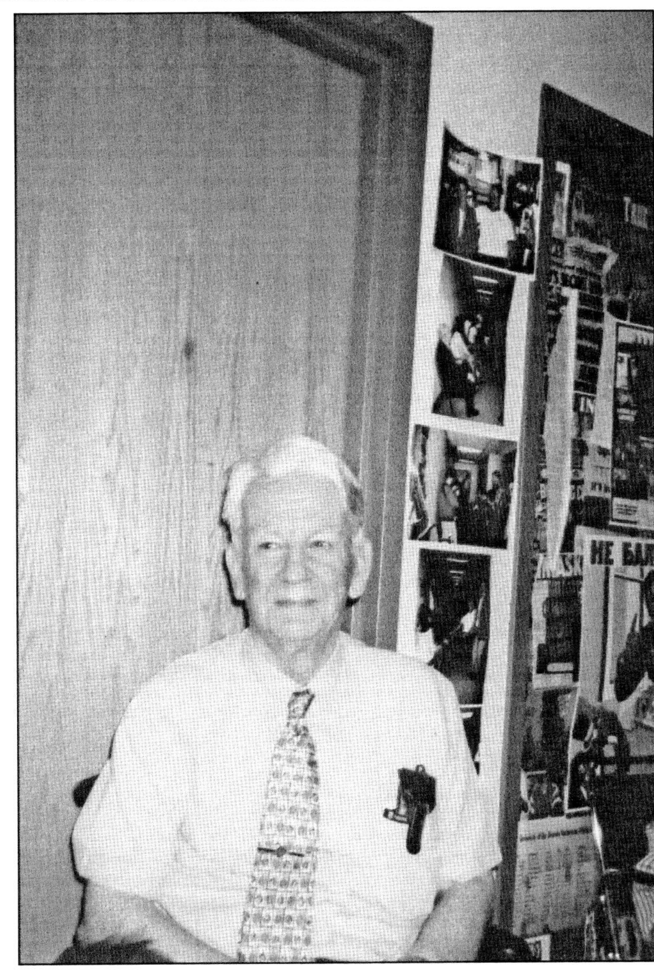

Evan Davis of Oak Hill's philanthropic endeavors have been extremely important to the University of Rio Grande in recent decades. His father, E.E. Davis, was a member of the board of regents and played an important role when the community college was formed; E.E. Davis is the namesake of the tech center. Several campus landmarks bear the names of Davis family members. Meanwhile, Evan Davis's service continues.

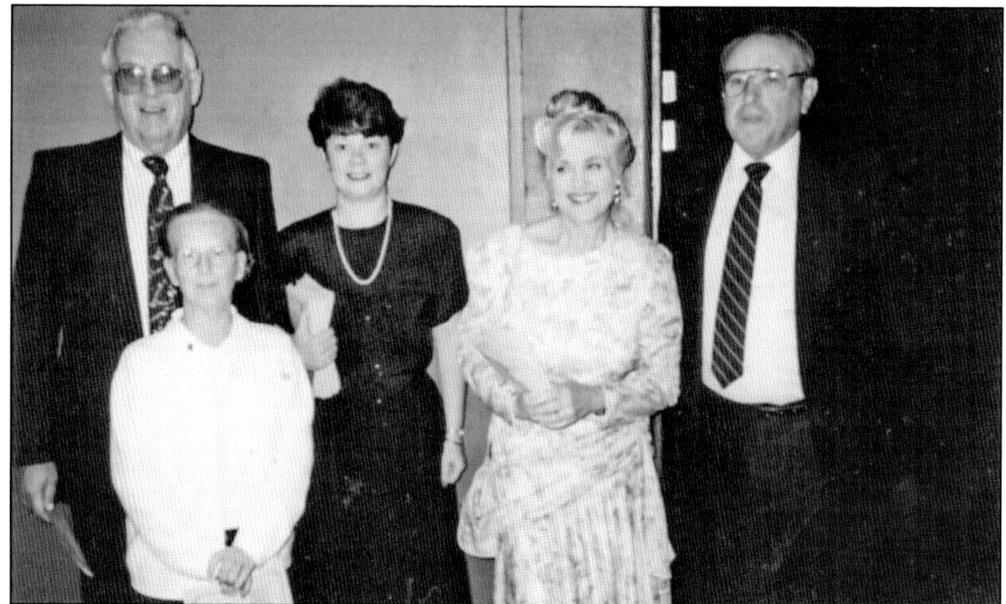

This photograph captures a quintet of University of Rio Grande staff members in the mid-1990s. In the foreground on the left is longtime Lyne Center secretary Patty Forgey. Behind her are, from left to right, education chair Paul Lloyd, presidential assistant Bev Crabtree, assistant professor of education Linda Bauer, and mathematics professor Ben Forshey.

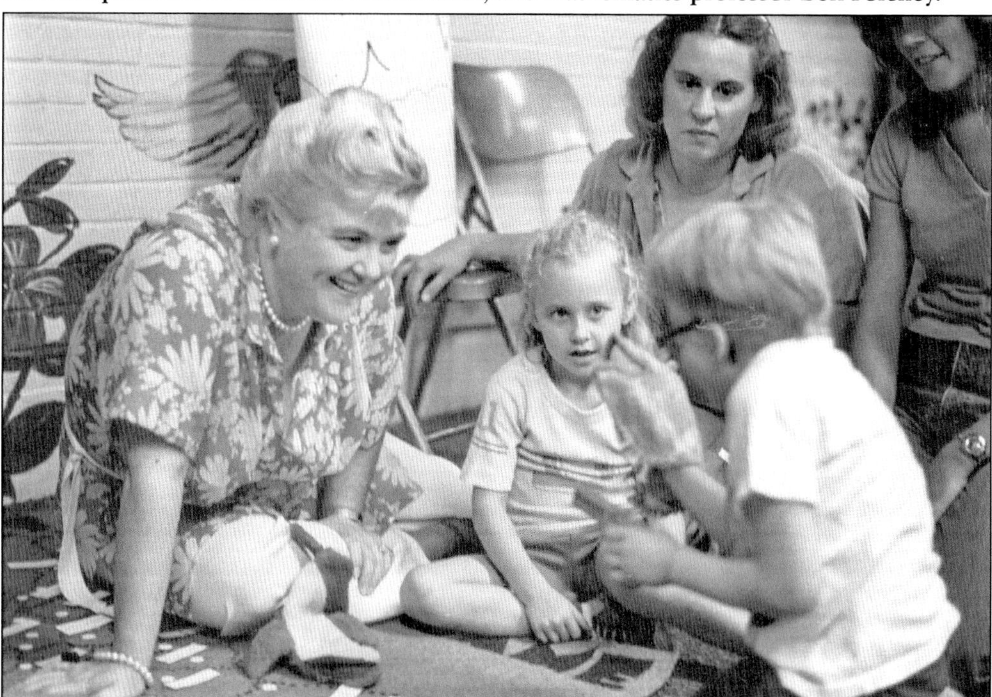

Linda Bauer entered Rio Grande in the Cadet Teacher Program in 1956 and after two degrees and varied experience joined the faculty in 1973, remaining until retirement in 2007. Linda specialized in early childhood education and stimulated her students to be creative. Widely admired, she continued living in Oak Hill following retirement.

Elaine Pleasants Armstrong (born 1946, class of 1986) became known as one of Rio Grande's most efficient and able staff members. She moved gracefully from the Crossroads Program to become a highly successful vice president for students until her retirement in 2007. Elaine and her husband, Gene Armstrong, also served as tireless workers promoting the Gallia County African American community.

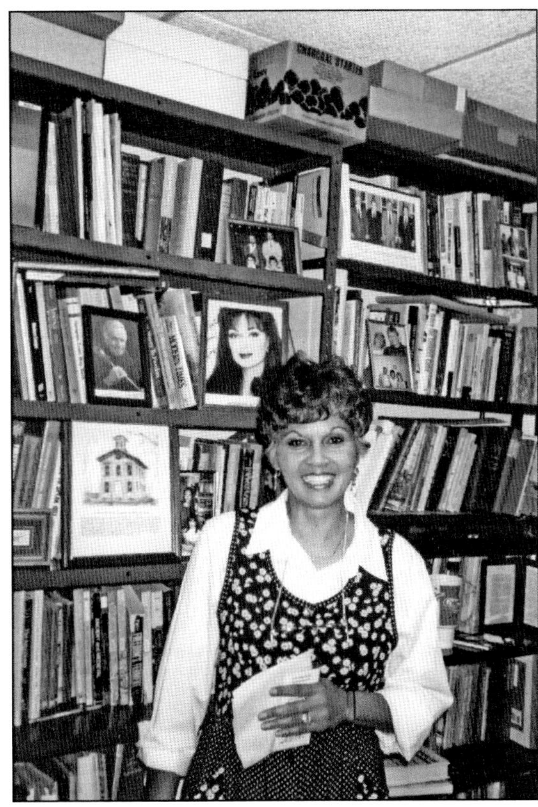

Dr. Herman Koby came to Rio in 1966 as dean of students and over the next 34 years held a wide variety of administrative posts, most especially as secretary-treasurer of the community college. After retirement, he spent several months as interim president of the community college at a crucial time. Koby is pictured here with his wife, Saundra.

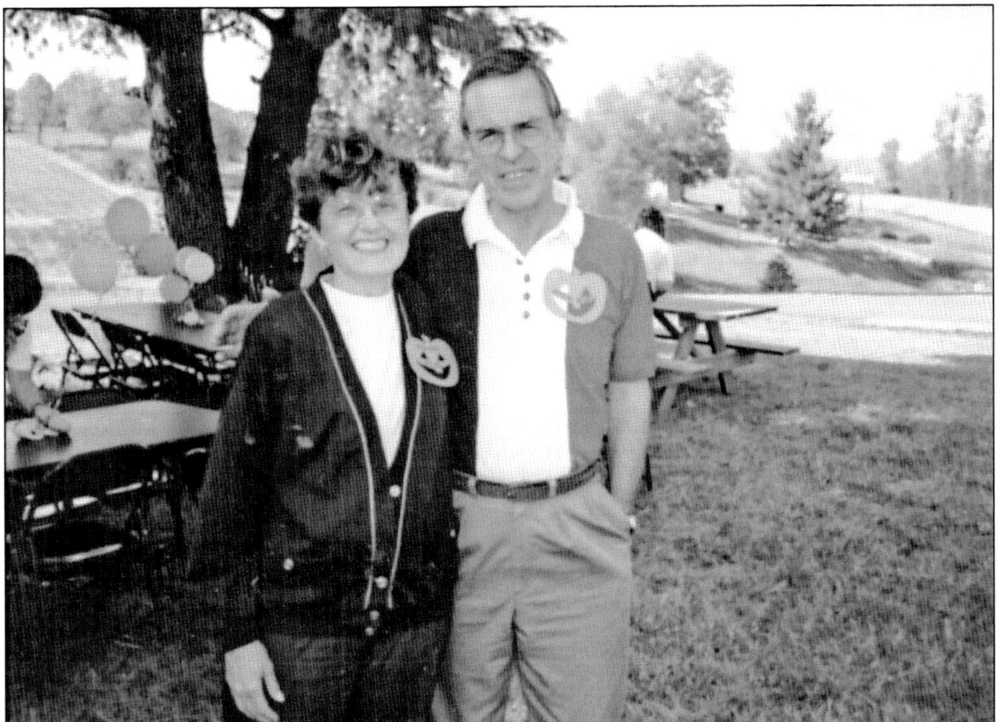

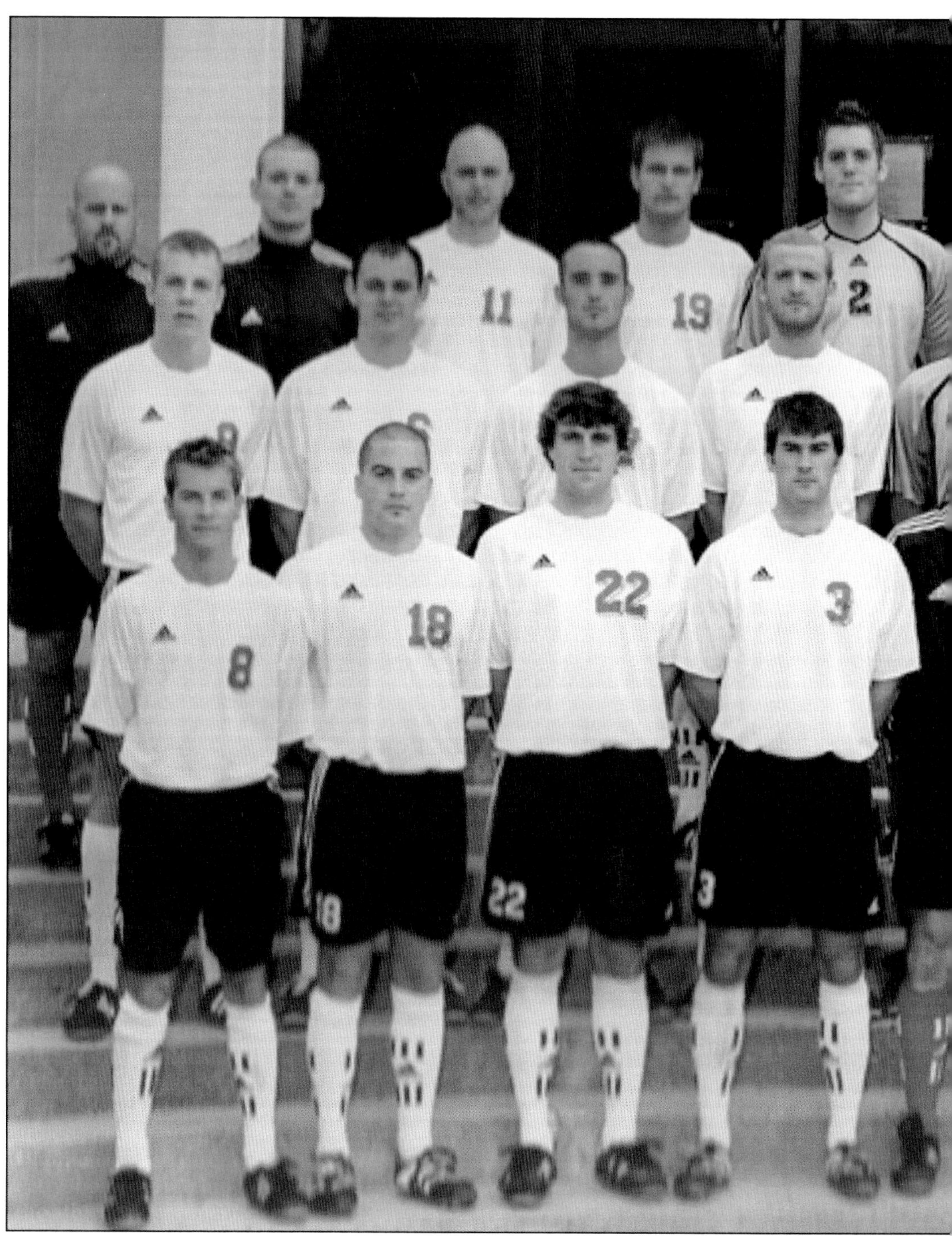

Rio's greatest soccer team (24-0-1) won the 2003 NAIA championship in Kansas City. From left to right are (first row) Ben Hughes, Nils Hocke, Kyle Gilbert, Jason Harvey, coach Scott Morrissey, Steven Kehoe, Paul Fiddler, Michael McManus, and Jared Bush; (second row) Ben Hunter, John Carroll, Ben Callan, Noel Monaghan, Tim Hart, Mark Fahey, Courtney Rimmer,

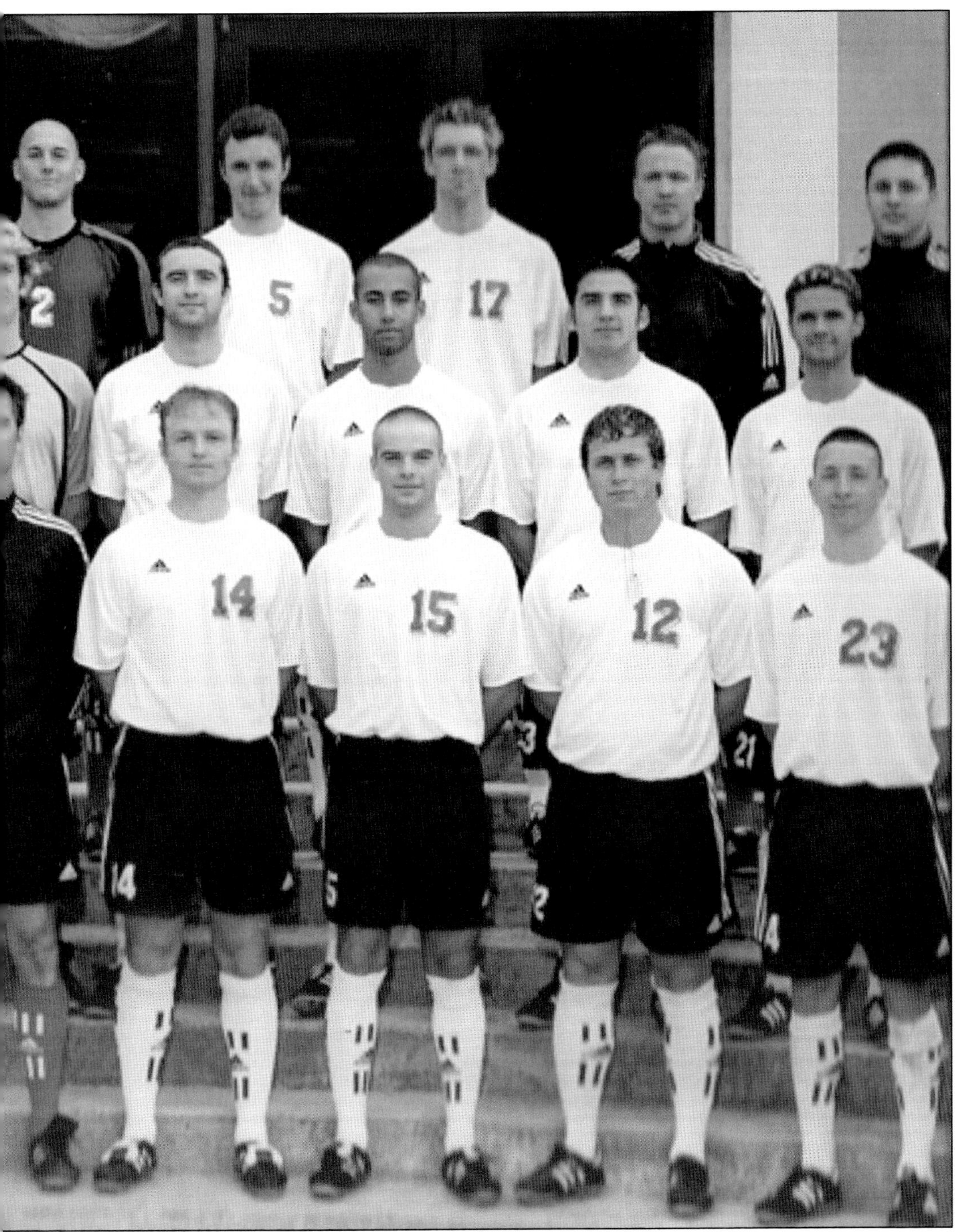

Phillip Lance, and Sean Wiseman; (third row) assistant coach Tony Daniels, Kevin McCloskey, Simon Carey, Guy Heywood, Oliver Sanders, Matt Eversole, Tony Griffiths, Conor Dawson, Kevin Peacock, and Jonathan Leonard.

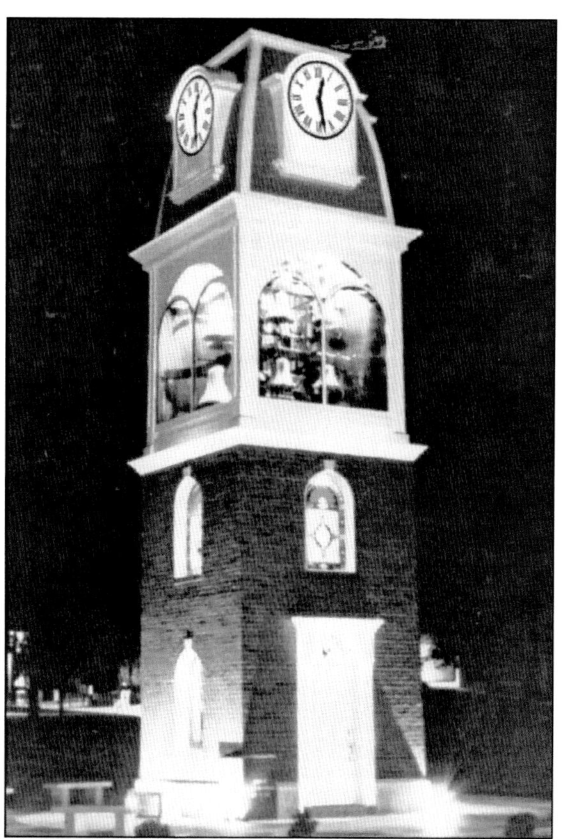

The Alumni Bell Tower, although not reaching the height of the original Atwood Hall Bell Tower, represented a major achievement of Barry Dorsey's presidency. It was dedicated as part of Rio Grande's 125th anniversary. The landscaping that surrounds it was a gift of retired Jackson schoolteacher Hope Leedy Keller (class of 1959).

On graduation weekend in 2002, the 125th-anniversary history *From Baptists and Bevo to the Bell Tower* came off the presses of the Jesse Stuart Foundation. The initial release book signing took place on Saturday with Pres. Barry Dorsey (far right) and coauthors Abby Gail Goodnite (class of 2001, left) and Ivan M. Tribe.

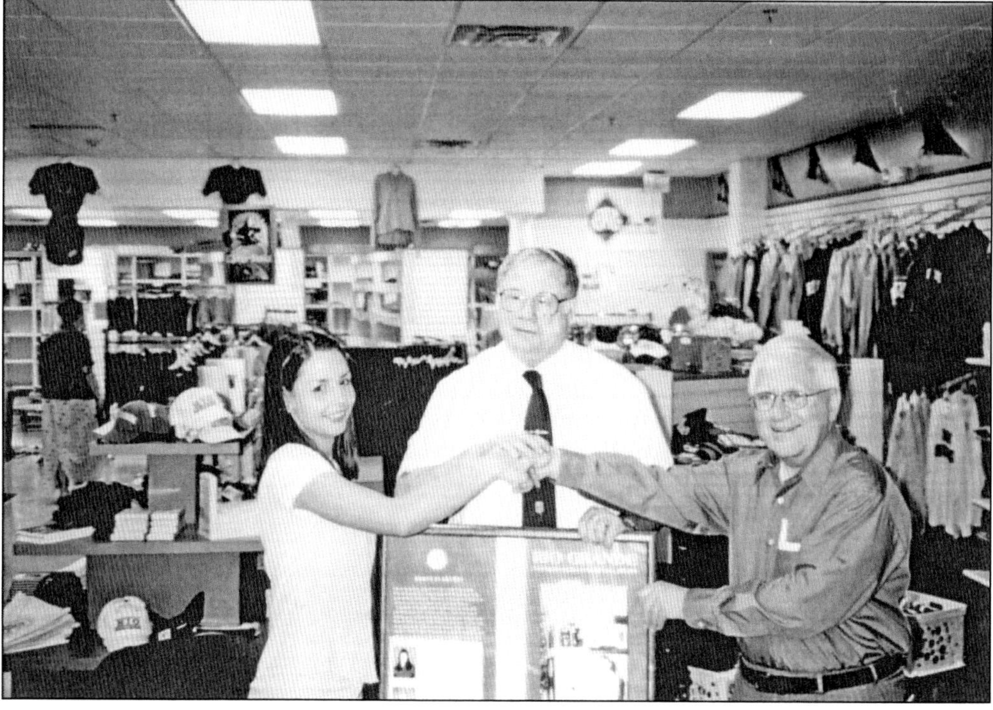

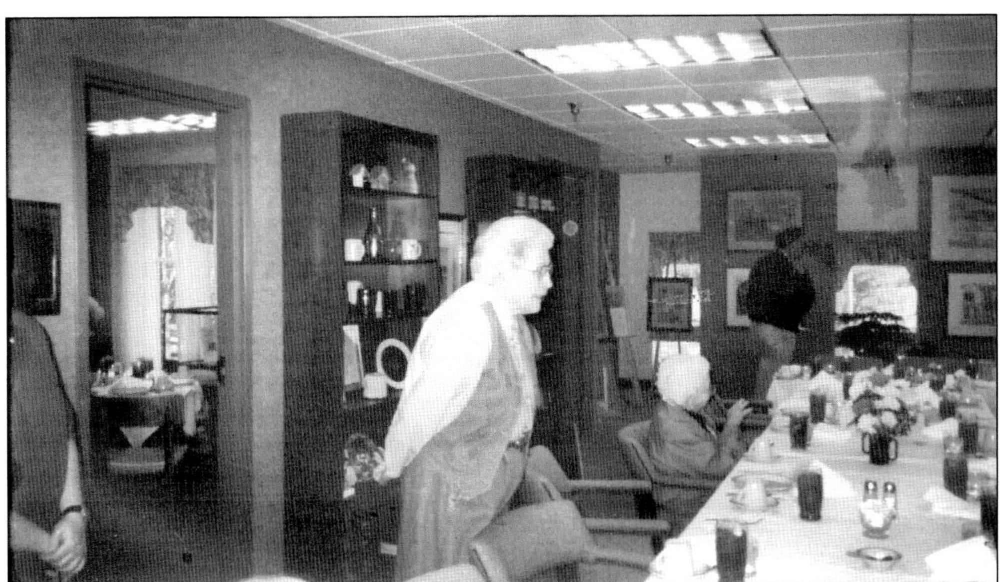

Jean Cooper (1924–2011) began her career at Rio Grande in 1948 as a member of the clerical staff. She became the secretary of the board of trustees and served in that capacity until she became ill in 2006. Jean's driving concern was always the history of Rio Grande and the vital role it played in southeastern Ohio. To honor her, the archives, when they moved from Davis Library to their current location in the Greer Museum, were named the Jean Lloyd Cooper Archives.

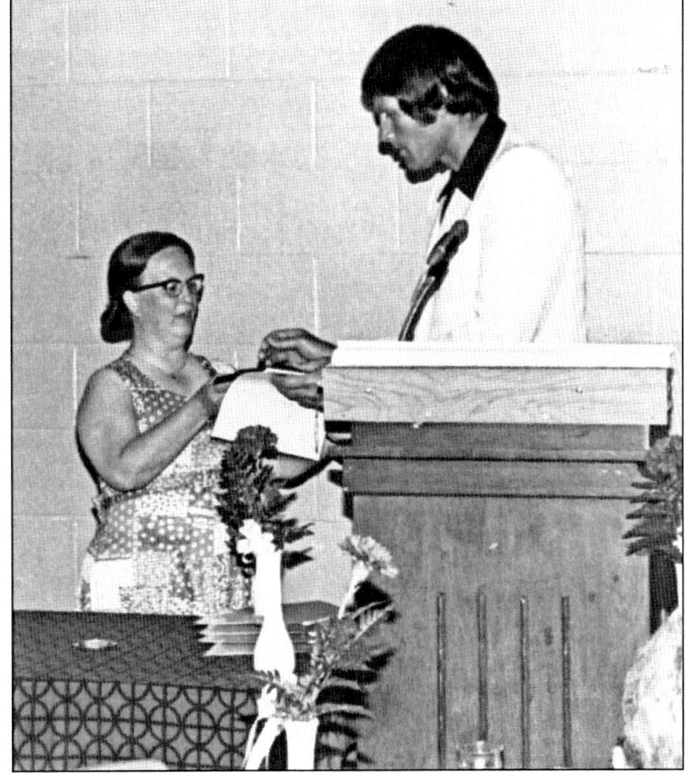

Patty Forgey (1940–2010, class of 1960) spent her entire life in her beloved Rio Grande. She began work at the college in 1962. Most of her career was spent as the secretary of the athletic department. Diminutive in stature, Patty loomed large in the athletic department. The cross-country team sponsors the Patty Forgey Invitational every fall, and a memorial was built to her outside of Lyne Center.

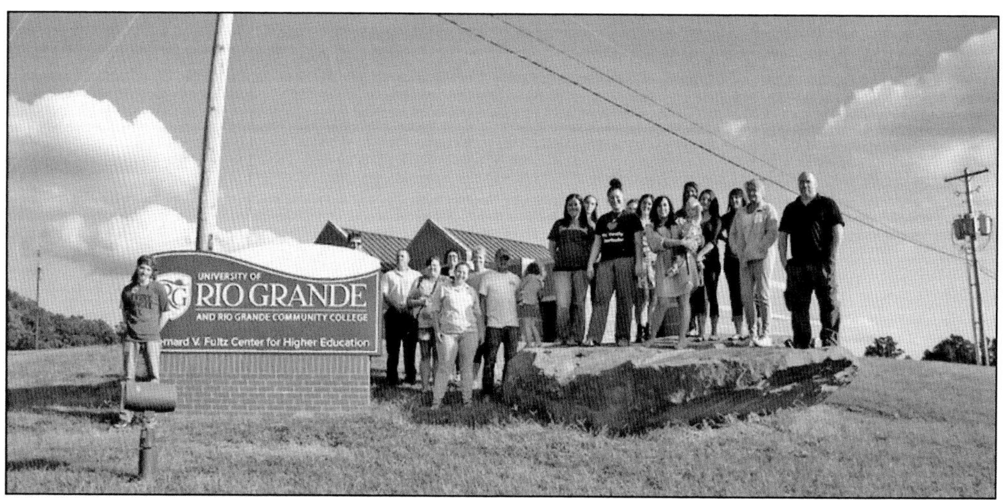

The Bernard V. Fultz Center for Higher Education in Meigs County opened in the fall of 2008. The 13,000-square-foot, state-of-the-art facility offers a safe and comfortable environment for students to learn and grow right in Meigs County. The Meigs Center moved from a rented space into the new building, and enrollment skyrocketed. Many students, including adults, were able to receive college instruction and still maintain busy schedules of job and family.

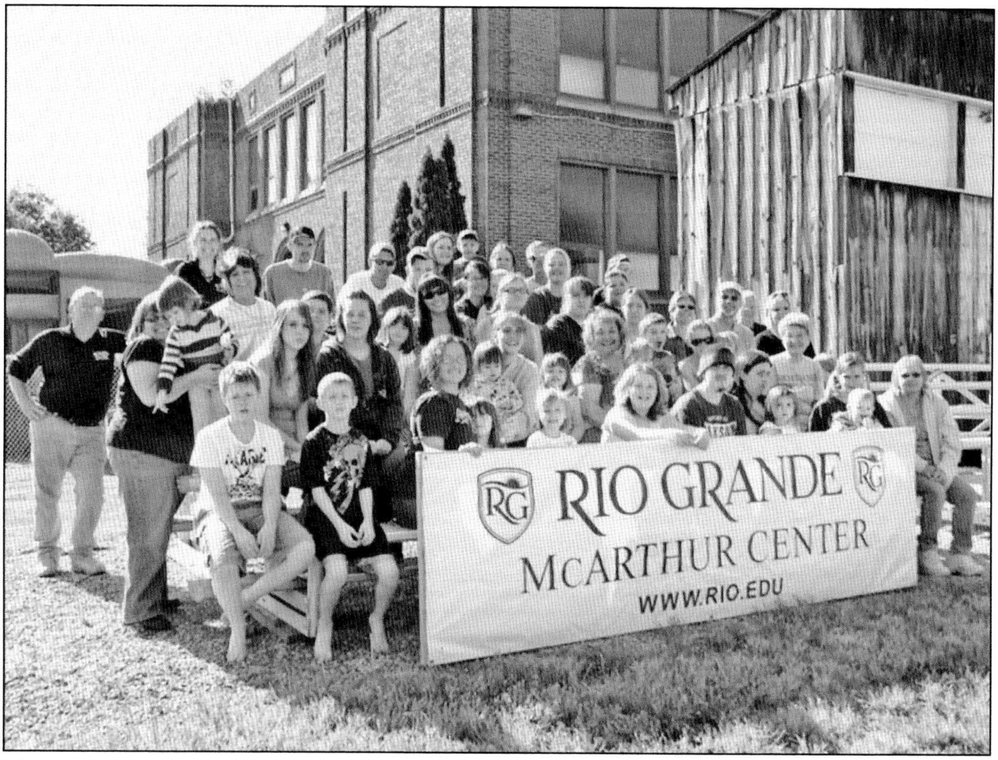

The Rio Grande McArthur Center opened in the fall of 2010 as a joint venture between Rio Grande and the Vinton County schools. The center is located in the Vinton County schools' administrative office building in McArthur, Ohio. The Rio Grande McArthur Center allows students to take general education courses in a comfortable atmosphere close to home. Plans are well under way to construct a new building to allow for expansion.

The Rio Grande Jackson Center launched in the summer of 2015 as part of a consortium funded by the Ohio Means Jobs–sponsored Industry Workforce Alliance Grant. Enrollment has grown so rapidly that plans are under way to move into a much larger facility and greatly expand course offerings. This move occurred in January 2017.

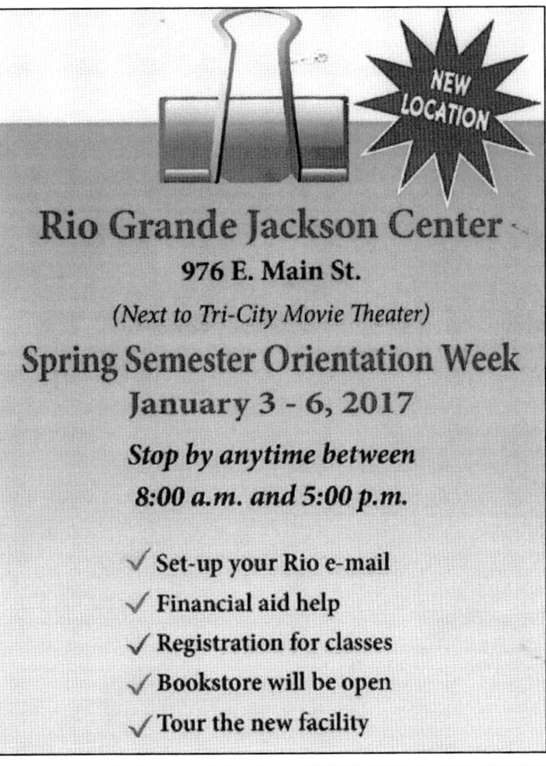

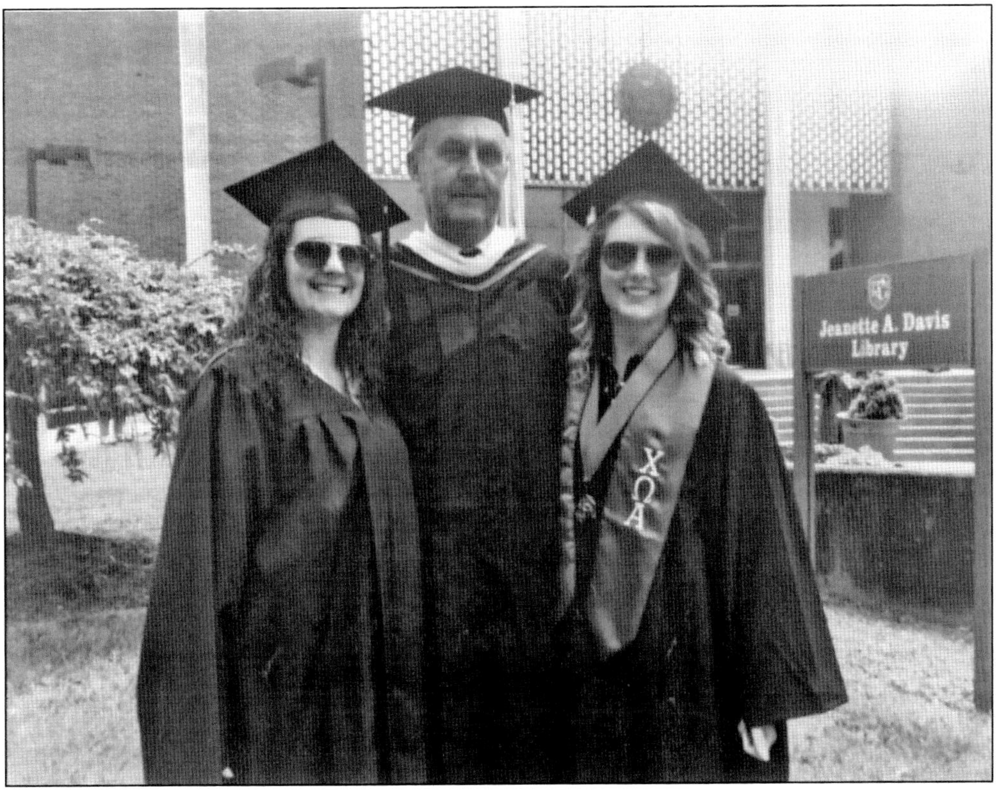

Graduation 2016 proved to be memorable for longtime speech professor Earl Thomas. It marked his last graduation before retirement. He is pictured here with daughter Rebecca Thomas Long (class of 1999, right), the vice president of administrative services, and his youngest daughter, Emily Thomas (class of 2016), who would soon be hired as a member of the admissions staff.

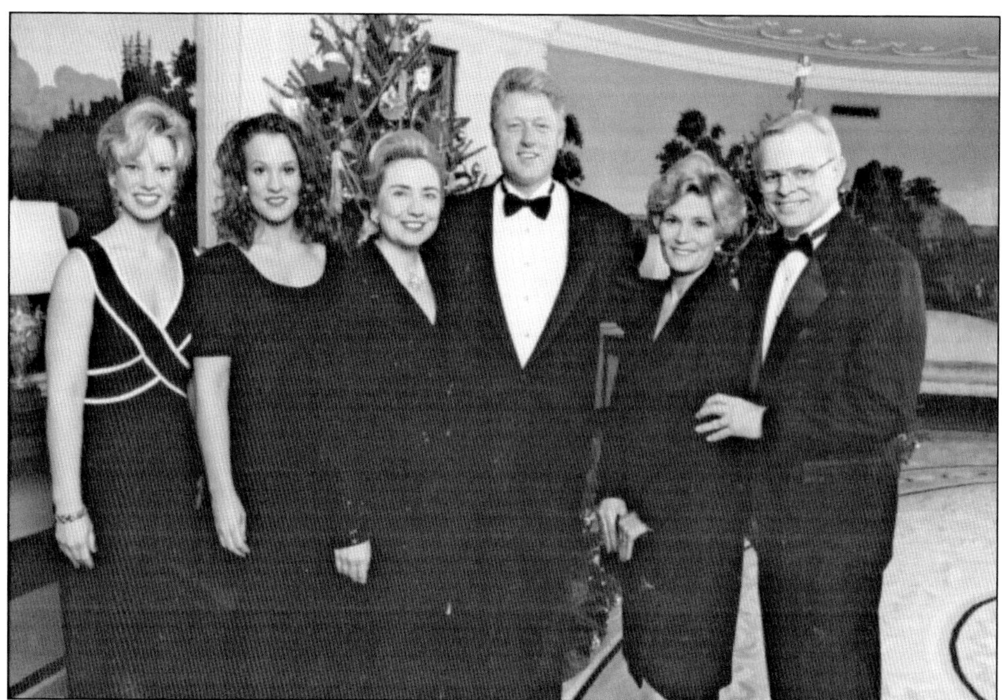
The late Frank Cremeans (class of 1967) is the only Rio Grande College alum to serve in Congress (1995–1997). He and his wife, Carol (a onetime Miss Ohio runner-up and Rio nursing student) are pictured at far right. Daughters Carrie (far left) and LeeAnn are to the left, with Pres. William J. Clinton and Hillary Clinton in the center. (Courtesy of Carol Cremeans.)

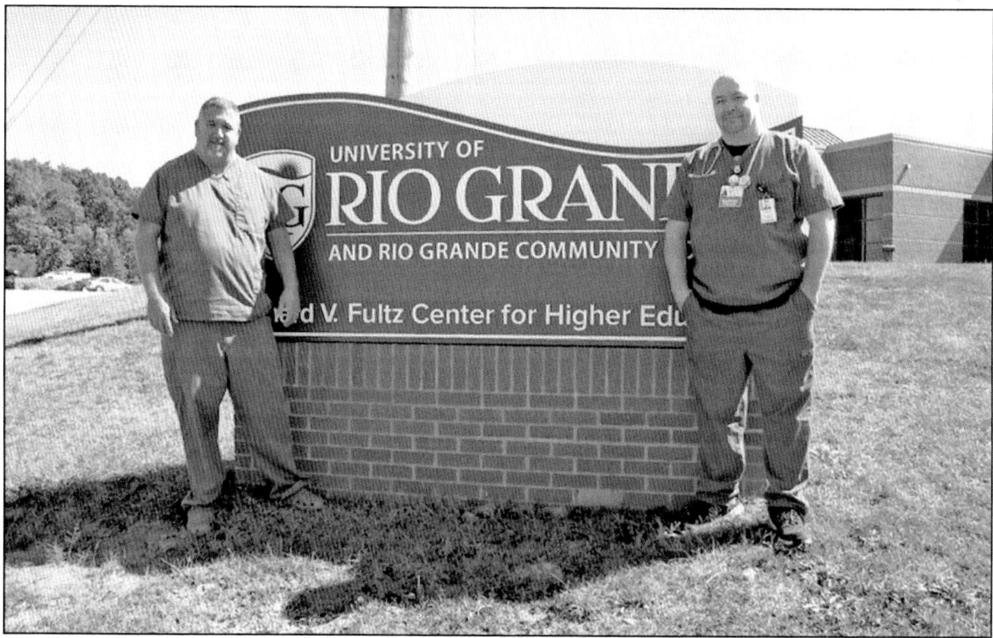

Chris Scherfel (class of 2014, left) and John Mount (class of 2014) are pictured at the Meigs Center. Enrolling as adults, they found the Meigs Center perfect for education close to their homes. Both are employed as respiratory therapists.

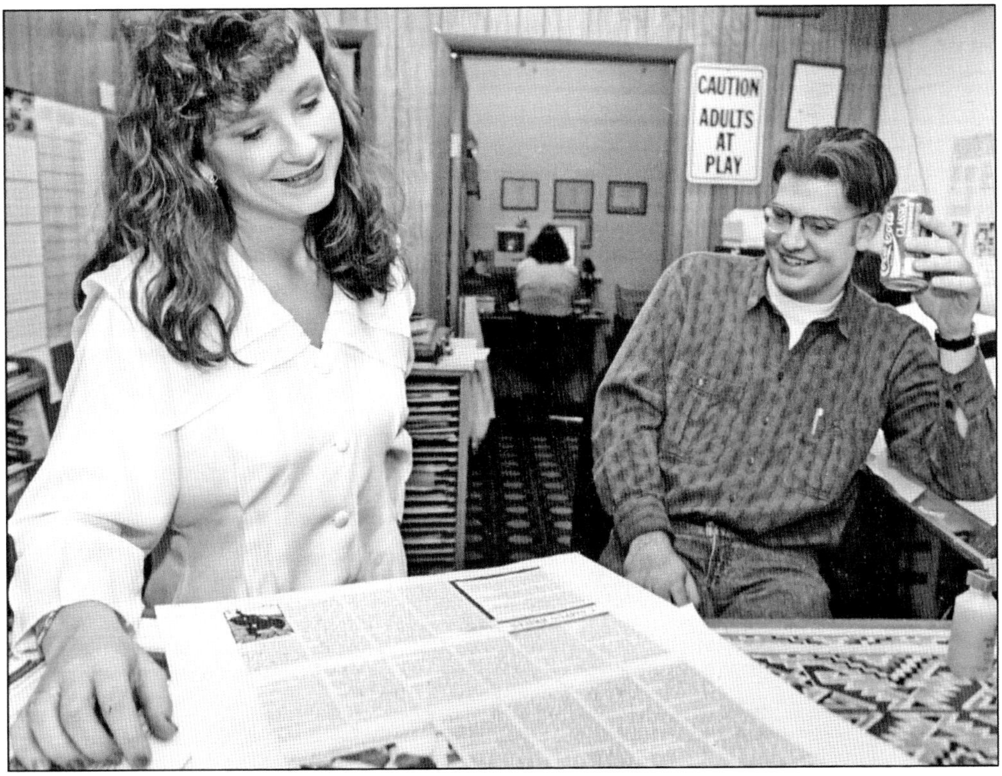

Chadrick Lambert (class of 1995) originated a comic strip character, Possum, several editions of which saw publication. Pictured here is the first issue, *Possum at Large*. Lambert served on the staff of *Signals* and subsequently married editor Angela Price (class of 1995). He has also enjoyed other successes, such as spending some years as producer of the nationally syndicated *Gary Burbank Show*. Lambert is an award-winning graphic novelist. (Courtesy of Chad and Angela Lambert.)

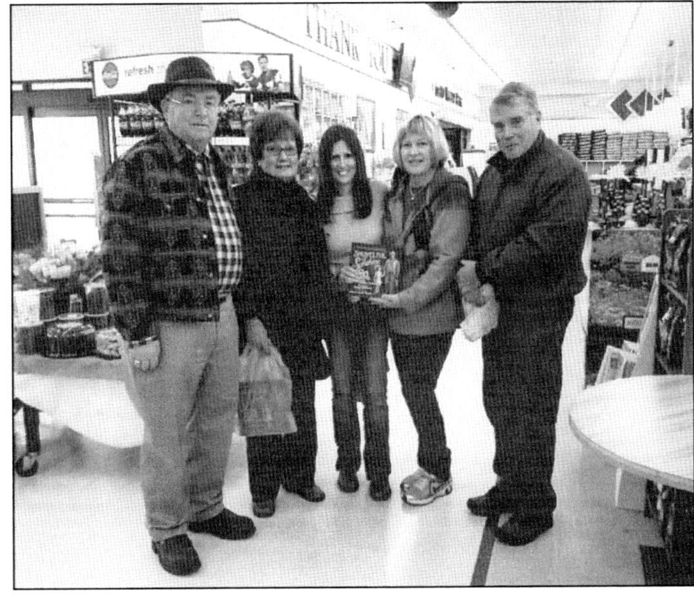

Stacy Vaughn-Hutton (class of 1994, center) of Torch, Ohio, majored in elementary education and taught for a time but followed her dream of writing children's literature. To date, her best-known work is *Shovelful of Sunshine* (2012), about a coal miner and his daughter. Vaughn-Hutton also serves on the URG Board of Trustees. She is pictured here at a book signing speaking to Steve Evans (far left) the son of Bob Evans. (Courtesy of Stacy Vaughn-Hutton.)

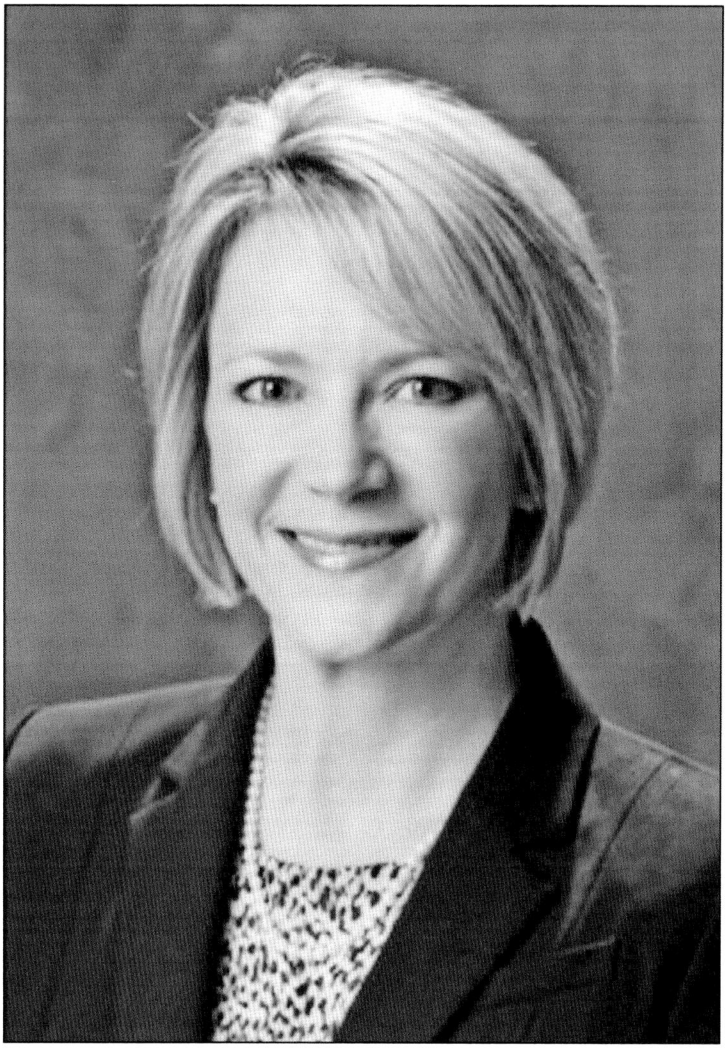

Michelle Johnston became the 22nd president of the University of Rio Grande in the fall of 2014. She came from Alabama's University of Montevallo and endeavored to create a more open, friendly atmosphere—following some years of indecisive leadership at Rio—while facing up to difficult financial challenges not of her making.

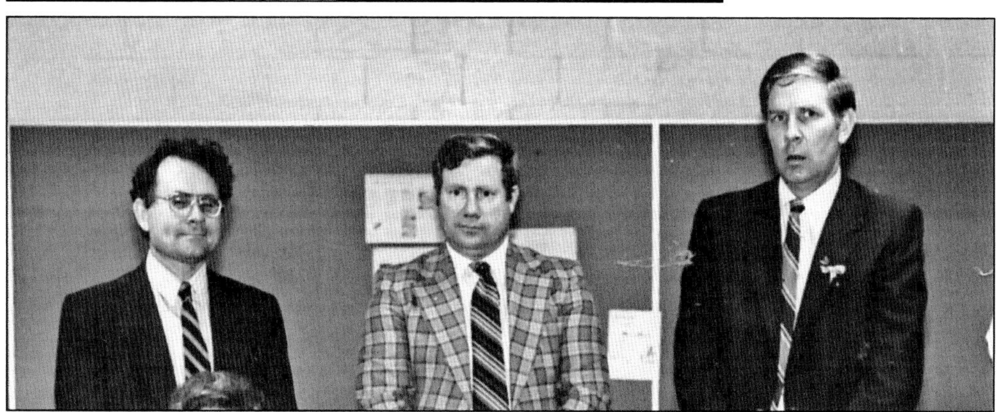

Dr. Ivan Tribe (center) is professor emeritus of history at Rio Grande. A prolific author and world-recognized authority on bluegrass music, he is pictured with his good friends Dr. Barry Thompson (right) and C. Robert Leith.

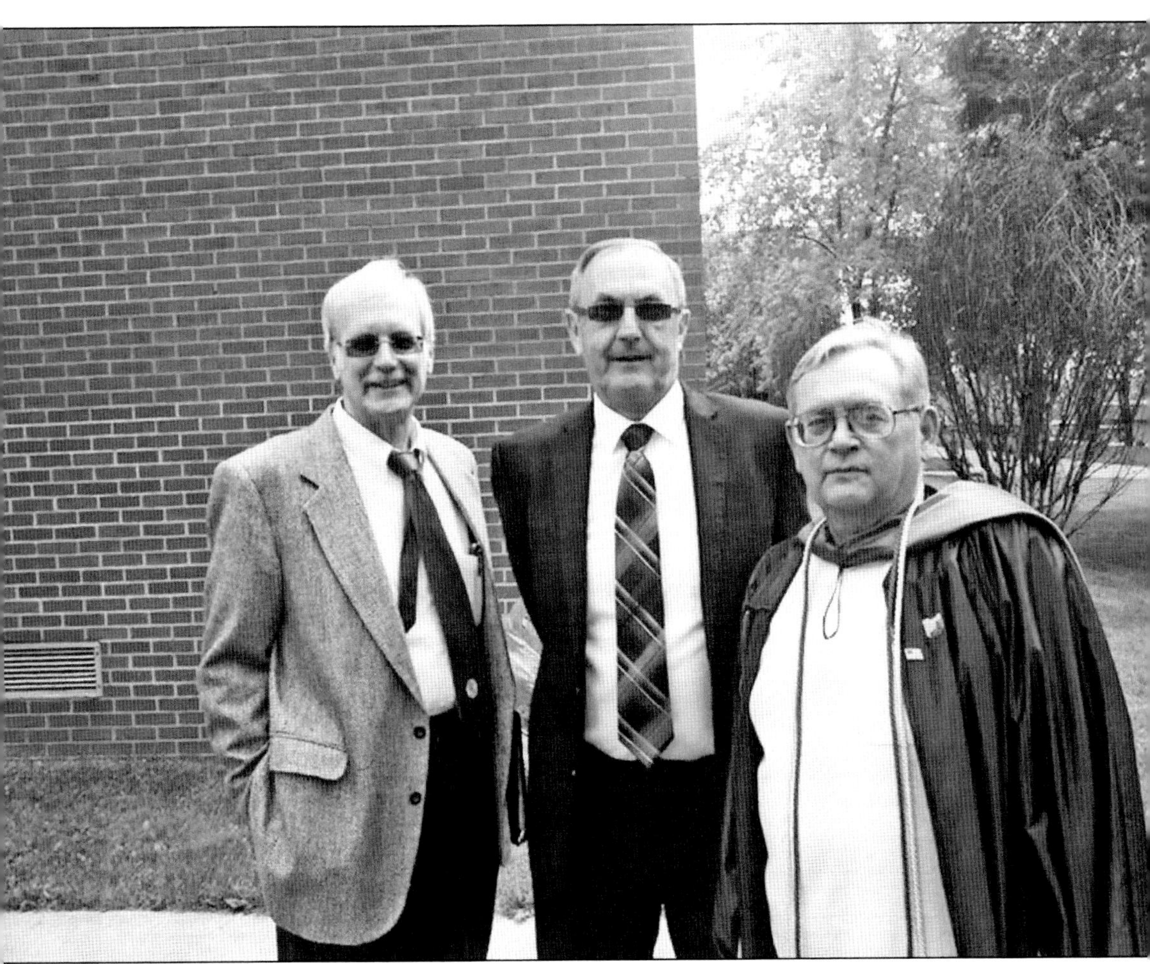

One of Rio Grande's longest-serving faculty members is Philadelphia-born Ray Matura (class of 1971, left), who began teaching sociology just after graduating and while pursuing a master's degree at Ohio University. Later, he took leave to obtain a doctorate at the University of Florida. Matura continues teaching a full load in the fall of 2016, specializing in gerontology. Earl Thomas (class of 1974, center) has been a key figure in Rio's communications program and in the success of the school's basketball teams. He spent many years as assistant coach and head coach of the Redmen cage squad, retiring from the faculty in 2016 after more than 32 years of service to the institution. Jake Bapst (class of 1975, right) came to Rio Grande College as a new student in 1971 and, except for the decade of the 1980s, has since held a variety of teaching and administrative posts as well as being an unofficial goodwill ambassador for Rio to many area schools. In recent years, he has been instrumental in both the Meigs and McArthur Centers as well as being coauthor of two Arcadia books. These friends of more than 45 years have only two words for readers: Go Rio!